WITH THE MASTER SHEPHERDING THE SHEEP

A Ladies' Bible Study of 1 Timothy

By
Susan J. Heck

With the Master Shepherding the Sheep
A Ladies' Bible Study of 1 Timothy
By Susan J. Heck

©2021 Focus Publishing, Bemidji, Minnesota
All rights reserved

Cover design by Amelia Schussman

ISBN 978-1-936141-60-9

Printed in the United States of America

Dedication

To the men in my family who are good shepherds of their sheep.

Charles Pack, my father

Doug Heck, my husband

Charles Heck, my son

David Gundersen, my son-in-law

Endorsements

Susan Heck is a sound and safe gifted women's teacher, a rare combination to find in our climate today. She respects the text and does not push a 'feminist' agenda as so many do. This volume on 1 Timothy is quite accessible and practically constructed for lay students with helpful, overview summaries and good questions to consider at the end of each chapter. These supplements enhance the value of this exposition for personal or interactive group studies.

Jim Andrews, Senior Pastor
Lake Bible Church, Lake Oswego, Oregon
Author and Bible Teacher,
The Final Word Radio

In the opening to this book, our sister quotes Jay Adams: "What is necessary to carry on a fruitful, faithful ministry of the Word is 'healthy teaching' given by trustworthy persons." Ladies, here is yet another healthy teaching given by a trustworthy Susan Heck.

Justin Bates, Pastor
Cambridge Baptist Church, Cambridge, Kansas

The tone of Paul's letters to Timothy is that of a seasoned shepherd discipling young men for ministry. Thus, teaching this book effectively begs a seasoned shepherd who has walked through a variety of ministry challenges. I know of few people better qualified to teach young women what it means to minister to others than my mother. Her expositions shared throughout this book come from decades of Scripture memorization and discipling hundreds of women. Read this book and you will be equipped for the work of the ministry.

Charles Heck, Teaching Pastor
Wichita Bible Church, Wichita, Kansas

Susan Heck's teaching has been a blessing to many ladies in my congregation through her Bible study courses and public speaking ministry. This study in 1 Timothy demonstrates why that is. Susan tackles controversial and difficult passages with grace and clarity. She is able to cut through the confusion and clatter that often accompanies small group Bible studies and focus on the author's intended meaning in the text. Her outlines and illustrations illuminate the meaning and the questions at the end of each chapter apply the truth. Doctrinal soundness, biblical faithfulness, and exegetical precision are the hallmarks of Susan's work in 1 Timothy. This will bless the teachable student of God's Word. I highly recommend it!

Jim Osman, Author
Pastor, Kootenai Community Church
Kootenai, Idaho

Table of Contents

Chapter 1

The Beginning of a
Letter from a Father to a Son

1 Timothy 1:1-2

One summer not long ago, my husband and I had the joy of having our children and their families come for a visit. During their stay, while my daughter and I were visiting, she asked me what women I was "hanging out" with. Her question opened up a dialogue in which I began to share with her how I was more and more valuing the time I could spend with my two mentors, who are now 72 and 82. I told her I realized they were both getting older and I had recently been struck by the fact that they could soon leave this life. I wanted to glean everything I could from them while they were still living. I will miss them greatly when the Lord takes them home. I have learned much from these two special women in my life; they are indeed two of my spiritual mothers.

You might be wondering, "What does this have to do with the book of 1 Timothy?" Well, as we begin our study of 1 Timothy, the relationships I've just described are to some extent where we find the apostle Paul and his son in the faith, Timothy. As Paul is writing, he has only a few years left to live and he wants to say some things to Timothy, whom he has mentored in the faith. (I don't know if my mentors plan on leaving me a letter, but I would value it if they did!)

Before we begin this wonderful letter from a spiritual father to his spiritual son, let's go over some of the background to this epistle so that we might better understand it as we study. First Timothy is one of three epistles that we call the Pastoral Epistles; the others are 2 Timothy and Titus. All three of these epistles are written by the apostle Paul, where he refers to Timothy and Titus as his sons in the faith (see 1 Timothy 1:2; 2 Timothy 1:2; and Titus 1:4). These three pastoral epistles differ from most of Paul's other letters in that they have a more personal note about them because they are written to two of his dearest friends. And while these three pastoral epistles do deal some with doctrinal issues, they are also very practical. Hopefully, you will see these things as we make our way through 1 Timothy.

The first question that comes to my mind when studying a book of the Bible is, "Who wrote it?" In this case, we don't have to go very far to discover the answer. The first word in 1 Timothy tells us that *Paul* wrote it. We also don't have to go very far to discover the answer to my second question: "To whom was it written?" Paul states in verse 2 that it is written *to Timothy*. But this epistle is also written to the entire church at Ephesus. The reason we know this is because in verse 3 Paul mentions to Timothy that he had urged him to remain in Ephesus that he might "charge some that they teach no other doctrine."

We might ask, "Where was Paul when he wrote this epistle?" It appears that Paul was in Macedonia, according to 1 Timothy 1:3. We know that 2 Timothy was written from a Roman prison right before Paul's death. In fact, he says in 2 Timothy 4:6-7, "For I am already being poured out as a drink offering, and the time of my departure is at hand. I have fought the good fight, I have finished the race, I have kept the faith."

We might be interested to know, "When was First Timothy written?" The probable date for this epistle's writing was between 62 and 66 A.D. But the question I am personally most eager to discover is the "Why?" question: "Why was First Timothy written?" As we've already mentioned, 1 and 2 Timothy and Titus are what are known as the Pastoral Epistles. One of the reasons they are referred this way is because Paul wrote these epistles to Timothy and Titus so that they would

- remember their responsibilities as pastors:
- know the importance of defending truth;

- learn practical instructions regarding the church and how it should be conducted;

- know the role of men and women;

- practice holy living.

This list is certainly not exhaustive, but these subjects are common in the Pastoral Epistles. Particularly in 1 Timothy, Paul reminds Timothy to remain at Ephesus, as is made clear in 1:3. The reason for this admonition was that evidently there were some false teachers in the church, as mentioned in 1:20; Timothy needed to remain in Ephesus in order to stand against these opposers, as well as any others who might be infiltrating the church. Interestingly enough, Paul says something very similar to Titus, in Titus 1:5: "For this reason I left you in Crete, that you should set in order the things that are lacking, and appoint elders in every city as I commanded you." And then, starting in verse 10 of that same letter, Paul says,

> For there are many insubordinate, both idle talkers and deceivers, especially those of the circumcision, whose mouths must be stopped, who subvert whole households, teaching things which they ought not, for the sake of dishonest gain. One of them, a prophet of their own, said, 'Cretans *are* always liars, evil beasts, lazy gluttons.' This testimony is true. Therefore rebuke them sharply, that they may be sound in the faith, not giving heed to Jewish fables and commandments of men who turn from the truth.

This is certainly one of the main roles of any pastor of any true church. True shepherds will protect their flocks from false teachers, and they will be willing to stand for truth and to confront anyone who is teaching anything other than sound doctrine.

This isn't the only reason that Paul wrote 1 Timothy. He mentions in 3:14-15 that he hopes to come to Ephesus soon, but if he is unable to, he is writing so that they will know how to behave in the house of God, and he reminds Timothy that God's house is the pillar and ground of the truth: "These things I write to you, though I hope to come to you shortly; but if I am delayed, I write so that you may know how you ought to conduct yourself in the house of God, which is the church of the living God, the pillar and ground of the truth." This seems to be another purpose for which Paul wrote 1 Timothy.

As we study this book, we will see that Paul instructs Timothy and the church not only regarding sound doctrine but also regarding the use of the law; the role of women in the church; the qualifications for leadership, along with what is a reasonable salary for them; doctrines of demons, which have crept into the church; the importance of using spiritual gifts; how to rebuke older women and older men; the qualifications for a widow; the importance of being content with food and clothing alone; and warning them of the love of money, along with a specific warning for those who are rich. Paul also writes regarding the depth of his own sin and how humbling it is that God would allow him to serve Him. He includes several doxologies in this epistle that exalt the high name of God. One man says about 1 Timothy, "As we begin to look at this pastoral epistle, let me alert you to a theme that runs throughout: What is necessary to carry on a fruitful, faithful ministry of the Word is 'healthy teaching' given by trustworthy persons."[1] This is a rich, yet warm letter that should challenge each of us! With that in mind, let's read the two verses together and see what we can glean from them.

1 Timothy 1:1-2

> Paul, an apostle of Jesus Christ, by the commandment of God our Savior and the Lord Jesus Christ, our hope, [2] To Timothy, a true son in the faith: Grace, mercy, and peace from God our Father and Jesus Christ our Lord.

Our outline for this lesson will include:

Who is this Father? What is He Known For? (v. 1)
Who is this Son? What is He Known For? (v. 2)
Who is Our Father? What is He Known For? (vs. 1, 2)

---

1   Jay Adams, *The Christian Counselor's Commentary: I & II Timothy and Titus* (Hackettstown: Timeless Texts, 1994), 3.

Who is Our Father? What is He Known For?

1 Timothy 1:1

Paul, an apostle of Jesus Christ, by the commandment of God
our Savior and the Lord Jesus Christ, our hope, (1 Timothy 1:1)

Paul begins his epistle by mentioning his name first. This is a very common practice in New Testament writings; correspondence in that day would begin with the name of the person who was writing. In our day, we do the opposite; we end our letters with the name of the one who is writing. But I think they might have had the better idea. In this case, progress doesn't necessarily mean a better way!

Who is this *Paul*? His name means little one, and we know from church history that he was short in stature, was bald-headed, and had a hooked nose and eyebrows which seemed to meet one another. So, he wasn't that great to look at! Even Paul says of himself, in 2 Corinthians 10:10, "For his letters, they say, are weighty and powerful, but his bodily presence is weak, and his speech contemptible." Acts 9 records for us how God saved Paul on the Damascus road, and how he would preach the gospel and suffer for Christ's sake. Paul's life was never the same, and he never seemed to get over the saving grace of God. He refers to himself as the chief of sinners and the least of the apostles, and he knew that it was only God's grace that enabled him to do anything.

After Paul mentions his name, he then reminds his readers of who he is: *an apostle*. What is an apostle? The Greek word is apostolos, and it means to be sent on a mission with a message. We know from Acts 9 that Paul's mission was to preach the gospel to the Gentiles, to kings, and to the children of Israel, and to suffer for Christ. Paul makes it clear that this apostleship was not from himself, but from *Jesus Christ*, and, specifically, *the commandment of God our Savior and the Lord Jesus Christ*. It's interesting that Paul uses the word *commandment* here, because in most of his letters he mentions that he is an apostle by the will of God, not by the commandment of

God. The word commandment has the idea of a command given by someone who was a king, as in the case of Esther 1. (This is the account in which King Ahasuerus commanded Queen Esther to parade before others so they could look on her beauty. She refused and lost her Queenship—the point being that commands were considered something to be obeyed in biblical times!) So, why would Paul use the phrase *commandment of God* instead of the will of God? Perhaps, as Paul is reflecting on the fact that he is coming to the end of his earthly life, he still remembers that he is to receive orders from someone else, that being the One who saved him. (That was another conversation my daughter and I had: how one confronts those who are older to keep them from becoming stagnant in their walk with Christ. Paul deals with this topic in chapter five).

Another reason, perhaps, that Paul mentions his apostleship as being by the commandment of God is that while Paul and Timothy enjoyed a very close relationship, Paul may have wanted to emphasize that he was an apostle and that his letter carried the authority of an apostle. It would also communicate that this letter wasn't only intended for Timothy but for the entire church at Ephesus; they may have needed to be reminded of the fact that Paul's apostleship wasn't something man-made, but rather by the command from God. This would give weight to what he writes, especially regarding doctrine, in the next few verses:

> As I urged you when I went into Macedonia—remain in Ephesus that you may charge some that they teach no other doctrine, nor give heed to fables and endless genealogies, which cause disputes rather than godly edification which is in faith. Now the purpose of the commandment is love from a pure heart, *from* a good conscience, and *from* sincere faith, from which some, having strayed, have turned aside to idle talk, desiring to be teachers of the law, understanding neither what they say nor the things which they affirm. (1 Timothy 1:3-7)

And then,

> This charge I commit to you, son Timothy, according to the prophecies previously made concerning you, that by them you

> may wage the good warfare, having faith and a good conscience, which some having rejected, concerning the faith have suffered shipwreck, of whom are Hymenaeus and Alexander, whom I delivered to Satan that they may learn not to blaspheme. (1 Timothy 1:18-20)

Perhaps you are thinking, "Well, isn't that rather mean of the Lord to command Paul to be an apostle?" When we grasp the truth that Jesus is ruler over our lives and that we are to submit joyfully to His Lordship, then no command of His is a burden for us (1 John 5:3). Also, when we consider the character of our Lord, as Paul will mention next, then why would we regard any command of His as being harsh? Paul says He is *our hope*! This commandment was given by One who is our hope! The word *hope* has the idea of Christ being our very substance, our foundation, the object of our hope. This is a certainty that Paul is referring to. You and I might say, "I hope to go on a vacation this year," or "I hope someday to get married or have children." None of these "hopes" are certainties; we can't bank on them. But Christ—our hope—is a certainty we can count on. Is He your hope? What is your hope? Who do you hope for, or what do you hope for? Is your hope in your marriage? A child? A person? Your financial future? Our hope should be in the Lord, my friend, and He alone is enough.

So, what does this verse tells us that Paul, the spiritual father of Timothy, is known for? He is an apostle of Jesus Christ. Who is our Heavenly Father? And what does this verse teach us that He is known for? He is God our Savior and He alone is our hope. In verse 2, Paul gives us a little glimpse into the character of his son in the faith, Timothy, along with a greeting.

Who is this Son? What is He Known For?
Who is Our Father? What is He Known For?

1 Timothy 1:2

> To Timothy, a true son in the faith: Grace, mercy, *and* peace from God our Father and Jesus Christ our Lord (1 Timothy 1:2)

Paul mentions the one to whom he is writing, and his name is *Timothy*. Who is Timothy? According to Acts 16:1-3, Paul met Timothy when Paul arrived in Derbe and Lystra:

> Then he came to Derbe and Lystra. And behold, a certain disciple was there, named Timothy, the son of a certain Jewish woman who believed, but his father was Greek. He was well spoken of by the brethren who were at Lystra and Iconium. Paul wanted to have him go on with him. And he took him and circumcised him because of the Jews who were in that region, for they all knew that his father was Greek.

Timothy accompanied Paul on his third missionary journey. We also know from 2 Timothy 1:5 that Timothy's mother's name was Eunice and his grandmother's name was Lois: "When I call to remembrance the genuine faith that is in you, which dwelt first in your grandmother Lois and your mother Eunice, and I am persuaded is in you also." Evidently, though Timothy's father was not a believer, his mother and his grandmother were. This should be encouraging to those of you who have unbelieving husbands, to know that as you train your children in the ways of God, they too might become a Timothy. It's also encouraging that even though Timothy's father was not a believer God provided a spiritual father for him in the apostle Paul. We do not have a record of Timothy's conversion, like we do Paul's, so we can only speculate at best; some think that Paul had something to do with Timothy's conversion, and yet, when we see the influence of his mother and grandmother, it could be assumed that somehow it was their influence that pressed the gospel upon his soul (see 2 Timothy 3:15). Paul mentions Timothy in all of his letters except for Galatians, Ephesians, and Titus. While this list of facts about Timothy is certainly not exhaustive, in the Questions to Consider I've given you the main passages for you to study and glean from on your own.

But, as we can see here in 1 Timothy 1:2, Paul gives us a small glimpse into who Timothy is as he calls Timothy *a true son in the faith. True* would be in the sense of not being false. The word *true* was often used in reference to children who were born in wedlock, in contrast to those who were born of out of wedlock, who were called illegitimate. This is much like what we read in Hebrews 12:5-9, where the writer to the Hebrews speaks of those whom God chastens:

> And you have forgotten the exhortation which speaks to you as to sons: 'My son, do not despise the chastening of the Lord, nor be discouraged when you are rebuked by Him; for whom the Lord loves He chastens, and scourges every son whom He receives, if you endure chastening, God deals with you as with sons; for what son is there whom a father does not chasten? But if you are without chastening, of which all have become partakers, then you are illegitimate and not sons.

Timothy was genuine, as opposed to those whom Paul mentions at the end of 1 Timothy 1. Perhaps that is why Paul emphasizes this fact at the very beginning of his letter; it may be that he wants the church at Ephesus to know that unlike those who have defected, Timothy is genuine.

Paul mentions not just that Timothy is a son but *a true son*, and not that he was a son in the flesh, which he wasn't, but a son *in the faith*. Spiritual family is true and, in many instances, more precious than physical family. I have one physical daughter who happens to be a spiritual daughter as well. But I am also privileged to be a mother to many spiritual daughters, and I am of all women most blessed to have had these relationships and to continue to have these relationships which stimulate me to love and good deeds. And Timothy isn't the only one Paul calls his true son in the faith; he also says the same thing of Titus in Titus 1:4.

It's important to clarify that this discipleship that went on between Paul and Timothy and Paul and Titus was nothing like what we see in most of our modern-day discipleship. Discipleship in New Testament times was serious business. The Greek word disciple, found in Matthew 28:18-20, is Jesus' great commission to go and makes disciples. It conveys the idea of a person who attaches himself or herself to a master with a commitment to follow that person's teaching and imitate that person's life. Even though discipleship is a teacher and student relationship, many times the teacher is the biggest learner as iron sharpens iron. In New Testament times, a disciple was someone who studied and learned with a view to obey what their master or mentor taught or commanded. This instruction would be both formal and informal, as the student would learn by oral questions and answers, along with memorization, which was the primary way of learning.[2] As you can see, this is quite different from the vast majority of modern-day discipleship relationships, where we get together for coffee and chit-chat. Discipleship was and should be serious business. No wonder Paul could entrust these men to pastor the churches he had started!

Having told us who Timothy is, Paul sends a greeting: *Grace, mercy, and peace from God our Father and Jesus Christ our Lord.* It's interesting to me that Paul only uses this triad in one other place and that is in his second epistle to Timothy, 2 Timothy. Usually Paul's greetings consist of just grace and peace—as we see in Romans, 1 and 2 Corinthians, Galatians, Ephesians, Philippians, Colossians, 1 and 2 Thessalonians, Titus, and Philemon—but here he adds mercy. We can only speculate as to why he adds mercy in this greeting, but as a pastor's wife I can tell you that pastoring requires a lot of mercy. To shepherd sheep necessitates a great deal of mercy and Paul knew that, because he had himself founded many churches; he knew that Timothy also would need mercy as a pastor, especially because of the false teachers invading the church at Ephesus.

Paul begins his triad with the greeting of *grace.* When Paul uses this word grace, it is in reference to God's free gift of salvation to depraved mankind. Paul certainly never got over the fact that God reached down and drew him to Himself. In his own estimation, Paul saw himself as the chief of sinners (see 1 Timothy 1:12-17; 1 Corinthians 15: 9-10; Ephesians 3:6-8). I fear that many of us have "gotten over" the fact that God saved us and many of us think we deserve salvation. My friend, nothing could be further from the truth! We should never get over the fact that God's grace has saved us.

2 Susan Heck, *A Call to Discipleship* (Bemidji: Focus Publishing, 2012), 3.

Paul mentions *mercy* in his greeting. Mercy is shown from one person to another and involves acts of pity directed toward someone in need. One man describes it as an "emotional response to a bad situation."[3] And, as we mentioned already, Timothy would need a lot of mercy in pastoring the church at Ephesus. They are the congregation John mentions in Revelation that lost their first love (Revelation 2:4). There is nothing more heartbreaking than to be in a church full of people who aren't passionate about their relationship with Christ.

Peace is the third part of Paul's greeting, and peace comes from knowing God. It isn't necessarily emotional, but it is a reality. Peace is a by-product of our salvation, and it is part of the fruit of the Spirit. As believers in Jesus Christ, it is essential that we have all three of these—grace, mercy, and peace—present in our lives, but it is especially essential for those in leadership because they desperately need these qualities as they shepherd the sheep. And note, these three things can only come *from God our Father and Jesus Christ our Lord.* As one man has said, "With these three terms, then, Paul greets Timothy and the church: grace—God's ongoing forgiveness and enabling, mercy—God's sympathy and concern, peace—God's tranquility and stability within and among them as individuals and as a Christian community."[4] It's also interesting that just as Paul is a spiritual father to Timothy, his son, God is the Father of His Son Jesus Christ. All four are mentioned in this opening of this letter!

So, who is this spiritual son and what do we learn about him? Timothy is Paul's spiritual son and we learn that he is genuine and that he is a believer in the Lord Jesus Christ. What do we learn about our Heavenly Father from this verse? We learn that grace, mercy, and peace come from Him, that He is God our Father, and that His Son is Jesus Christ our Lord.

---

3 William D Mounce, *Word Biblical Commentary* (Nashville: Thomas Nelson Publishers, 2000), 3.

4 George W. Knight III, *The New International Greek Testament Commentary: The Pastoral Epistles* (Grand Rapids: Wm. B. Eerdmans Publishing Co., 1996), pg 67.

Summary

As we close this first lesson on this letter to a spiritual son from a spiritual father, a number of questions come to mind: Who are your spiritual mothers, and what have you gleaned from them? Who are your spiritual daughters, and what have you gleaned from them? If you were facing your final days, what things would you want to pass on to those whom you have poured your life into? What things would be most important to you to pass on to those whom you disciple?

For the apostle Paul, the important issues to pass on to Timothy are those of eternal value. In fact, Paul will write to Timothy in 2 Timothy 2:1-2, "You therefore, my son, be strong in the grace that is in Christ Jesus. And the things that you have heard from me among many witnesses, commit these to faithful men who will be able to teach others also." For Paul, he wants to leave Timothy instructions for things that matter:

- Instead of warning him about how to survive a natural disaster should one occur, Paul warns Timothy about how to survive false teachers and how to confront them.

- Instead of building Timothy's self-esteem, Paul writes about how humbling it is that God would choose any of us.

- Instead of exalting himself and all his accomplishments as an apostle, Paul exalts and lifts up the King eternal, the only wise God.

- Instead of writing political jargon about how corrupt the government is, Paul writes about our biblical responsibility to pray and give thanks for it.

- Instead of writing about how Timothy needs to get with the seeker-friendly church, Paul writes about the importance of the God-given roles of males and females within the church.

- Instead of telling Timothy to just pick any warm body to lead the church, Paul gives specific guidelines regarding how to choose godly men for leadership.

- Instead of telling Timothy to make sure he follows the latest health fads, diet trends, and exercise techniques so he can be in shape for the pastorate, Paul warns Timothy of the danger of promoting these types of things and calls them doctrines of demons.

- Instead of encouraging Timothy to minimize his sin and give in to culture change, Paul charges Timothy to be an exemplary example by waging war against sin.

- Instead of encouraging him to put older people in nursing homes, Paul gives instruction on how the church is to care for the aged.

- Instead of telling Timothy to make sure he climbs the success ladder in ministry and sends his resume to the finest churches so that he can live in luxury, Paul warns Timothy of the dangers of riches and the love of money.

- Instead of telling Timothy he will never be happy unless he accumulates more and better material stuff, Paul lovingly tells Timothy that food and clothing are really all he needs for genuine contentment.

All these things, and much more, are written by a loving spiritual father to his true son in the faith. Paul genuinely loves his son. And Paul loves the churches that he started, specifically here the church at Ephesus. And he knew that Timothy would need these specific helps as he goes about the work of "With the Master Shepherding the Sheep."

Questions to Consider

1 Timothy 1:1-2
The Beginning of a Letter from a Father to a Son

1. (a) Read 1 Timothy and write down what you think is the theme of the book. (b) If you were Timothy, what thoughts might you have as you read this epistle from your father in the faith, the apostle Paul?

2. Memorize 1 Timothy 1:1-2.

3. (a) When did Paul first meet Timothy, according to Acts 16:1-3? (b) What do you learn about Timothy from this passage?

4. (a) What else do you learn about Timothy from the following passages? Acts 17:14-15; 18:5; 19:22; 20:4; Romans 16:21; 1 Corinthians 4:14-17; 16:10; 2 Corinthians 1:1, 19; Philippians 1:1; 2:19-22; Colossians 1:1; 1 Thessalonians 1:1; 3:2; 3:6; 2 Thessalonians 1:1; 1 Timothy 1:1-3, 18; 6:20; Philemon 1:1; and Hebrews 13:23. (b) After reading these verses, how would you describe Timothy?

5. (a) Paul calls Timothy a true son in the faith. Who do you consider to be your "daughters in the faith," and what have you learned from them? (b) Who do you consider to be your "mothers in the faith," and what have you gleaned from them?

6. Paul makes it clear in the introduction to his epistle that Christ is our hope. Is Christ alone your hope? Have you made that commitment to follow His Lordship and to place your trust in Him alone? Are you relying on Him alone for your redemption? If He was all you had in this life, would He be enough?

7. What would you like to gain from this study? Please write down your desire in the form of a prayer request to share with your group. (I would also encourage you to memorize this precious and rich epistle, as it is written toward the end of Paul's life from the heart of a father to his son in the faith, Timothy.)

Chapter 2

What Good is the Law Anyway?

1 Timothy 1:3-11

Charles Haddon Spurgeon once said that "new doctrine is dangerous doctrine."[5] As we consider the many new and novel ideas that are popular within the church today, most would fall under the category of "dangerous." Most of these ideas are not from God but from man, tickling the ears and promoting selfish thinking and living. There's the emergent movement, the postmodern movement, the seeker-friendly movement, the narcissistic movement, and on and on with all the "movements" making headway into the church. In fact, it is almost impossible to keep up with all the trends.

As we reflect on these trends, we may be prone to think that these new and novel ideas are things the church hasn't yet faced, but nothing could be further from the truth; new, novel, and false ideas are as old as Adam and Eve. What is going on in the church today is no different than what was going on in the church at Ephesus in the days of Paul and Timothy. It is the same false doctrine, packaged a little differently than it was in the 1st century. In this letter, Paul warns Timothy and the church at Ephesus regarding these nonsense ideas and what happens to those who buy into them. But Paul also encourages those who are true to sound doctrine by reminding them that their lives will produce something that is pure, genuine, and real—love. Let's listen in to what Paul has to say in 1 Timothy 1:3-11.

1 Timothy 1:3-11

> As I urged you when I went into Macedonia—remain in Ephesus
> that you may charge some that they teach no other doctrine,

---

5 Charles Haddon Spurgeon, *Metropolitan Tabernacle Pulpit*, 39:434.

> ⁴nor give heed to fables and endless genealogies, which cause disputes rather than godly edification which is in faith. ⁵ Now the purpose of the commandment is love from a pure heart, from a good conscience, and from sincere faith, ⁶from which some, having strayed, have turned aside to idle talk, ⁷desiring to be teachers of the law, understanding neither what they say nor the things which they affirm. ⁸But we know that the law is good if one uses it lawfully, ⁹knowing this: that the law is not made for a righteous person, but for the lawless and insubordinate, for the ungodly and for sinners, for the unholy and profane, for murderers of fathers and murderers of mothers, for manslayers, ¹⁰for fornicators, for sodomites, for kidnappers, for liars, for perjurers, and if there is any other thing that is contrary to sound doctrine, ¹¹according to the glorious gospel of the blessed God which was committed to my trust.

As we consider these verses, we will see that Paul writes regarding two main themes:

The Wrong Use of the Law (vs 3-7) and
The Right Use of the Law (vs 8-11).

As we consider false teaching versus sound teaching, we have to keep in mind that those who teach anything other than the truth of God's Word are teaching false doctrine and are using the law—which is everything God has said—in a wrong way, an evil way. However, those who are teaching sound doctrine are using the law of God in the right way. Let's begin by looking at the wrong use of the law.

The Wrong Use of the Law

1 Timothy 1:3-7

> As I urged you when I went into Macedonia—remain in Ephesus that you may charge some that they teach no other doctrine (1 Timothy 1:3)

As mentioned in our last lesson, Paul and Timothy were ministering together at Ephesus. We're not certain of why Paul went into

Macedonia, but when we read Acts 19, we learn that there had been quite a bit of confusion since people were turning from their idols to God because of Paul's teaching. The makers of those idols were upset because their means of earning income seemed to be coming to a halt. There was a huge uproar in Ephesus regarding the goddess Diana, and Acts 20:1 says, "After the uproar had ceased, Paul called the disciples to himself, embraced them, and departed to go to Macedonia." Paul did not take Timothy along but wanted him to remain in Ephesus. He said, *"I urged you"* Timothy, even though I had to leave Ephesus and go to Macedonia, to *"remain in Ephesus"* and minister there. The word *urged* means to beg, entreat, implore. We might think it a bit odd that Paul had to beg Timothy to stay in Ephesus and minister there, but remember that Timothy was young at this time, perhaps between 25-35 years of age (see 4:12, "let no one despise your youth"), and he also had an issue with fear. This is evident from 2 Timothy 1:7, where Paul says, "For God has not given us a spirit of fear, but of power and of love and of a sound mind." It is possible that Timothy's fear was what gave him stomach problems; Paul tells him in 5:23, "No longer drink only water, but use a little wine for your stomach's sake and your frequent infirmities." For these two reasons, youth and fear, and perhaps others, Timothy may have felt inadequate to handle the challenges of ministry in Ephesus. Ministering in Ephesus had the potential to be a little bit frightening for Timothy, but Paul continued to write to him about how this should be done. In fact, in chapter five, Paul instructs Timothy regarding how to go about confronting those who are older than he: "Do not rebuke an older man, but exhort him as a father, younger men as brothers, older women as mothers, younger women as sisters, with all purity."

Paul tells Timothy that he is leaving him in Ephesus for the purpose of refuting sound doctrine. He says *charge some that they teach no other doctrine. Charge* means command, and, specifically, it's the command from a superior to an inferior. The word *some* here refers, more than likely, to the elders at Ephesus. Paul will mention two of them in verse 20. (Remember, Paul had warned the leaders at Ephesus that *some* of them would get caught up in false teaching;

17

Acts 20:29-31 says, "For I know this, that after my departure savage wolves will come in among you, not sparing the flock. Also from among yourselves men will rise up, speaking perverse things, to draw away the disciples after themselves. Therefore watch, and remember that for three years I did not cease to warn everyone night and day with tears.") He wanted Timothy to not be fearful, and neither should we! Timothy needed to be bold, and even though his mentor wasn't there, this was a charge he needed to fulfill. Mentors are God-given and rich blessings, but there does come a time when we all have to stand on our own spiritual feet, just as in the physical realm there comes a time when we have to let go of our children so they can learn to stand alone. Paul gives a similar charge to Titus, another son in the faith, in Titus 1:10-16:

> For there are many rebellious people, mere talkers and deceivers, especially those of the circumcision group. They must be silenced, because they are ruining whole households by teaching things they ought not to teach—and that for the sake of dishonest gain. Even one of their own prophets has said, 'Cretans are always liars, evil brutes, lazy gluttons.' This testimony is true. Therefore, rebuke them sharply, so that they will be sound in the faith and will pay no attention to Jewish myths or to the commands of those who reject the truth. To the pure, all things are pure, but to those who are corrupted and do not believe, nothing is pure. In fact, both their minds and consciences are corrupted. They claim to know God, but by their actions they deny him. They are detestable, disobedient and unfit for doing anything good.

In verse 4 of our text, Paul goes on to say what kind of false doctrine they were teaching.

> nor give heed to fables and endless genealogies, which cause disputes rather than godly edification which is in faith. (1 Timothy 1:4)

Evidently these false teachers were caught up in *fables and endless genealogies*. Fables, of course, are not founded on facts, and yet those who heed them would claim them to be true. In reality, such fables are superstitious and man-made; we might call them "old wives' tales." Their *genealogies* are *endless*, Paul says. One man helps us here by describing how this would happen:

> It is a known fact from early times the rabbis would 'spin their yarns' and endless yarns they were!—on the basis of what they considered some 'hint' supplied by the Old Testament. They would take a name from a list of pedigrees (for example, from Genesis, 1 Chronicles, Ezra, Nehemiah), and expand it into a nice story. Such interminable embroideries on the inspired record were part of the regular bill of fare in the synagogue, and were subsequently deposited in written form in that portion of *The Talmud* which is known as *Haggadah*.[6]

Jews prided themselves in their genealogies, but as you can imagine, keeping records was not always perfect and precise and so they would be endless. "Are you related to so and so?" "Are you in the lineage of Messiah?" Can you imagine the endless questions that would come up that would lead to nothing but vanity?

Paul mentions this to Titus as well in Titus 3:9 where he warns, "But avoid foolish disputes, genealogies, contentions, and strivings about the law; for they are unprofitable and useless." This type of nonsense only leads to vain pursuits and pride. Maybe you're wondering why this is harmful or wrong for a believer. Why can't we pursue these types of things? Paul says because they *cause disputes rather than godly edification which is in faith*! Fables and endless genealogies are not based on Scripture and lead to arguing and not to godly edification. We may not be that concerned about fables and genealogies, but our age has its own novelties, whether it be all the people who claim to have gone to Heaven and back; the Da Vinci Code; the prosperity gospel; mysticism; prayer circles; or the like. I think a good principle to keep in mind when participating in anything would be to ask if it leads me to sinful responses or does it promote godliness? James gives us some food for thought in James 3:13-18,

---

6 William Hendriksen, *New Testament Commentary: Exposition of the Pastoral Epistles* (Grand Rapids: Baker Book House, 1957), 58-59.

> Who is wise and understanding among you? Let him show by good conduct that his works are done in the meekness of wisdom. But if you have bitter envy and self-seeking in your hearts, do not boast and lie against the truth. This wisdom does not descend from above, but is earthly, sensual, demonic. For where envy and self-seeking exist, confusion and every evil thing are there. But the wisdom that is from above is first pure, then peaceable, gentle, willing to yield, full of mercy and good fruits, without partiality and without hypocrisy. Now the fruit of righteousness is sown in peace by those who make peace.

The scribes and Pharisees were a good example of this; Jesus mentions in Matthew 23 that they wiggled out of their vows, their responsibilities to their parents, and the like, in order to justify their religious duties. Jesus tells them that they omitted the real use of the law, that of mercy, justice, and faith. My dear sister, be aware and be watchful, as Christendom is looking for the new and novel—as if we have mastered the 66 books in the sacred library! Seriously! Instead of being caught up in such nonsense, Paul tells us what genuine believers should be about in verse 5.

> Now the purpose of the commandment is love from a pure
> heart, from a good conscience, and from sincere faith,
> (1 Timothy 1:5)

Verse 5 is in sharp contrast to verse 4. Instead of teaching false doctrine, instead of talking about stuff that is foolish and creates strife, here we have those who have pure hearts, good consciences, and sincere faith. This is *the purpose of the commandment*, which is *love*. The *purpose* of the law—which, by the way, is not just the 10 commandments, but all of God's Word—is not to create disputes but to create love.

Notice here that love produces three things: *a pure heart* and *a good conscience* and *sincere faith*. *A pure heart* refers to a man's moral affection. Jesus says in the Sermon on the Mount, in Matthew 5:8, "Blessed are the pure in heart, for they shall see God." *A good conscience* is a conscience that is free from guilt. Even Paul, in Acts 24:16 said he strove to have a good conscience before God and man. *Sincere faith* is faith that is not hypocritical. False teachers do not possess these things but instead have impure hearts, soiled consciences, and false faith, as Jude says: "These are sensual persons, who cause divisions, not having the Spirit" (Jude 19). It is obvious from Paul's next sentence that this is indeed true, that not all have love from a pure heart and not all have a good conscience,

> from which some, having strayed, have turned aside to idle talk
> (1 Timothy 1:6)

The *some* mentioned in verse 3 are the same *some* who have *strayed*, according to verse 6. Strayed means to have missed the mark. "They are like marksman who miss their target, like travelers who never reach their destination because they have taken the wrong turn and have failed to look for familiar signs along the road."[7] (Again, it's like the scribes and Pharisees whom Jesus calls blind guides, hypocrites, and fools in Matthew 23.) These false teachers have missed out on the proper use of God's Word and instead *have turned aside to idle talk*, or idle chatter. These are words that are of no profit and make no sense, which goes back to what Paul has just said about their fables and endless genealogies. That indeed is the speech of a false teacher.

Not long before I wrote this lesson, I had this very thing illustrated to me when my then 96-year-old father suffered a series of strokes. I noticed that most of what he said to me made no sense and was only mumbled words, but every once in a while, his words made sense to me. I don't know about you, but it's the same thing I think when I listen to a false teacher! Most of what they're saying makes no sense to me, but every once in a while, they say a sentence or two that seems logical. Idle talk isn't the only thing they're involved in. They also want to be teachers when they have no business being teachers of God's Word, as Paul says in verse 7.

> desiring to be teachers of the law, understanding neither what
> they say nor the things which they affirm. (1 Timothy 1:7)

---

7 Ibid, 63.

They want to be recognized as Rabbis, which is what *teachers of the law* are. They want the praise of men more than the praise of God. No wonder James says, in James 3:1 that we should not rush into the office of a teacher! Paul says here what he just said in verse 6, only in a different way, that is, *understanding neither what they say nor the things which they affirm*. I don't know about you but when I tune in to listen to a false teacher, which isn't often, I find myself thinking, "What are they saying?! They make no sense!" and that's usually followed up with, "I can't believe all those people in the audience drinking this nonsense like water!" And then I remind myself of what Peter says in his second epistle: "Many follow their pernicious ways!" (2 Peter 2:2). The wrong use of the law can be summed up as this: using it to get caught up in foolish talk and foolish pursuits which only lead to foolish arguments.

We might wonder, "If so many are using the law wrongly, why don't we just abandon it altogether?" Perhaps Paul even predicts this argument; he moves on to remind his audience that the law is good if it is used rightly. Isn't that the way it is with a lot of things? Used rightly, a great many things are good, but those very things can go bad when used wrongfully (i.e., food, sex, social media, etc.).

The Right Use of the Law

1 Timothy 1:8-11

> But we know that the law is good if one uses it lawfully,
> (1 Timothy 1:8)

But is a word of contrast. Paul says that the *law is good*, but it must be used right. I remember, a while back, I was taking my dad somewhere in the car and ran a stop sign in a parking lot. My dad graciously asked, "Since when did a stop sign cease to be a stop sign?" The law is good if you use it lawfully; but if you don't use it, you wind up in trouble! In contrast to those who are saying things they don't understand or can't affirm, we have those who *use* the law *lawfully*. What does it mean that *the law is good if one uses it*

lawfully? It means to use the law for what it was intended for—to bring us to Christ. It is not to be used to place us in bondage, as the Judaizers taught, and it is not to be used for fables and endless questions, which only lead us to arguments; it is intended to lead us to Christ. Paul explains in the next verse.

> knowing this: that the law is not made for a righteous person, but for the lawless and insubordinate, for the ungodly and for sinners, for the unholy and profane, for murderers of fathers and murderers of mothers, for manslayers, (1 Timothy 1:9)

This is what Paul wants us to know: *the law is not made for a righteous person.* What does that mean? It means that the law is not for those who are *righteous*; it is made for sinners, and all of us are sinners. We might understand this better with this illustration: The laws of the land are indeed for all of us, but who needs them the most? Those whose hearts are corrupt and whose motives are evil. Those who murder, steal, and otherwise break the law. They need the law so that they can be caught and punished for what they've done. In the same way, God's law is intended for those who are unrighteous. Paul gives a long list of those for whom the law is made. First, it is made for those who are *lawless and insubordinate.* The *lawless* are those who do not want to be bound by any law and act as if there is no law. The *insubordinate* are those who live and act as if they are under no authority. It is also *for the ungodly and for sinners.* The *ungodly* are those who do not honor God. *Sinners* are those who transgress the law or commit any type of sin. It's also for *the unholy and profane. The unholy* means those who are unclean, and *profane* means those who are scoffers, those who are careless of their responsibilities towards God. The law is also *for murder of fathers and murders of mothers.* To murder one's parent is unthinkable, and yet we are certainly seeing more and more of this in our age. The way the Greek reads here is "murderers of fathers and yet, as low as it is, even murderers of mothers." To kill the very one who gave birth to you is unthinkable! And then Paul adds *manslayers*; yes, the law is for them too. If this isn't enough, Paul goes on to others who need the law in verse 10.

> for fornicators, for sodomites, for kidnappers, for liars, for perjurers, and if there is any other thing that is contrary to sound doctrine, (1 Timothy 1:10)

A *fornicator* is one who commits any act of sexual sin, and a *sodomite* is a homosexual. *Kidnappers* are those who steal people; the word literally means to "catch a man by the foot." *Liars* are those who tell untruths, and *perjurers* are those who swear falsely. Maybe you're thinking, "Wow, I don't do any of that stuff!" Well, the bar is raised higher with the next phrase: *and if there is any other thing that is contrary to sound doctrine.* Every sin is a sin against sound doctrine, because as every sin we commit is opposed to God's law. *Sound doctrine* has the idea of healthy doctrine, healthy teaching, that promotes our spiritual health. Oh, my friend, how can we not think that sound doctrine is essential for believers?! Paul knows it's essential; he knows how precious it is, as evidenced by what he says in the next verse.

> according to the glorious gospel of the blessed God which was committed to my trust. (1 Timothy 1:11)

"By calling it 'the gospel of glory,' that is, 'the glorious gospel,' he sharply rebukes those who labored to degrade the gospel, in which God displays His glory."[8] Paul is saying that if you want to be a teacher of the law, the best way to explain the law is to preach the gospel and live the gospel. How can we degrade the glorious gospel by using it for such nonsense like fables and endless genealogies?! Paul writes in Galatians 1:8 that if anyone teaches anything but this glorious gospel, they are cursed! The One who invented the law is the very One who sent His Son to fulfill the law—and this was committed to Paul's trust (see 1 Corinthians 9:17; Galatians 2:7; 1 Thessalonians 2:4). And Paul never seemed to get over this, as we'll see in our next lesson.

---

8   John Calvin,*Calvin's Commentaries, Volume XXI* (Grand Rapids: Baker Book House Co., 1981), 33.

Summary

When we put all of this together, we see: *The Wrong Use of the Law* (vs 3-7) is using it for the purpose of getting caught up in foolish talk and foolish pursuits, which lead only to foolish arguments. We see this today, and it's expanding rapidly. For example, more and more people are using the Bible for their own means and, in so doing, making Christians look like fools.

Let me ask you, my friend, are you guilty of being enticed by new and novel ideas in the church today? Do you spend as much time in God's Word as you do in reading people's blogs and books? Are you guilty of spending your time in foolish pursuits which lead to arguments and dissension? How much time do you spend on social media, meddling in other people's business, in comparison to getting face to face with the living God in His Word and in prayer?

We also see: *The Right Use of the Law* (vs 8-11) is using it for the purpose of getting caught up in wise talk and loving others, which leads to godly edification. Let me ask you, again, dear one, are you using the law in a righteous manner by reading it, studying it, memorizing it, talking about it day and night to your children and to those with whom you come in contact? Is your speech that of the Proverbs 31 woman, who speaks with wisdom and kindness? Does your speech and do your works lead to godly edification? Are you in a church that is teaching sound doctrine?

We have a choice to make: We can echo with our brother, Charles Spurgeon, that new doctrine is dangerous doctrine, and the result will be our pursuing God's Word and obeying it, leading to eternal life. Or we can echo with someone who is not our brother, who is likely in eternal hell right now, Sigmund Freud, who said, "Religious doctrines are illusions," and the result will be our pursuing foolish things, which will only lead us to destruction! May our Good Shepherd help us as we pursue a right use of God's Word for His glory and for the edification of the body of Christ!

Questions to Consider

What Good is the Law Anyway?
1 Timothy 1:3-11

1. Read 1 Timothy 1:3-11, along with 1 Timothy 4:12. Then read Acts 19:21-20:1, which is the account of what happened before Paul left Timothy at Ephesus. What do you think was going through Timothy's mind as he read these words from Paul in 1 Timothy 1?

2. Memorize 1 Timothy 1:5-6.

3. (a) In these verses, Paul emphasizes the importance of avoiding fables and genealogies. What are the dangers of getting caught up in these things, according to 1 Timothy 6:3-4; 6:20; 2 Timothy 2:14-19; and Titus 1:10-16; 3:9-11. (b) What should we be doing instead, according to 1 Timothy 4:7; 6:20; 2 Timothy 2:14-19; 4:2-5; Titus 1:10-16; 3:9-11; and Hebrews 13:9. (c) How do you avoid novel ideas that well-meaning Christians try to convince you of? (d) What are some practical ways we can pursue sound teaching instead of these false ideas?

4. (a) Read 1 Timothy 1:8-11, along with Exodus 20:1-17. What similarities do you notice between these passages? (b) What do you think Paul meant, in 1 Timothy 1:9, when he said that the law was not made for a righteous man?

5. (a) Paul calls the gospel "glorious" in 1 Timothy 1:11. What else is the gospel called in Matthew 4:23; Romans 1:9, 16; 2:16; 10:15; 15:16; 2 Corinthians 2:12; Galatians 1:6; Ephesians 6:15; 1 Thessalonians 2:2; Revelation 14:6? (b) How would you describe the gospel?

6. (a) Is it a loving thing to confront those who are caught up in fables and idle chatter? Why or why not? (b) Do you think pastors should publicly confront false teachers? Why or why not?

7. Do you know anyone who has been caught up in erroneous teaching? Will you lovingly confront them and show them the truth from God's Word?

8. Are you shunning all forms of false teaching? Are you pursuing sound doctrine? Please write any need in the form of a prayer request.

Chapter 3

Amazing Grace that Saved
a Wretch like Paul!

1 Timothy 1:12-17

Many years ago, while my son was attending seminary, he and some of his friends decided that they would "check out" Robert Schuller's church to see what it was all about. Robert Schuller was a televangelist, pastor, and motivational speaker. His ministry was housed in a great crystal cathedral in California in the last century. I remember discussing with my son what took place in the service, and he related to me how the congregation had been led in a song about how great they were! How great I am?! Of course, this isn't at all surprising when we consider Roberts Schuller's "theology." He didn't believe in sermons about sin because he felt they were offensive. He deliberately avoided condemning people for sin; in fact, Schuller defined sin as any act or thought that robs myself or another human being of his or her self-esteem. He also encouraged Christians (and non-Christians) to achieve great things through God and to believe in their dreams; he believed that if you can dream it, you can do it! He defined salvation as a change from a negative self-image to a positive self-image—from inferiority to self-esteem, from fear to love, from doubt to trust. This is quite a contrast from what the apostle Paul says about sin, about himself, and about salvation! Let's read 1 Timothy 1:12-17 and notice the stark contrast between the apostle Paul and Robert Schuller!

1 Timothy 1:12-17

> And I thank Christ Jesus our Lord who has enabled me, because He counted me faithful, putting me into the ministry, [13]although I was formerly a blasphemer, a persecutor, and an insolent man but I obtained mercy because I did it ignorantly in unbelief. [14]And the grace of our Lord was exceedingly abundant, with

faith and love which are in Christ Jesus. [15]This is a faithful saying and worthy of all acceptance, that Christ Jesus came into the world to save sinners, of whom I am chief. [16]However, for this reason I obtained mercy, that in me first Jesus Christ might show all longsuffering, as a pattern to those who are going to believe on Him for everlasting life. [17]Now to the King eternal, immortal, invisible, to God who alone is wise, be honor and glory forever and ever. Amen.

In this lesson, we will see:

Paul's Thankful Heart (v 12);
Paul's Wicked Past (v 13);
God's Abundant Grace (vv 14-16); and
God's Awesome Attributes (v 17).

Paul's mention of the glorious gospel, in the previous verses, reminds him of the fact that this glorious gospel saved him and gave him a purpose: giving back to the Lord by serving Him! You might think it odd that Paul shares a personal testimony of his salvation sandwiched between writing about false teachers. But when you take some time to consider it, you find that it's not so strange. It's as if Paul is telling Timothy that the right use of the law—the glorious gospel—transforms one's life; it certainly does not lead one to getting caught up in false teaching. Paul knows that the gospel transforms one's life because before Christ saved him, Paul's life certainly fit the list of sins we looked at in our last lesson. False teachers know nothing of the grace of God that Paul had experienced. And because of that grace, Paul's heart is filled with thanksgiving, as we can clearly see in his opening statement:

Paul's Thankful Heart

1 Timothy 1:12

And I thank Christ Jesus our Lord who has enabled me, because He counted me faithful, putting me into the ministry, (1 Timothy 1:12)

Notice, first of all, who Paul is thankful to—*Christ Jesus our Lord*. Rarely do we hear false teachers giving thanks to God; more often than not, their praise goes to themselves for their own abilities or cleverness. But not so with Paul. He is thankful to the *Lord*, and the Greek rendering indicates that this is a continual thankfulness Paul is expressing. We should be in a continual attitude of thankfulness for our salvation and for what God has done in our lives. Paul says it was the Lord who *enabled* him and put him *into the ministry*. To *enable* means to empower or to give one ability or strength. Paul knew this enabling did not come from some inner strength he possessed but from God alone. By the way, do you know the ministry that God has called you to and are you thankful for it? What a joy to be called by the Lord and to be counted as faithful for His service!

Paul writes that he was *counted faithful*, which means that he was considered as trustworthy. This does not mean that God chooses us based on our worthiness. As Augustine said, "God does not choose anyone who is worthy, but in choosing him renders him worthy."[9] Of course, there is a sense in which, after conversion, we are faithful to do the work that God has called us to do. In fact, in his second epistle to Timothy, Paul will exhort Timothy to pass on to faithful men the things that he has learned from Paul (2 Timothy 2:2). Faithfulness is essential in the work of the Lord. My friend, can God say that about you—that you are faithful? Do others say that about you? Are you faithful?

Paul was also trustworthy in the ministry. This *ministry* Paul speaks of is service; it is waiting on others, like waiters wait on tables. There is nothing self-glorifying in that! Our ministry is to benefit others, not ourselves. Jesus Himself said, in Mark 10:45, "For even the Son of Man did not come to be served, but to serve, and to give His life a ransom for many." Are you pouring your life out in whatever the Lord wants you to do? We should think often of our life before Christ, remembering our wretchedness, remembering where we have come from and what God has done to save wretches

---

9 Mounce, William D.; Word Biblical Commentary, Volume 46; (Nashville, Thomas Nelson Publishers, 2000); pg. 51.

like us; this will keep our lives in proper perspective for faithful service to the Lord and to others. Do you also have a thankful heart? Paul certainly had a thankful heart, and he evidently reflected often on his life before Christ. In verse 13, he moves from expressing his thankful heart to explaining his wicked past.

Paul's Wicked Past

1 Timothy 1:13

> although I was formerly a blasphemer, a persecutor, and an insolent man; but I obtained mercy because I did it ignorantly in unbelief. (1 Timothy 1:13)

We should make a serious notation here that Paul says he was *formerly* involved in all these things and not currently involved in them! Oh, my friend, how we need to remember that we are not bound to sin, that Christ has come to set us free from sin. Sin no longer has mastery over us because the gospel has transforming power over us! Paul makes it clear in numerous places that if we think we can retain our sin and possess everlasting life, then we are mistaken! He says in Galatians 5:19-21,

> Now the works of the flesh are evident, which are: adultery, fornication, uncleanness, lewdness, idolatry, sorcery, hatred, contentions, jealousies, outbursts of wrath, selfish ambitions, dissensions, heresies, envy, murders, drunkenness, revelries, and the like; of which I tell you beforehand, just as I also told you in time past, that those who practice such things will not inherit the kingdom of God.

And again, in 1 Corinthians 6:9-11,

> Do you not know that the unrighteous will not inherit the kingdom of God? Do not be deceived. Neither fornicators, nor idolaters, nor adulterers, nor homosexuals, nor sodomites, nor thieves, nor covetous, nor drunkards, nor revilers, nor extortioners will inherit the kingdom of God. And such were some of you. But you were washed, but you were sanctified,

but you were justified in the name of the Lord Jesus and by the Spirit of our God.

Here in 1 Timothy, Paul lists some of the sins from which Christ came to save him. The first sin Paul mentions is that he was *a blasphemer*, which is one who slanders and abuses others with their speech. Paul's blaspheming was toward the Lord. Just the week before I wrote this lesson, there was a satanic black mass in a nearby city. The local newspaper ran an article explaining what would take place there: there would be a denouncing of Jesus Christ, a swearing of allegiance to the devil, and blasphemy against Christ. This, Paul says, is what he was before Christ. Second, Paul says that he was *a persecutor*. This word is only used here in the New Testament, and it describes someone who chases Christians like they would wild animals. Luke tells us, in Acts 8:3, that Paul actually went from house to house dragging men and women out of their homes and putting them in prison. He chased after them like wild animals. Third, Paul says he was *an insolent man*. This is the strongest of the three terms, and it means that Paul was proud, malicious, and outraged. When he was standing before King Agrippa, in Acts 26, Paul says this about himself, in verses 9-11:

> Indeed, I myself thought I must do many things contrary to the name of Jesus of Nazareth. This I also did in Jerusalem, and many of the saints I shut up in prison, having received authority from the chief priests; and when they were put to death, I cast my vote against them. And I punished them often in every synagogue and compelled them to blaspheme; and being exceedingly enraged against them, I persecuted them even to foreign cities.

We might read this and think this guy needs to be locked up in prison somewhere. He sounds like he's ready to join a terrorist organization; they seem to enjoy killing Christians. It certainly doesn't sound like there's any hope for this guy. But with Christ there is always hope! There is no sin too enormous for God to forgive.

This very thing was illustrated to me in a physical sense the day I wrote this lesson, while I was at the doctor's office with my husband.

He was receiving his first injection in his eye, in the hope that it would prevent him from going blind. While we were conversing with the doctor's assistant, she explained to us that before this new drug came out, they could offer no hope for patients with my husband's condition. They would simply tell them that they were going blind and that they would need to stop driving. But then she said, "Now we can offer hope." Ladies, the same is true in the spiritual sense; before Christ came to die for our sins, there was no hope! We were blind, but now we see!

Paul, like many of us, *obtained mercy*, he says, because he *did it ignorantly in unbelief.* Paul is not excusing his sin; he, himself, would say that he is the chief of sinners and the least of all the apostles. He is saying that he really did not know what he was doing; he was ignorant. In Romans 10:3-4, Paul defines this: "For they being ignorant of God's righteousness, and seeking to establish their own righteousness, have not submitted to the righteousness of God. For Christ is the end of the law for righteousness to everyone who believes." This is similar to what Jesus said on the cross, in Luke 23:34, "Father, forgive them, for they do not know what they do." Or, as Paul says regarding those who killed Jesus in 1 Corinthians 2:8, "which none of the rulers of this age knew; for had they known, they would not have crucified the Lord of glory." They were ignorant and in unbelief, just as Paul had been. But Paul knew that where sin abounds grace abounds even more, so he goes on to write about God's abundant grace in verses 14-16.

God's Abundant Grace

1 Timothy 1:14-16

> And the grace of our Lord was exceedingly abundant, with faith and love which are in Christ Jesus. (1 Timothy 1:14)

Grace was shown to Paul, just as it has been shown to you and to me. *Grace* is God's undeserved favor shown to a guilty sinner. The songwriter put it well: "Marvelous grace of our loving Lord, grace that exceeds our sin and our guilt."[10] Paul says God's grace was not just abundant, but *exceedingly abundant*, which means that it was super-abundant. Along with this grace was the *faith and love which is in Christ Jesus*. It is interesting that Paul mentions three of his gross sins back in verse 13 and now three of God's gracious attributes here in verse 14. Paul clarifies this grace of God, in verse 15.

> This is a faithful saying and worthy of all acceptance, that Christ Jesus came into the world to save sinners, of whom I am chief. (1 Timothy 1:15)

This is a true saying and worthy for everyone to accept. What is this *faithful saying*, this true saying, which is *worthy of all acceptance*? *That Christ Jesus came into the world to save sinners, of whom I am chief.* It is believed that this verse, along with 1 Timothy 3:1 and 4:9-11; 2 Timothy 2:11-13; and Titus 3:8 were sayings or portions of hymns that the early church would sing. In 1 Timothy 3:1, we read, "This is a faithful saying: If a man desires the position of a bishop, he desires a good work." First Timothy 4:9-11 says, "This is a faithful saying and worthy of all acceptance. For to this end we both labor and suffer reproach, because we trust in the living God, who is the Savior of all men, especially of those who believe. These things command and teach." Second Timothy 2:11-13 says, "This is a faithful saying: For if we died with Him, We shall also live with Him. If we endure, we shall also reign with Him. If we deny Him, He also will deny us. If we are faithless, He remains faithful; He cannot deny Himself." And Titus 3:8 reads, "This is a faithful saying, and these things I want you to affirm constantly, that those who have believed in God should be careful to maintain good works. These things are good and profitable to men."

Paul's statement here is much like John's statement, in John 1:29, when he sees Jesus; he says, "Behold! The Lamb of God who takes away the sin of the world!" Both John and Paul are a far cry from our culture, which minimizes and rationalizes its sin. Paul mentions yet another aspect of God's grace, in verse 16.

10   Words by Julia H. Johnston (1911)

> However, for this reason I obtained mercy, that in me first
> Jesus Christ might show all longsuffering, as a pattern to
> those who are going to believe on Him for everlasting life.
> (1 Timothy 1:16)

Paul *obtained mercy* for this reason: that *Jesus Christ might show all longsuffering* to those who will *believe on Him*. Obviously, this is not the only reason that Paul obtained mercy, but it is the reason he mentions here. The *longsuffering* of Christ refers to his forbearance. Paul writes of God's patience in many places, but Romans 2:4 specifically emphasizes this longsuffering of our Savior: "Or do you despise the riches of His goodness, forbearance, and longsuffering, not knowing that the goodness of God leads you to repentance?" Even Peter mentions Paul's writing of this, in 2 Peter 3:15: "and consider that the longsuffering of our Lord is salvation—as also our beloved brother Paul, according to the wisdom given to him, has written to you." Paul wasn't saved for Paul's glory but for God's glory, that His longsuffering might be revealed to all. God's patience is clearly seen in the salvation of a wretch like Paul—and in wretches like us, I might add.

Paul adds that his experience of God's longsuffering is *a pattern to those who are going to believe on Him for everlasting life*. A *pattern* is a sample, and this would certainly be an encouragement to those who, in the future, would believe. As they look at the life of Paul, they will see and be encouraged to learn that God saves even murderers! If God can save Paul, God can save anyone. If God can save David, a murderer and an adulterer, God can save us! If God can save Rahab, a prostitute, then God can save us! In Romans 15:4, Paul says, "For whatever things were written before were written for our learning, that we through the patience and comfort of the Scriptures might have hope." The lives of people like Rahab, David, and Paul are strong examples that bring us hope. If God can save them, He can save us, and He can save all those who will believe in the future. Jesus even mentions those who, in the future, will believe on Him, in His High Priestly Prayer, in John 17:20; He says, "I do not pray for these alone, but also for those who will believe in Me through their word." This belief is only *on Him*; He is the only way to *everlasting life*, which is life eternal. This life eternal, Jesus says, is to know the only true God and Jesus Christ (John 17:3). As Paul reflects on this great salvation that was offered to him, he breaks out into a doxology of praise to this glorious God and mentions several of God's awesome attributes.

God's Awesome Attributes

1 Timothy 1:17

> Now to the King eternal, immortal, invisible, to God who alone is wise, be honor and glory forever and ever. Amen. (1 Timothy 1:17)

It is worthy to note that God gets all the glory for Paul's Damascus road experience. True as it may be that God uses men and women to share the gospel, they are only mouth pieces for Him; He gets all the glory for saving anyone. Notice that Paul doesn't say now unto me but *now to the King*! He doesn't say how great am I but how great is He. This *King* is *eternal*, which means that He has no beginning and no end. He is also *immortal*, which means that He is imperishable and incorruptible and will not decay. Paul mentions also that He is *invisible*, which means that no one can see Him. The Bible is clear: no man has seen God at any time (1 John 4:12). He can, however, be seen through creation, as Paul says in Romans 1:20, "For since the creation of the world His invisible attributes are clearly seen, being understood by the things that are made, even His eternal power and Godhead, so that they are without excuse." Paul also says, here, *to God who alone is wise*, which actually reads "the only God." There is no other. To this God alone, Paul ends his doxology, to Him *be honor and glory forever and ever. Amen.* Forever. For all eternity. For Paul, he would experience life everlasting with the One who alone receives glory forever, the King Eternal.

Summary

Paul's Thankful Heart (v 12): Paul's heart showed forth through Paul's mouth, in giving thanks to God for what He had done in granting Paul such rich salvation. Do you have a thankful heart, especially as it relates to the fact that God has saved you? If your heart is not thankful, your mouth will not be thankful either, because the Scriptures say that out of the abundance of the heart the mouth speaks (Luke 6:45). When was the last time you thanked God for saving your soul?

Paul's Wicked Past (v 13): Paul mentions that before Christ saved him, he was a blasphemer, a persecutor, and an insolent man. What was your life like before Christ saved you? Liar? Cheater? Thief ? Rebel? Sexually perverse? Murderer? Whatever it was, be assured of this: no sin is too awful for God's mercy.

God's Abundant Grace (vs 14-16): God's grace was super-abundant in Paul's life and, my friend, it is also super-abundant in your life. Do you think about that? Do you dwell on God's grace toward you?

God's Awesome Attributes (v 17): Paul finishes expressing his journey in salvation by praising God for His attributes: eternal, immortal, and invisible. What attributes of God stand out in your mind as you dwell on your redemption?

Paul's heart is a far cry from the heart of Robert Schuller and many other false teachers. Paul's heart revealed that it had been thoroughly changed and transformed by the power of God. Paul understood the amazing grace of God that saved a wretch like him. Most of us know that John Newton wrote those words: "Amazing grace—how sweet the sound—that saved a wretch like me! I once was lost but now am found, was blind but now I see." John Newton, like Paul, never got over the wonderful reality that God had saved a wretch like him. He said,

Until the time of his death at the age of 82, John Newton never ceased to marvel at the grace of God that transformed him so completely. Shortly before his death he is quoted as proclaiming with a loud voice during a message, "My memory is nearly gone, but I can remember two things: That I am a great sinner and that Christ is a great Saviour!"[11]

11 Kenneth W. Osbeck, *Amazing Grace* (Grand Rapids: Kregel Publications, 1990), 170.

Questions to Consider

Amazing Grace that Saved a Wretch like Paul!
1 Timothy 1:12-17

1. (a) As you read 1 Timothy 1:12-17, write down all the names of God and attributes of God that you find in the text. (b) What are some of God's other attributes, according to the Scriptures? (Please provide the Scripture reference.) (c) When you combine all these and consider them together, what should be our response to this awesome One who has saved such wretched sinners like us?

2. Memorize 1 Timothy 1:16.

3. (a) Paul mentions briefly what his life was like before Christ, in 1 Timothy 1:14. What do the following passages tell us about the things that Paul participated in before his conversion? Acts 7:57-8:4; 9:1-9; 22:1-5; 26:1-11. (b) How do these Scriptures help you in understanding Timothy 1:12-17?

4. (a) Paul speaks of his life before Christ by saying that he was formerly a blasphemer, a persecutor, and an insolent man. How would you describe your life "before Christ" in three words? (b) How would you describe your life "after Christ" in three words?

5. (a) Pick one of the attributes of God that you see mentioned in 1 Timothy 1:12-17. Using a concordance, look up at least 10 other verses in God's Word that mention that same attribute. What do you learn about this particular attribute of God from what you have looked up? (b) Why do you think it is important to study the attributes of God?

6. (a) How could you use the passage we have studied to encourage someone who perhaps thinks he or she is too wicked for God to save? (b) What other passages could you also use to give that person hope that no sin is too great for God to forgive?

7. Write a prayer of thanksgiving to God for saving you! (You might want to include some of your thoughts from your answer to question 4b.)

Chapter 4

Wage War or Suffer a Shipwreck?

1 Timothy 1:18-20

On April 16, 2014, a South Korean ship sank with hundreds of children on board, many of whom did not grasp the urgency of the situation. Retrieved from the phone of 17-year-old Park Su-hyeon were audio and video recordings which revealed students in a cabin on the ship. On those recordings, one student asks: "Am I going to die?" Another says: "I should leave my final words before I die." Park tells him: "Okay, go ahead now. Here, leave them as my phone is recording." He says: "Please, if only I could live. Mum, dad, I love you." In the background, an announcement can be heard: "Do not move from your current location and be prepared for a dangerous situation." At one point in the clip, a student can be heard asking: "Why are you getting your life jacket?" The child who was putting on the life jacket responds: "You're stupid. We don't want to die. We don't want to die." Three minutes later, another voice can be heard saying: "These are the pictures we need to take as our last memories." At one point, you can even hear them joking with one another, saying "It's like the Titanic," before they proceeded to hum the theme from the 1996 film based on the disaster. When the Titanic sank on April 15, 1912, more than 1500 people perished. April 16, 2014, oddly enough, was the date the Korean ferry sank. There were 475 people on board, 325 of whom were students on a school trip. 302 people died in the disaster.[12]

As tragic as these two disasters are, both of which involved shipwrecks at sea, there is a disaster which is far worse: the shipwreck of one's faith. As Paul writes to his spiritual son Timothy, he mentions two men who suffered such spiritual shipwreck.

1 Timothy 1:18-20

12 http://www.mirror.co.uk/news/world-news/south-korea-ferry-video-inside-3486916#ixzz39v1tRDfx

> This charge I commit to you, son Timothy, according to the prophecies previously made concerning you, that by them you may wage the good warfare, [19]having faith and a good conscience, which some having rejected, concerning the faith have suffered shipwreck, [20]of whom are Hymenaeus and Alexander, whom I delivered to Satan that they may learn not to blaspheme.

In this lesson, we will see:

> *The Mandate to Wage Good Warfare* (v 18);
> *The Means to Wage Good Warfare* (v 19a); and
> *The Misery of Not Waging Good Warfare* (vv 19b-20).

As he ends 1 Timothy 1, Paul still has on his heart the false teachers that are present in the church at Ephesus, and so he reminds Timothy in verse 18 of the charge that had been given to him. He does not want Timothy to defect as others had done. Let's look at the mandate to wage good warfare.

The Mandate to Wage Good Warfare

1 Timothy 1:18

> This charge I commit to you, son Timothy, according to the prophecies previously made concerning you, that by them you may wage the good warfare, (1 Timothy 1:18)

As we begin verse 18, we notice that this is not the first time Paul has given a charge to Timothy. He used the same Greek word back in verse 3 when he mentioned to Timothy the need to charge some to teach sound doctrine. It is interesting that both of these charges have to do with false teachers and doctrine. The word *charge*, remember, is a command; it is not an option. It also has the sense of urgency. And Paul says this charge *I commit to you*, Timothy. The word *commit* has the idea of committing something to someone for the purpose of keeping it safe, like putting a deposit in the bank. It also has a secondary meaning of passing it on to others. In this way, it is like what Paul says to Timothy in 2 Timothy 2:2:"And the things that you have heard from me among many witnesses, commit these to faithful men who will be able to teach others also."

Before he goes on to remind Timothy of what this charge is, Paul calls Timothy his *son*. This is a reminder to Timothy that Paul is his spiritual mentor and has both the authority and the fatherly love and compassion to help his son in the faith. This charge, Paul reminds Timothy, was *according to the prophecies previously made concerning you*. Some have wondered what these prophecies were. It may have been a prophecy given during the apostolic age regarding Timothy; if there was such a prophecy, we have no recording of it in the Bible as we have of the prophecy Christ gave to Paul in Acts 9 on the Damascus road. More than likely, the prophecy mentioned here was Timothy's call to the ministry in Acts 16. In Acts 16:1-5 Luke writes,

> Then he came to Derbe and Lystra. And behold, a certain disciple was there, named Timothy, the son of a certain Jewish woman who believed, but his father was Greek. He was well spoken of by the brethren who were at Lystra and Iconium. Paul wanted to have him go on with him. And he took him and circumcised him because of the Jews who were in that region, for they all knew that his father was Greek. And as they went through the cities, they delivered to them the decrees to keep, which were determined by the apostles and elders at Jerusalem. So the churches were strengthened in the faith, and increased in number daily.

This was the point at which Timothy was called into the ministry, so it could just simply be Paul prophesying (heralding the truth) that Timothy was indeed called into the ministry.

Paul tells Timothy that he is to *wage the good warfare*. My friend, we are in a war. As Warren Wiersbe says, "The Christian life is not a playground; it is a battleground." What is *good warfare*? A person who wages good warfare is someone who does so for righteous reasons, who obeys his Master, who is courageous, who isn't slothful, who never forsakes his post. In fact, Paul gives Timothy other instructions about this warfare in 2 Timothy 2:3-4, when he says, "You therefore must endure hardship as a good soldier of Jesus Christ. No one engaged in warfare entangles himself with the affairs of this life, that he may please him who enlisted him as a soldier." Paul also instructs the church at Corinth about this warfare, and they were certainly in need of this instruction, as they were known for their carnality. In 2 Corinthians 10:3-4, Paul says, "For though we walk in the flesh, we do not war according to the flesh. For the weapons of our warfare are not carnal but mighty in God for pulling down strongholds." In fact, Paul will leave Timothy with these words at the end of this epistle we're studying; in 1 Timothy 6:12, he says, "Fight the good fight of faith, lay hold on eternal life, to which you were also called and have confessed the good confession in the presence of many witnesses." And we know Paul heeded his own advice because right before he was beheaded by Nero, he writes, "I have finished *my* course (KJV). Each one of us should be running our own race and endeavoring to reach the finish line knowing we have fought a good fight and have kept the faith. Having given him the mandate, Paul moves on to give Timothy the means by which he is to wage this warfare. How does one fight in a spiritual battle? In verse 19b, Paul gives us two means by which we can wage good warfare.

The Means to Wage Good Warfare

1 Timothy 1:19a

having faith and a good conscience, (1 Timothy 1:19a)

In the Questions to Consider, you looked at all the armor we are to put on as Christians, in Ephesians 6. Here we see only two things mentioned: *faith and a good conscience*. Why are there only two mentioned here? One man suggests, "whereas in Ephesians 6:10-17 Paul describes in detail the Christian's armor, he confines himself here to two items of equipment which embrace the fundamental aspects of doctrine and practice."[13] But it is certainly interesting that

---

13   Donald Guthrie, *The Pastoral Epistles* (Grand Rapids: Wm. B. Eerdmans Publishing Company, 1979), 68.

Paul's Epistle to the Ephesians is written to the church at Ephesus, and so is 1 Timothy; I guess they got a double teaching!

The two means Paul mentions here of waging good warfare are *faith* and *a good conscience*. The questions come to mind: What is *faith*? Is Paul using it as a term of salvation, or does it mean to be steadfast or trustworthy? The Greek word for *faith* means having moral conviction, especially reliance upon God for salvation. Also, given the context, it is plain to see that Paul is talking about salvation because he goes on to say that some have rejected this faith and he has delivered them over to Satan. These guys were never in the faith! If we are going to be good soldiers, if we're going to wage a legitimate war, then it is imperative that we know what we are fighting for and who we're fighting against. We can't even begin to understand the armor Paul mentions in Ephesians 6 if we don't possess genuine faith. As we already mentioned, Paul will go on to say in the next few verses that some have rejected this faith and have suffered shipwreck. Matthew 13 speaks of those who are interested in spiritual things but when persecution, trials, the cares of this world, or the love of money get in their way, they defect from the faith. They don't fight the good fight of faith; they don't lay hold on eternal life. I know people like this; some of them are my physical family. This is a sobering reminder of my own need to wage war and to have a mentor like Timothy.

Secondly, Paul mentions to Timothy that if he is going to wage war, he must have a *good conscience*. *Conscience* refers to that inner judge that bears witness. Practically speaking, having a good conscience looks something like going through our day asking, "Would Christ do this?" or "Would Christ say this?" or "What does His Word say about this situation?"—and then obeying what we know to be right! It makes sense that if we have the right faith, we will have the right behavior. Right? What we believe dictates how we live. Dear friend, if we are redeemed, we will be sensitive to the Holy Spirit, we will not quench Him or grieve Him, and thus we will not desensitize our consciences. One man tells the following story, entitled "Wrecked through Losing a Good Conscience."

I had a friend who started in commercial life, and as a book merchant, with a high resolve. He said, "In my store there shall be no books that I would not have my family read." Time passed on, and one day I went into his store and found some iniquitous books on the shelf, and I said to him, "How is it possible that you can consent to sell such books as these?" "Oh," he replied, "I have got over those puritanical notions. A man cannot do business in this day unless he does it in the way other people do it." To make a long story short, he lost his hope of Heaven, and in a little while he lost his morality, and then he went into a mad-house. In other words, when a man casts off God, God casts him off.[14]

Not all fight the good fight of faith to lay hold on eternal life; some become castaways and make shipwreck of their faith. So, we turn from the means of waging a good warfare to the misery of not waging good warfare, in the remainder of verse 19 and in verse 20.

The Misery of Not Waging Good Warfare

1 Timothy 1:19b-20

which some having rejected, concerning the faith have suffered shipwreck, (1 Timothy 1:19b)

Paul puts it like this: *some having rejected, concerning the faith have suffered shipwreck.* Some have rejected this faith; some have intentionally not pursued a good conscience. What does it mean that they have *rejected* these things? The word has the idea of thrusting this faith away and implies a willful defiance of their conscience. When you are fighting in a battle you can't throw away your shield or your armor or you'll be defeated. There are some who do this in our day, and there were some who did this in Paul's day. The aged, old apostle John writes about this in 1 John 2:19; where he says, "They went out from us, but they were not of us; for if they had been of us, they would have continued with us; but they went out

---

14 T. De Witt Talmage, "Wrecked Through Losing a Good Conscience" The Biblical Illustrator, Electronic Database. Copyright © 2002, 2003, 2006, 2011 by Biblesoft, Inc. All rights reserved. Used by permission. BibleSoft.com

that they might be made manifest, that none of them were of us." There will always be people who apostatize from the faith. And as we get closer to the end, which I believe we are, we will see a great falling away, as Paul describes in 2 Thessalonians 2:3. Personally, I think it's likely that we are already there, as young and old alike are quickly vacating the church.

Not only are some rejecting the faith and a good conscience, but Paul goes on to say that *concerning the faith* they *have suffered shipwreck.* Paul now shifts from the analogy of fighting in a ground war in the army to that of being in the navy. What does it mean to *suffer shipwreck*? It means to break a ship completely to pieces. It's like the Titanic that struck an iceberg, or the Korean ship that was overloaded; both were destroyed, without any possibility of either being rebuilt. Paul understood the devastation of a shipwreck; he mentions in 2 Corinthians 11:25 that he was shipwrecked three times and even spent a day and night out in the sea. In Acts 27, he gives a fairly detailed description of one of those shipwrecks. But, as bad as Paul's shipwrecks were, or the Titanic or that Korean ship, none were as devastating as a spiritual shipwreck. There is nothing more sobering than to see one destroy their faith by being tossed about by every wind of doctrine, by defiling their conscience, by not waging war against sin, or by any other tactic of the evil one. As Paul closes chapter one of his epistle, he specifically names two men who suffered such shipwreck of their faith. It is indeed a sobering end to this chapter. He says,

> of whom are Hymenaeus and Alexander, whom I delivered to
> Satan that they may learn not to blaspheme. (1 Timothy 1:20)

Evidently, these two men had been leaders in the church. The first one mentioned is *Hymenaeus*, whom Paul also mentions in 2 Timothy 2:16-19:

> But shun profane and idle babblings, for they will increase to
> more ungodliness. And their message will spread like cancer.
> Hymenaeus and Philetus are of this sort, who have strayed
> concerning the truth, saying that the resurrection is already

past; and they overthrow the faith of some. Nevertheless the solid foundation of God stands, having this seal: "The Lord knows those who are His," and, "Let everyone who names the name of Christ depart from iniquity."

The second man Paul mentions is *Alexander* in 2 Timothy 4:14: "Alexander the coppersmith did me much harm. May the Lord repay him according to his works. You also must beware of him, for he has greatly resisted our words." We've already noted from 2 Timothy 2 that Hymenaeus was saying that the resurrection was already past and thereby causing many to shipwreck their faith. This could have been Alexander's error as well. In Matthew 22, Jesus confronts the Sadducees regarding their error concerning the resurrection; He tells them that they're mistaken and do not know the Scriptures nor the power of God. My dear friend, we must be women of the Word! We must not be tossed about by every new and novel idea! It might just be that such teaching could lead to our spiritual devastation, our spiritual shipwreck.

Paul says that he *delivered* these guys *to Satan* so that they would *learn not to blaspheme*. What does it mean that they were *delivered to Satan*? Paul uses this same terminology in 1 Corinthians 5:1-5; there, he says,

> It is actually reported that there is sexual immorality among you, and such sexual immorality as is not even named among the Gentiles—that a man has his father's wife! And you are puffed up, and have not rather mourned, that he who has done this deed might be taken away from among you. For I indeed, as absent in body but present in spirit, have already judged (as though I were present) him who has so done this deed. In the name of our Lord Jesus Christ, when you are gathered together, along with my spirit, with the power of our Lord Jesus Christ, deliver such a one to Satan for the destruction of the flesh, that his spirit may be saved in the day of the Lord Jesus.

This is the process of church discipline, in which one who is willfully unrepentant is excommunicated from the church in hopes that they can be prompted toward repentance and be restored back into the fellowship of the church. In Matthew 18:15-20, Jesus outlines the steps of this process; we won't take time to study that process now, but suffice it to say that this is something all of God's people should follow and all true churches should implement. Unfortunately, we allow many shipwrecked people to sit in our pews while we fail to confront sin and remove the leaven from out of the church. My friend, this does nothing but demoralize the church and weaken the resolve of its members to live in holiness. Ananias and Sapphira, in Acts 5, are two examples of those having been delivered over to Satan. Peter even says to Ananias in verse 3 of that chapter, "Ananias, why has Satan filled your heart to lie to the Holy Spirit and keep back part of the price of the land for yourself?" Judas is another example of one being delivered over to Satan for the destruction of his flesh. In fact, John 13:2 says that Satan put it into Judas' heart to betray Jesus. This is such a sad state! And yet in the years my husband has been pastoring churches, I have witnessed numerous people being given over to Satan for the destruction of their flesh.

Paul says he does this so *that they may learn not to blaspheme*. In other words, so that they will no longer blaspheme the name of God and His Word. This is similar to what Paul tells older and younger women in Titus 2:3-5, where he says,

> the older women likewise, that they be reverent in behavior, not slanderers, not given to much wine, teachers of good things— that they admonish the young women to love their husbands, to love their children, to be discreet, chaste, homemakers, good, obedient to their own husbands, that the word of God may not be blasphemed.

When we as God's daughters do not live out the standards of Titus 2, we blaspheme the Word of God and make it unattractive. There are too many in the church today who are guilty of such blasphemy, who are professing Christ but not living Christ. In our last lesson, remember, Paul called himself a blasphemer; he knew the danger of blaspheming and knew that it was a sin worthy of eternal judgment.

Summary

The Mandate to Wage Good Warfare (v 18). Paul reminds Timothy of the charge to wage war. Are you waging war against sin? Are you fighting the good fight of faith? Do you have a Paul in your life who is frequently reminding you of the importance of pressing on toward the prize?

The Means to Wage Good Warfare (v 19a). The means by which we wage warfare are faith and a good conscience. Do you know for sure that your faith is genuine? Is it possible that you are not an authentic believer? Will you be among those whom John says went out from us for they were never of us, for if they had been of us they would have continued with us? Is your conscience clean and undefiled? Are you making every effort to keep short accounts with God and with man? Is there anyone with whom you need to make restitution?

The Misery of Not Waging Good Warfare (vv 19b-20). What is the misery we risk by not waging good warfare? Rejecting one's faith; suffering disastrous spiritual shipwreck; and being handed over to Satan. Oh, my friend, this is not how you want your life to end; believe me! Being handed over to Satan is being handed over to an eternity in the lake of fire, where there will be weeping and gnashing of teeth.

As dreadful as the disasters of the Titanic and the Korean ships are to us, there is a shipwreck that is far more sobering, the shipwreck of one's faith, one's soul. How fares it with you, my friend? Are you waging war, or are you close to suffering shipwreck? I know some will read these warnings and say, "Well, God is sovereign in salvation." Yes, He is sovereign in salvation, but man is responsible as well, and we would do well to make sure of our own redemption and compel others to make sure of theirs. The time is short!

The Rev. E. S. Ufford, well known as a Baptist preacher, lecturer, and evangelist, was witnessing a drill at the life-saving station on Point Allerton, Nantasket Beach, when the order to throw out the life-line and the sight of the apparatus in action, combined with the story of a shipwreck on that spot, left an echo in his mind until it took the form of a song-sermon. Returning home, he penciled the words of this rousing hymn, and sat down to his instrument to match the lines with a suitable air. ... In fifteen minutes the hymn-tune was made.[15]

Throw out the life line across the dark wave;
There is a brother whom someone should save;
Somebody's brother! O who then will dare
To throw out the life line, his peril to share?

Refrain
Throw out the life line! Throw out the life line!
Someone is drifting away;
Throw out the life line! Throw out the life line!
Someone is sinking today.

Throw out the life line with hand quick and strong:
Why do you tarry, why linger so long?
See! he is sinking; oh, hasten today
And out with the life boat! away, then away!
Refrain

Throw out the life line to danger fraught men,
Sinking in anguish where you've never been;
Winds of temptation and billows of woe
Will soon hurl them out where the dark waters flow.
Refrain

Soon will the season of rescue be o'er,
Soon will they drift to eternity's shore;
Haste, then, my brother, no time for delay,
But throw out the life line and save them today.
Refrain

---

15 Theron Brown and Hezekiah Butterworth, *The Story of the Hymns and Tunes* (New York: American Tract Society, 1907), 374.

This is the life line, oh, tempest tossed men;
Baffled by waves of temptation and sin;
Wild winds of passion, your strength cannot brave,
But Jesus is mighty, and Jesus can save.
Refrain

Jesus is able! To you who are driv'n,
Farther and farther from God and from Heav'n;
Helpless and hopeless, o'erwhelmed by the wave;
We throw out the life line, 'tis "Jesus can save."
Refrain

This is the life line, oh, grasp it today!
See, you are recklessly drifting away;
Voices in warning, shout over the wave,
O grasp the strong life line, for Jesus can save.[16]

Please, dear one, I beg you to fight the good fight of faith; lay hold
on eternal life!

---

16 Words by Edwin S. Ufford, 1988

Questions to Consider
Wage War or Suffer a Shipwreck?
1 Timothy 1:18-20

1. (a) Read chapter one of 1 Timothy. What things are repeated in this chapter, and why do you think they are mentioned more than once? (b) How would you outline this chapter and what title would you use? (c) How would you summarize this chapter in three sentences?

2. Memorize 1 Timothy 1:18-19.

3. (a) What do you notice about the conscience, according to the following passages? John 8:9; Romans 2:15; 13:5; 1 Corinthians 8:7-12; 1 Timothy 3:9; 4:2; Titus 1:15; Hebrews 9:14; 10:22. (b) What does Paul say about his conscience in Acts 23:1 and 24:16? (c) Why do you think it's important to do what Paul says regarding one's conscience? (d) How do you keep your conscience good and pure?

4. (a) In 1 Timothy 1:18, Paul tells Timothy to wage good warfare. How does one do this, according to what Paul writes in Ephesians 6:10-20? (b) What can happen if we as believers don't fight with the armor provided for us? (c) What have you found to be helpful as you wage spiritual warfare?

5. What advice would you give someone who tells you that the Christian life is too difficult and is close to defecting from the faith?

6. Do you know anyone who was delivered unto Satan like Alexander and Hymenaeus? What sobering lessons did you learn? (Please be discreet about using names, unless they have been publicly put out of the church!)

7. Are you waging war against sin? Do you have a good conscience? Please write a prayer request based on your answer to the above questions.

Chapter 5

Godly Incentives to Pray for our Leaders

1 Timothy 2:1-8

Evil leadership is as old as time. We can start back at the beginning of the Old Testament and read about wicked leaders like Lot, Abimelech, Jezebel, Manasseh, and many others. In fact, you can read through 1 and 2 Kings and 1 and 2 Chronicles and discover multiple kings who, one after another, caused Israel to do yet more evil with each generation. The New Testament isn't exempt from wicked leadership either. There, we find Herod Antipas, Herodias, Herod the Great, and others. Within the pages of history books, we discover wicked rulers like Hitler, Stalin, and Fidel Castro. More recently, wicked leaders have done unthinkable evil; North Korea's leader Kim Jong Un is said to have killed millions of North Koreans, either by starvation or by sending them to die in concentration camps. Saddam Hussein was said to have killed a quarter to half a million people during his reign. There have been wicked leaders since the beginning of time, and there will continue to be wicked leaders until the Lord returns.

As we begin our study of chapter two of Paul's first letter to Timothy, we might ask ourselves the question, "Could it be that some of the evil carried out by past and present kings, rulers, and presidents might be in some measure the fault of God's children, who have failed to obey the command to pray for their leaders?" I think you might be a bit surprised and challenged by what we discover as we study 1 Timothy 2:1-8.

Remember, as Paul is writing this letter, Nero is in power in the Roman Empire. This is the Nero who burned Rome down only to blame the Christians for it. This is the Nero who killed Christians by setting them on fire as living torches for his gardens at night. This is the Nero who killed Christians by sewing them to the skins of dead animals, then letting wild animals tear them apart limb by limb. This is the Nero who executed his own mother and poisoned his step-brother. This is the Nero who would soon behead the writer of this very epistle, the apostle Paul, and then commit suicide not long after. And yet, Paul begins chapter two with these words:

1 Timothy 2:1-8

> Therefore I exhort first of all that supplications, prayers, intercessions, and giving of thanks be made for all men, [2]for kings and all who are in authority, that we may lead a quiet and peaceable life in all godliness and reverence. [3]For this is good and acceptable in the sight of God our Savior, [4]who desires all men to be saved and to come to the knowledge of the truth. [5]For there is one God and one Mediator between God and men, the Man Christ Jesus, [6]who gave Himself a ransom for all, to be testified in due time, [7]for which I was appointed a preacher and an apostle—I am speaking the truth in Christ and not lying—a teacher of the Gentiles in faith and truth. [8]I desire therefore that the men pray everywhere, lifting up holy hands, without wrath and doubting;

Our outline for this lesson will include:

> *The Mandate to Pray* (vs 1-2a, 8) and
> *The Motivations to Pray* (vs 2b-7).

Let's look at the mandate to pray, beginning in verse 1.

The Mandate to Pray

1 Timothy 2:1-2a, 8

> Therefore I exhort first of all that supplications, prayers, intercessions, and giving of thanks be made for all men, for kings and all who are in authority, (1 Timothy 2:1-2a)

Paul starts out by saying *I exhort*, which means I beseech you or I beg you, and Paul's exhorting here is not just to Timothy but for the whole church at Ephesus. Since Paul is writing this epistle in order that they might know how to behave themselves in the house of God, this begging may pertain to the need for public prayer. Paul begins by addressing the men, as we see in verse 8, and then he will address the women in verse 9 and following.

Why does Paul say *first of all*? It could be that he is just saying that the first thing he is writing about is the need for prayer in public worship, or he could be saying that prayer in public worship is of utmost priority. It seems to me that he must be writing first of all about the need for public praying because he writes to the church at Ephesus that the church is for the equipping of the saints (Ephesians 4:12) and he writes to the church at Corinth regarding church order and in neither of those places does he say that prayer is the primary thing the church is to focus on (1 Corinthians 11-14). Having said that, prayer is and should be a priority in the local church and, unfortunately, it is not. Ample time should be given to public praying in the assembly as well as in other times of prayer.

I remember when I was growing up in a minister's home, that Wednesday night was devoted to "prayer meeting." Few would come, but nonetheless it was a priority. Even now, in the church my husband pastors, we have a brief time of prayer before our morning worship; sadly, only a handful of people are regularly there and see it as a priority. As one man has said, "If I were to put my finger on the greatest lack in our Christianity, I would point to the need for an effective prayer life among laity and ministers."[17]

Paul uses four terms to describe prayer: *supplications, prayers, intercessions, and giving of thanks*. The term for *supplications* means petitions, which means to fill needs. This would include praying for certain needs; it might be needs for your particular church, a particular person, or something along those lines. *Prayers* is a broad term which includes drawing near to God with boldness and can be used to describe even a place of prayer. *Intercessions*

---

17 E. F. & L. Harvey, *Kneeling We Triumph: Book One* (Shoals: Old Paths Tract Society, Inc., 1982), 16.

describes pleading on the behalf of others. We can understand this word when we consider Hebrews 7:25, which says, "Therefore He is also able to save to the uttermost those who come to God through Him, since He always lives to make intercession for them." Jesus, whoever lives, is interceding for us; He is pleading at the right hand of the Father. This should encourage us as God's children to plead for the souls of others, especially our leaders in government! The fourth term Paul uses for prayer is *giving of thanks*, which means being grateful. First Thessalonians 5:18 tells us that we are to give thanks in everything, so this is something that should be included in our praying, especially for our leaders—even if they are evil. These four terms certainly encompass a lot of elements that should be present as we pray. I find it interesting that Paul uses these terms again in Philippian 4:6, where he says, "Be anxious for nothing, but in everything by prayer and supplication, with thanksgiving, let your requests be made known to God." (While it's another topic for another time, we women would do well to heed this verse when we're struggling with anxiety!)[18]

Paul goes on to say that these prayers should *be made for all men*. This does not mean that we should pray for every individual who has ever lived or ever will live—that would be humanly impossible— but, rather, that we should pray for all men in the sense of all kinds of people, regardless of race, size, gender, authority, etc. In regard to those in authority, Paul specifically draws attention to that category of people in the next verse as he expounds upon those for whom we should pray. He says we should pray *for kings and all who are in authority*. *Kings* would be a reference to those who are supreme in rule. Keep in mind that Nero is the one in power over the Roman Empire at the time Paul is writing. I've already cited several facts regarding Nero's character, so you can imagine the challenge it would be for believers to pray for him. But Paul doesn't stop with the exhortation to pray for kings; he adds that we must also pray for *all who are in authority*. In biblical times, this would include the high priest, governors, Pharisees, Sadducees, and others. In the form

18 See chapter 22 of *With the Master in Fullness of Joy*, by Susan Heck (Bemidji: Focus Publishing, 2011).

of government we live under in the United States, that would include the president, vice president, senators, representatives, governors, various court justices, police officers, and so on.

This command to pray for those in authority over us should cause us to ponder the potential outcome of obeying in this area. We ought to ask ourselves, "If we put as much energy into praying for our leaders as we often do in complaining about them, might we see some significant changes being made?" God is certainly sovereign in salvation, but I wonder how much change there would be in Washington if God's people would spend as much time on their knees as they spend protesting about the government and its leaders.

> The meaning here is, that while all people should be the subjects of prayer, those in authority should be particularly remembered before the throne of grace. So much depends on their character and plans—the security of life, liberty, and property. God has power to influence their hearts, and to incline them to what is just and equal; and hence we should pray that a divine influence may descend upon them. The salvation of a king is of no more importance than that of a peasant or a slave; but the welfare of thousands may depend on him, and hence he should be made the special subject of prayer.[19]

The Motivations to Pray

1 Timothy 2:2b-7

> that we may lead a quiet and peaceable life in all godliness and reverence. (1 Timothy 2:2b)

In verses 2-7, Paul explains four specific motivations for why we should pray. He begins with his first motivation as to why we should pray for our leaders, by saying *that we may lead a quiet and peaceable life*. What does that mean? *Quiet* indicates an outer tranquility, while *peaceable* indicates an inner tranquility. My friend, does this not motivate you to pray for your leaders?! We should desire that

---

19 Albert Barnes, *Barnes' Notes: Ephesians to Philemon* (Grand Rapids: Baker Book House,1873), 129.

inner peace in our soul but also the outer peace of our nation. I was thinking about this recently, in light of the turmoil in our world right now, and thought that if we would just pray about these things, we might experience a little more peace. In fact, as I was studying these verses, I was reminded of King Jehoshaphat in 2 Chronicles 20, when God sent a great army against him. Jehoshaphat didn't know what to do, so he called the nation to prayer. God defeated the army in a supernatural way, and in 2 Chronicles 20:30 we read, "Then the realm of Jehoshaphat was quiet, for his God gave him rest all around."

Paul goes on to say this quiet and peaceable life is *in all godliness and reverence. Godliness* refers to our attitudes and actions toward others; *reverence* refers to our attitudes and actions toward God. When we as God's people pray for our rulers, it promotes a quiet and peaceable life that is manifested in holy living toward God and others. When things are in turmoil, it is difficult to focus on godly and holy living. This was illustrated to me quite clearly while I was studying this passage. I had just taken a break from my studies and was watching the news with my husband. That week, there had been serious unrest in the city of Ferguson, Missouri, due to the shooting of an 18-year-old by a police officer, with looting and rioting continuing for some time. Because the unrest wasn't dying down, a press conference was called in which the governor of Missouri declared a state of emergency and instituted a mandatory curfew. They had this press conference in a church, no less, and yet there were mobs of people in upheaval, screaming and yelling and out of control, to the point that the reporters' questions couldn't even be heard. This is not quiet and peaceable, and it does not promote godly or reverent living toward God and man. The second motivation to pray, then, is that it promotes godly and reverent attitudes and actions toward God and man. This brings Paul to yet a third motivation to pray for our leaders in verse 3.

> For this is good and acceptable in the sight of God our Savior,
> (1 Timothy 2:3)

The third motivation for praying for our leaders is that *this is good and acceptable in the sight of God our Savior*. What is *good and acceptable*? God considers it *good*—which means He considers it excellent, beautiful, and admirable—to pray for our leaders. It is also *acceptable* in His sight, which means that He receives it gladly and with satisfaction. Our prayers for our leaders are well-pleasing to God; they're viewed by Him as a good thing. We often think of our holiness as well-pleasing to God, our submission to our husbands as well-pleasing to God, our using of our spiritual gifts well-pleasing to God, but do we stop and think that our prayers for our leaders are also well-pleasing to Him? You might be asking, "Why is this so?" Paul gives us the answer to that question in the next verse.

> who desires all men to be saved and to come to the knowledge
> of the truth. (1 Timothy 2:4)

I know that for some of you, your theology might be making you wiggle right about now. And you can wiggle all you want. John Calvin himself said, "God wishes that the gospel should be proclaimed to all without exception."[20] God *desires* that the gospel be proclaimed to all types of men, even those who are in authority. This is very similar to what we just saw in verse 1. Just as we cannot possibly pray for all people, but we can pray for all kinds of people, so it is with salvation. All men will not be saved, we know this to be a fact, but it is God's desire that all kinds of men will be saved. Just as Peter says in his epistle that God is not willing that any should perish but that all should come to repentance (2 Peter 3:9). Regardless of your theology, we can bank on this: God wants men of all types to be saved and to come to the knowledge of the truth of the gospel—even wicked rulers! God came to save sinners! Remember, Paul has already written about himself as being a blasphemer, a persecutor, and an insolent man (1 Timothy 1:13). This is the fourth motivation to pray: God wants people to be saved! And, my friend, He does listen to the prayers of His saints and He does answer those prayers! Andrew Murray once said, "The man who mobilizes the

---

20 John Calvin, *Calvin's Commentaries: Volume XXI* (Grand Rapids: Baker Book House, 1981), 54-55.

Christian church to pray will make the greatest contribution to world evangelization in history." And such prayer is necessary, Paul says, because there is only one way for all men to be saved, even awful leaders.

> For there is one God and one Mediator between God and men, the Man Christ Jesus, (1 Timothy 2:5)

There is only one way by which anyone will be saved, rich or poor, slave or free, fat or skinny, male or female, actors and actresses and, yes, even kings and presidents. Jesus said, in John 14:6, "I am the way, the truth, and the life. No one comes to the Father except through Me." It's not through Mary and it's not through the Pope, but it is through *the Man Christ Jesus* that we are saved. He is the *one Mediator between God and men*. The word *mediator* indicates a middle person whose job it is to bring together two people who are at war with one another so that they are made to be at peace with one another. Before salvation, we were at war with *God*; we were His enemies. Paul puts this well in his letter to the Ephesian church; in Ephesians 2:14-18, he writes,

> For He Himself is our peace, who has made both one, and has broken down the middle wall of separation, having abolished in His flesh the enmity, that is, the law of commandments contained in ordinances, so as to create in Himself one new man from the two, thus making peace, and that He might reconcile them both to God in one body through the cross, thereby putting to death the enmity. And He came and preached peace to you who were afar off and to those who were near. For through Him we both have access by one Spirit to the Father.

So, what did this mediator do for those He saved? Paul says,

> who gave Himself a ransom for all, to be testified in due time, (1 Timothy 2:6)

Jesus *gave Himself a ransom for all*. What does the word *ransom* mean? It refers to that which is given in exchange for another person for the price of that person's redemption. And Paul says that this ransom was given *for all* (who will be saved). Scripture teaches that Christ *gave Himself* for all types of people, including evil kings and wicked leaders. And Paul says that this is *to be testified in due time*. This is a difficult phrase to interpret, but it means that in its proper time, when God deems best, this ransom will be made known to all men. I take the view that this goes along with what Paul tells the church at Philippi in Philippians 2:10-11: "that at the name of Jesus every knee should bow, of those in heaven, and of those on earth, and of those under the earth, and that every tongue should confess that Jesus Christ is Lord, to the glory of God the Father." In other words, one day all will recognize Jesus as Lord, whether they have done so in this life unto salvation or wait to do so on that final day, when they will be cast into the lake of fire.

There is also another possible meaning of this being testified in due time; it could refer to the fact that at the proper time God gave Himself to be a ransom. This would be like what Paul writes in Galatians 4:4-5: "But when the fullness of the time had come, God sent forth His Son, born of a woman, born under the law, to redeem those who were under the law, that we might receive the adoption as sons." Whichever interpretation is correct, it is clear that Paul is overcome at this point, as he reflects on the reality that he has been called to be a preacher of this marvelous truth of God's plan of salvation for mankind, the giving of His Son to be a ransom.

> for which I was appointed a preacher and an apostle—I am speaking the truth in Christ and not lying—a teacher of the Gentiles in faith and truth. (1 Timothy 2:7)

Paul says for this reason he was set apart, *was appointed a preacher and an apostle*: to be *a teacher of the Gentiles*. Remember, on the Damascus road, when Paul met Jesus, he said to Paul,

> But rise and stand on your feet; for I have appeared to you for this purpose, to make you a minister and a witness both of the things which you have seen and of the things which I will yet reveal to you. I will deliver you from the Jewish people, as well as from the Gentiles, to whom I now send you, to open their eyes, in order to turn them from darkness to light, and from

the power of Satan to God, that they may receive forgiveness of sins and an inheritance among those who are sanctified by faith in Me.

This was Paul's calling, as he records it in Acts 26:16-18: to be a teacher of *faith* and *truth* to the Gentiles.

Paul also mentions here that he is *speaking the truth* and is *not lying*. Why does he need to say this? Evidently, there were some in Ephesus who were challenging Paul's apostolic authority. When we began studying chapter one, we saw in verse 1 that Paul said he was "an apostle of Jesus Christ, by the commandment of God our Savior and the Lord Jesus Christ, our hope." We learned then that Paul wanted to emphasize that he was indeed an apostle and that this epistle carried the authority of an apostle. It also emphasizes the fact that the church at Ephesus needed to be reminded of Paul's apostleship due to the problems that they were having with doctrinal issues and with false teaching. Here, Paul reminds them again that his apostleship is not something man-made; rather, he is an apostle because God *appointed* him to that role. This gives yet further weight to what he writes to them, especially in regard to doctrine. Paul then ends this section with a mandate again for prayer in verse 8.

The Mandate to Pray

1 Timothy 2:1-2a, 8

I desire therefore that the men pray everywhere, lifting up holy hands, without wrath and doubting; (1 Timothy 2:8)

Chapter 2 of Paul's letter to Timothy starts with a command to pray in verse 1 and ends with a command to pray in verse 8. Only this time Paul adds *that the men should pray everywhere*, which literally means that they should pray in all places. We don't just pray in church; we pray everywhere in all places and in all times. The list of places in which we can pray is unlimited, and the list of times during which we can pray is unlimited. We are to be a praying people.

Paul adds that men are to do this by *lifting up holy hands, without wrath and doubting*. The practice of *lifting up* one's *hands* in prayer was very common to the Jew; it would indicate honor toward God, as well as humility before Him. Lifting our hands to Heaven communicates that we know our help comes from Him. It's like a child who lifts up his hands to his parent (or grandparent) because he wants to be picked up! He knows that's where the help comes from. But notice that Paul says that they are to be *holy hands*, hands that are pure and unpolluted by sin. The Scriptures are clear in Psalm 66:18, "If I regard iniquity in my heart, the Lord will not hear." We cannot come to the Lord in prayer and be holding on to sin in our lives. We must come to Him with clean hands and clean hearts.

Paul adds that we are to pray in this manner *without wrath and doubting*. This *wrath and doubting* would be directed toward God, and it would go along with the holy hands. We cannot come to God with *wrath* or anger in our hearts toward Him and expect Him to hear our prayers. Likewise, there should be no *doubting* as we approach God. James speaks of this in his epistle; when we're going through trials, we are to pray in faith with no doubting (James 1:6). In the context here, it is easy to see what might bring about this wrath and doubting—*wrath* that God would save or would want to save wicked leaders, and *doubt* that He could save such sinful men! This was Jonah's problem, remember? He didn't want God to save the Ninevites because they were a wicked people! But we must remember that we, too, were once enslaved to sin and enemies of the cross of Christ.

Summary

The Mandate to Pray (vs 1, 8) is that men are to pray all kinds of prayers for all kinds of men in all kinds of places. They are to do so with holy hands, without anger, and without doubting. Does this describe you? Are you a woman of prayer? Matthew Henry says, "I love prayer. It is all which buckles on the Christian's armor."[21] As

---

21 Matthew Henry, *Taking Hold of God*, edited by Joel R. Beeke and Brain G. Najapfour (Grand Rapids, Reformation Heritage Books, DATE), 141.

our last lesson taught us, we must be waging war, but, my sister, as we do so we must be praying! Maybe you are not praying as you ought to and you need some motivation, especially in praying for your leaders.

Paul gives *The Motivations to Pray* (vs 2-7). First, we pray so that we may lead a quiet and peaceable life. I don't know about you, but I certainly desire a quiet and peaceable life, and I find this to be a great motivation to pray. Second, we pray because it promotes godly and reverent attitudes and actions toward God and man. Dear sister, this should be the desire of all of God's children and a great motivation to pray. Third, we pray because this is good and acceptable in the sight of God our Savior. Again, it should be our desire to please our Father, and what joy it must be to Him to have us obey in this area. Last, we pray because God wants people to be saved. We should be praying for all kinds of people in all kinds of places and for all kinds of things! Are you a woman of prayer? Oswald Smith once said,

> found time to shut herself in her room for a full hour Oh, how few find time for prayer. There is time for everything else, time to sleep and time to eat, time to read the newspaper and the novel, time to visit friends, time for everything else under the sun, but—not time for prayer, the most important of all things, the one great essential! Think of Susannah Wesley who, in spite of the fact that she had nineteen children, each day, alone with God. My friends, it is not so much a case of finding time as it is of making time. And we can make time if we will.[22]

---

22 Harvey, *Kneeling We Triumph*, 62.

Questions to Consider

Godly Incentives to Pray for our Leaders
1 Timothy 2:1-8

1. (a) What does Paul command in 1 Timothy 2:1-8? (b) What are the reasons for this command?

2. Memorize 1 Timothy 2:1-2. (You'll want to obey it, too!)

3. (a) Paul admonishes the church at Ephesus to pray for their rulers. For whom else are we to pray, according to Matthew 5:44 and James 5:16? (b) Do you think there is anyone for whom we should not pray? (Use Scripture to back up your answer.)

4. (a) First Timothy 2:4 states that God desires all men to be saved and to come to the knowledge of the truth. Along with this verse, read Titus 2:11 and 2 Peter 3:9. What do these verses indicate? (b) Now read John 15:16-19; Romans 8:29-30; Ephesians 1:4-5; and 1 Peter 1:2. What do these verses indicate? (c) How do you reconcile these truths? (d) What do you think 1 Timothy 2:4 means?

5. (a) Do you find it difficult to pray for your governing leaders? (b) Why do you think it's important for us to pray for our leaders? (c) What things should we pray regarding them?

6. Take note this week how much time you spent complaining about the government and its leaders compared to how much time you spent praying for the government and its leaders. What did you discover? What will you change?

7. Please write a prayer for the leaders of our nation. Also, please include thanksgiving for those in authority over us!

Chapter 6

A Woman's Attire and Attitude in the House of God

1 Timothy 2:9-15

In recent years, the church of Jesus Christ has been in a battle over what the role of the woman is in the church and in the home. It has divided many biblical institutions, churches and even good friends. I have often wondered, "What is all the fuss about when the Scriptures are crystal clear?" What does the Bible have to say? Well, let's consider one of the key passages in the Word of God as we come to 1 Timothy 2:9-15.

1 Timothy 2:9-15

in like manner also, that the women adorn themselves in modest apparel, with propriety and moderation, not with braided hair or gold or pearls or costly clothing, ¹⁰but, which is proper for women professing godliness, with good works. ¹¹Let a woman learn in silence with all submission. ¹²And I do not permit a woman to teach or to have authority over a man, but to be in silence. ¹³For Adam was formed first, then Eve. ¹⁴And Adam was not deceived, but the woman being deceived, fell into transgression. ¹⁵Nevertheless she will be saved in childbearing if they continue in faith, love, and holiness, with self-control.

In this lesson, we will consider

The Woman's Clothing in the Church (v 9);
The Woman's Character in the Church (v 10);
The Woman's Conduct in the Church (vs 11-12);
The Woman's Created Order (vs 13-14); and
The Woman's Calling (v 15).

As we began our last lesson, we saw the mandate to pray, followed by four motivations to pray for our leaders. Paul addressed the men in verses 1-8, and now he addresses the women in verses 9-15. What is the woman's role in the church of God? To answer that question, Paul first deals with the clothing that she should wear as a woman who belongs to the household of God. Let's consider verse 9.

The Woman's Clothing in the Church

1 Timothy 2:9

> in like manner also, that the women adorn themselves in modest apparel, with propriety and moderation, not with braided hair or gold or pearls or costly clothing, (1 Timothy 2:9)

What does Paul mean when he says *in like manner also*? The phrase could mean two things. It could mean that women should pray in the same manner as the men, without wrath and doubting. Or it could refer to how a woman is to conduct herself in public worship. Paul has addressed the men and their role and responsibility in public worship, and now he addresses the women and their role and responsibility in public worship. Both views are accurate and the implication or application is the same.

Paul goes on to say that women are to *adorn themselves in modest apparel*. The word *adorn* means to arrange or to put in order. It would indicate that a woman's clothing should be arranged in some sort of order. *Modest* means a sense of shame, so it would indicate that a woman should not dress in such a way that she feels a sense of guilt over what she is wearing. She should not want to cause anyone who sees her at church to sin because of the way she is dressed. In fact, the word *apparel* means a dress, something let down, a flowing garment or robe. Women in biblical times wore robes or mantles. This does not mean, as some have taken it to mean, that we all should purchase togas for public worship. It does mean that a woman should dress for church with the thought in mind that she is going to worship God; she should dress to meet the Lord!

Paul further describes the way she should dress as being with *propriety and moderation*. *Propriety* is soundness of mind, or good sense. *Moderation* indicates that women should not be extreme in their dress. A woman in the church should not make any effort to show off her body or the latest fashions by the way that she is dressed. She should not be seeking to draw attention to herself. Indeed, the women in Paul's day did just that with their braided hair, gold, pearls and costly clothing.

The first way they overdid their outward adorning was with *braided hair*. You might be a bit puzzled by this, wondering, "Are braids sinful?" "Can I not braid my hair?!" That is not what Paul is saying. One man helps us understand Paul's words here; he says,

> No expense was spared to make clothing dazzling. They actually sparkled. The braids were fastened by jeweled tortoise-shell combs, or by pins or ivory or silver. Or the pins were of bronze with jeweled heads, the more varied and expensive the better. The pin-heads often consisted of miniature images (an animal, a human hand, an idol, the female figure, etc.) Braids, in those days, often represented fortunes. They were articles of luxury. The Christian woman is warned not to indulge in such extravagance.[23]

As you can see, braids in Paul's day were expensive and gaudy. Christian women are to avoid this type of extravaganza. Now, this doesn't give license to us to come to church with our hair looking like we stuck our finger in an electrical socket. Our hair should be becoming and not fixed to draw attention to ourselves.

The second outlandish adornment was *gold* and *pearls*. The same man helps us understand this:

> Similarly, a woman who is a believer must not try to make herself conspicuous by a vain display of ornaments of gold. Also, she will not yearn for pearls, obtained (at that time) from the Persian Gulf or from the Indian Ocean. These were often

---

23 William Hendriksen, *New Testament Commentary: I-II Timothy* (Grand Rapids: Baker, 1957), 107.

fabulously priced and thus way beyond the purchasing power of the average church-member. In order to obtain a pearl of great value a merchant might have to sell all his possessions. Yet someone who was living in Paul's day said, "I have seen Lollia Paulina [wife of emperor Caligula] covered with emeralds and pearls gleaming all over her head, hair, ears, neck, and fingers, to the value of over a million dollars."[24]

Again, this does not mean that women cannot wear jewelry to church, but it does mean that jewelry should be worn in such a way as to not draw attention to oneself. It should be attractive and becoming.

Lastly, Paul mentions that women should not wear *costly clothing* to church. Some women in Paul's day would wear dresses costing up to 7000 denarii, which is equivalent to about 140,000 U.S. dollars in our day. When we come to worship the Lord, we should not show off our bodies, our jewelry, or our clothing. When we dress in the morning for worship, we should be mindful of dressing to please God! We should not dress to attract the attention of men, or other women, but to show the inner attitudes of our hearts. We should not allow our culture to dictate to us what is appropriate for our dress, we should not worry about what others think of us, but we should dress to please the Lord. We should not be like the woman in Proverbs 7:10, of whom Solomon says, "And there a woman met him, with the attire of a harlot, and a crafty heart." Our outer dress reflects our inner hearts, and because of that, we would be wise to be conscious of how we dress in places other than the church gathering as well.

Paul moves from talking about the clothing women should wear to church to the character they should wear to church. And, by the way, women should wear this character at all times; to do so only in church is hypocrisy. As Charles Spurgeon says, what you are at home is what you are.

---

24   Ibid, 107

The Woman's Character in the Church

1 Timothy 2:10

… but, which is proper for women professing godliness, with
good works. (1 Timothy 2:10)

But is a word of contrast. Instead of dressing provocatively, we dress
properly. Instead of dressing ostentatiously, we dress moderately.
Paul puts it like this: that *which is proper for women professing
godliness*. In other words, that which is appropriate for women who
say they are God-fearing women. *Professing* means to convey with
a message that is loud and clear. Women today are dressing with a
message that is loud and clear, but for the most part it's a far cry from
godliness! I sometimes dread going out to the store and other places
(and sometimes churches!) knowing that there will be women who
are not appropriately dressed. I feel for the men of the world today
and the temptation that is ever before them because of women who
go about flaunting their bodies and dressing seductively.

Having said that, I will also say that a godly woman should look
nice at church, but she does not have to have the latest fashions in
order to do so. She doesn't need to shop all week spending money
on jewelry and the latest trends so that she can shock everyone at
church on Sunday. She realizes that all that will burn up some day,
and her heart is not set on her outward appearance but on her inner
attitude, that of a meek and quiet spirit which is precious in the sight
of God. Paul puts it like this: *professing godliness, with good works.*
Notice that he doesn't say good looks, but *good works*! It should
be a woman's good works that are her adornment; that should
be what attracts the attention of those she worships with, not her
clothes, jewelry, makeup, or hair! Hopefully, as you worked on your
homework lesson this week, you saw some of those good works.

I specifically think of Dorcus, in Acts 9:36, and what Luke says
about her: "This woman was full of good works and charitable deeds
which she did." In fact, before Peter raised her from the dead, the

widows were weeping and showing Peter all the clothes she'd made for them. A woman of God will focus on her good works, and that is what she will spend her time on. One man says of Paul's instructions here, "It reflects a right attitude of mind, for Paul was shrewd enough to know that a woman's dress is a mirror of her mind."[25] "A woman's adornment, in short, lies not in what she herself puts on, but in the loving service she gives out."[26] As Peter instructs us in his epistle, in 1 Peter 3:3-4, "Do not let your adornment be merely outward—arranging the hair, wearing gold, or putting on fine apparel—rather let it be the hidden person of the heart, with the incorruptible beauty of a gentle and quiet spirit, which is very precious in the sight of God." Paul moves from the subject of a woman's character to that of her conduct, in verses 11-12.

The Woman's Conduct in the Church

1 Timothy 2:11-12)

> Let a woman learn in silence with all submission.
> (1 Timothy 2:11)

This is a subject Paul also addresses when he writes the church at Corinth. He writes in 1 Corinthians 14:34-35, "Let your women keep silent in the churches, for they are not permitted to speak; but they are to be submissive, as the law also says. And if they want to learn something, let them ask their own husbands at home; for it is shameful for women to speak in church." To better understand what Paul is saying here, we need to understand that church services in New Testament times were far less formal than ours are today; it was commonplace for people to stand up and speak out and dialogue with one another in the midst of the service. In fact, Paul ends that very chapter, 1 Corinthians 14, by saying that everything needed to be done decently and in order.

We also need to understand that in Paul's day it was unheard of

---

25 Donald Guthrie, *The Pastoral Epistles* (Grand Rapids: Wm. B. Eerdman's Publishing Co., 1979), 74.
26 Ibid, 75.

in the Jewish world for a woman to even attend public worship. Women were also discouraged from learning and were encouraged to remain at home. Women didn't even come to meals with men and never appeared alone in public. Those who call Paul a male chauvinist do not realize what was going on in the biblical world at this time or that Paul is actually commending women to come and learn in the church service. There is no male or female; rather, we are all one in Christ Jesus.

With that said, there are distinct roles for each of us, both men and women, to which we must adhere. Paul says *let a woman learn in silence. Learn* means to listen to what is being taught. She listens under someone else's teaching. Does *silence* imply that she is to be muzzled? No! Rather, it means to remain clam. Women should come to church to listen and not to teach. And women should do this *with all submission*, that is, with utmost respect for those in authority over them. A woman should not be rebellious, in her heart or in her actions, that her calling in life as a woman comes with limitations, as a man's does. Can she teach women and children? Can she talk to people at church? Of course, she can! There are many, many things that women can do in the public assembly. Her limitations have to do with men, as Paul explains in the next verse.

> And I do not permit a woman to teach or to have authority over
> a man, but to be in silence. (1 Timothy 2:12)

Some of the questions that I am most asked about as I speak at women's conferences and retreats are, "What is the woman's role in the church?" and "Why can't there be women pastors?" I've received quite a bit of criticism for my answers, and I've even made some men angry because I wouldn't allow them to stay in the audience while I was teaching. I usually end up saying something like, "The Scriptures are clear on this matter," and I go on to quote this verse. And then I usually say, "These are my biblical convictions and also those of the elders of my church."

Paul says *do not permit a woman to teach* a man. I'm not sure what the opponent's issues are with this verse, because this is a command and not an option. Remember, Paul is talking about how we are to behave ourselves in the house of God, as he said in 1 Timothy 3:15; he's writing about public worship, the local assembly, and how women should conduct themselves in it. She is not *to teach or to have authority over a man* in church. Interestingly, the words *have authority* mean to play the master. She is not the authority and she is not to interrupt the preacher, thus evidenced by the next words: *but to be in silence.* The question might come to mind: Can a man learn from a woman? Of course, he can! Acts 18 records the incident in which Apollos was in error regarding baptism. He was speaking boldly in the temple, and verse 26 says that when Aquila and Priscilla heard him, they took him aside and explained the way of God more perfectly to him. The Greek order indicates that Priscilla did most of the talking. Men can learn from women, but women are not to teach in the public assembly. This is the second time the word *silence* is mentioned in this passage, so it must be important. Again, silence does not mean to be muzzled; rather, it means to be peaceable, quiet, and calm. In recent years in our own church, we actually had to exercise church discipline toward a woman who was being disruptive in the church service, along with other sinful behaviors. This is not what women should be doing. You might respond to all this by saying, "Well, Paul is a male chauvinist. He sure makes me angry!" No, he's not a male chauvinist, and I am sorry that he makes you angry, but he clearly gives a reason in verse 13 as to why women are to behave this way in the church, and it has to do with her created order, as he mentions in verses 13-14.

The Woman's Created Order

1 Timothy 2:13-14

For Adam was formed first, then Eve. (1 Timothy 2:13)

The first reason women are to be silent in the church is because *Adam was formed first*, not Eve. This is the order of creation. The head of the home was created *first*. Paul says very clearly in 1 Corinthians

11:3, "But I want you to know that the head of every man is Christ, the head of woman is man, and the head of Christ is God." Later on, he says in 1 Corinthians 11:8-9, "For man is not from woman, but woman from man. Nor was man created for the woman, but woman for the man." Woman was taken out of man's side to be his companion. She is not to be his master or his lord; she is not his Holy Spirit or his mother. Paul gives a second reason why women should not teach men in the local assembly.

> And Adam was not deceived, but the woman being deceived,
> fell into transgression. (1 Timothy 2:14)

The second reason woman is not to exercise authority over a man by teaching in the local assembly is because she was deceived in the garden. The word *deceived* means having been completely deceived, wholly seduced. Consider Genesis 3:1-7:

> Now the serpent was more cunning than any beast of the field which the Lord God had made. And he said to the woman, "Has God indeed said, 'You shall not eat of every tree of the garden'?" And the woman said to the serpent, "We may eat the fruit of the trees of the garden; but of the fruit of the tree which is in the midst of the garden, God has said, 'You shall not eat it, nor shall you touch it, lest you die.'" Then the serpent said to the woman, "You will not surely die. For God knows that in the day you eat of it your eyes will be opened, and you will be like God, knowing good and evil." So when the woman saw that the tree was good for food, that it was pleasant to the eyes, and a tree desirable to make one wise, she took of its fruit and ate. She also gave to her husband with her, and he ate. Then the eyes of both of them were opened, and they knew that they were naked; and they sewed fig leaves together and made themselves coverings.

Adam disobeyed God, but the woman was deceived by the serpent. In 2 Corinthians 11:3, Paul says, "But I fear, lest somehow, as the serpent deceived Eve by his craftiness, so your minds may be corrupted from the simplicity that is in Christ." In fact, he will write in 2 Timothy 3:6 regarding false teachers and how they prey on women who are easily deceived: "For of this sort are those who creep into households and make captives of gullible women loaded down with sins, led away by various lusts." What Adam did, he did on his own, with a willful choice, fully knowing what he was doing. Eve, however, was deceived, and because of that she fell into transgression. As women, we should recognize our weakness in this area. Satan knew that Eve would be easier to tempt than Adam, and so he targeted her with his deception and she fell into sin. She is the weaker vessel, Peter says 1 Peter 3:7. As women, we should realize that Eve was the one who was deceived and, because of that, adopt a humble attitude. Does all of this sound pretty bleak to you? My friend, it truly is not. Paul leaves us with the wonderful perspective of verse 15 as he shares with us the woman's high calling.

The Woman's Calling

1 Timothy 2:15

> Nevertheless she will be saved in childbearing if they continue in faith, love, and holiness, with self-control. (1 Timothy 2:15)

This is one of the most difficult verses to interpret in this epistle! Paul says *she will be saved in childbearing*. We know for certain that this cannot mean that women are spiritually saved by bearing children because salvation is by grace alone through faith alone, not through childbearing alone (Ephesians 2:8-9). The word *salvation* can refer to being saved from our sins in an eternal, saving sense, but it can also refer to being delivered or set free from something in a temporal sense. In other words, women can be delivered from the stigma of Eve's sin in the Garden of Eden by raising up children to the glory of God. John MacArthur says, "The pain associated with childbirth was the punishment for the woman's sin (Genesis 3:16), but her joy and privilege of child rearing delivers women from the stigma of that sin."[27] Paul will write later on in 1 Timothy 5:14, "Therefore I desire that the younger widows marry, bear children, manage the house, give no opportunity to the adversary to speak reproachfully."

---

27 John MacArthur, *The MacArthur New Testament Commentary: 1 Timothy* (Chicago: Moody Press, 1995), 88.

A Christian woman's role is not to be a female pastor but to be a female parent by raising godly children. She must, however, just like a man, *continue in faith, love, and holiness, with self-control.* This triad of faith, love, and holiness is what Paul begin his epistle with in chapter 1, verse 5: "Now the purpose of the commandment is love from a pure heart, from a good conscience, and from sincere faith." *Faith* would refer to faith in the Lord; *love* would be love to all, and *holiness* would mean that she is set apart. And she does all this with *self-control*, which means to be of sound mind, to be sober. This is a high calling, one that Paul reiterates in Titus 2 when he mentions that older women are to teach younger women how to be self-controlled.

Summary

The Woman's Clothing in the Church (v 9): Women are to dress in modest clothing and jewelry which are becoming in the profession of her faith in Christ. What about you? What about the way you dress to come to worship? Do you stop to look at yourself in the mirror and ask if what you are wearing pleases the Lord? Would you dress in that manner if Christ were going to visit your church this Sunday morning? Well, let me tell you, He is! Are you secretly trying to draw attention to yourself by the way that you dress? What about what you're wearing right now? Are your jeans too tight? Is your blouse too low? Are you in attire right now that would attract a man to desire something in you that you cannot righteously fulfill? Do you purposely dress seductively in tight-fitting clothes and low-cut blouses so as to attract the attention of a man? For those of you who are married, you might consider asking your husband before you leave the house whether he thinks you are appropriately dressed. And for those of you with daughters, please make sure that they are dressed appropriately.

The Woman's Character in the Church (v 10): Women are not to focus on their good looks but on their good works. How much time have you spent this past week focusing on your inner heart? How much time have you spent in the Word, in prayer, and in fellowship with God's people, in comparison to the time that you've spent shopping, or on social media, or searching the internet? How much time is spent on your inner woman versus your outer woman? What good works have you done this week for the Master?

The Woman's Conduct in the Church (vs 11-12): Women are to learn with all calmness and submission to those in authority over them. Are you guilty of overstepping your boundaries in this area? Do you secretly wish you could be the preacher in the pulpit?

The Woman's Created Order (vs 13-14): Have you embraced the God-given truth that woman was created second for the purpose of being a helper to her husband? Do you dwell on the untruth that you are a second-class Christian? Or do you rejoice in the fact that God has created you to be a woman?

The Woman's Calling (v 15): We are called to be delivered from the stigma of Eve's sin by rearing children to the glory of God and by continuing in faith, love, and holiness. And we are to do all of this with a serious mindset. For those of you with children, are you rearing your children for God's glory? Do you take your parenting seriously, and are you rearing your children in the nurture and admonition of the Lord? Does your life exhibit faith, love, and holiness? Would others say that you have your senses about you, that you are sober-minded and calm in your spirit?

Instead of being known as women with bobbed hair, who are bossy wives and women preachers, how about we endeavor to be known as women who properly dress, live godly lives, and rear children who bring glory to God.

Questions to Consider

A Woman's Attire and Attitude in the House of God
1 Timothy 2:9-15

1. (a) As you read 1 Timothy 2:9-15, write down all the characteristics of godly women. (b) Do these describe you? (c) Summarize 1 Timothy, chapter two, in three sentences.

2. Memorize any verse of 1 Timothy 2:8-15.

3. (a) What is the woman's role in the church, according to 1 Corinthians 11:1-6; 14:34-35; and 1 Timothy 2:9-15? (b) Do you think women should teach a co-ed Sunday school class? Can women teach children? How about singing or giving a testimony in church? Can women teach other women? Would it be okay for a woman to take the offering, read Scripture, or pray in church? (Please back up your answers with Scripture.)

4. (a) Paul mentions in 1 Timothy 2:10 that women are to profess godliness with good works. What are some of those good works that we as women should be manifesting, according to Proverbs 31:10-31 and Titus 2:3-5? (b) Does your life manifest these things?

5. What do you think Paul means in 1 Timothy 2:15, when he says that women are saved in childbearing?

6. (a) What do you think is appropriate attire for women to wear to church? (b) How would you use what you have learned to speak to a woman who consistently comes to church indecently dressed? (c) How can you or did you train your daughters to be modest in their dress?

7. Reread your answers to Questions 1b and 4b and write a prayer request asking God to help you in any areas of weakness.

Chapter 7

Is Your Pastor Qualified According to His Boss?

1 Timothy 3:1-7

In the weeks before I wrote this lesson, I heard of two men who were forced to step down from the office of "pastor," one due to infidelity and the other because of drunkenness, abusing his wife and children, and embezzling money from his church. It's sad to say, but this is becoming commonplace in the church today. I am certainly grieved, as I am sure you are, but how much more is our Father in Heaven grieved! Men who have been entrusted with the privilege and responsibility of shepherding the sheep are committing heinous sins and thereby disqualifying themselves. Such things send confusion throughout the body, weaken everyone's resolve to live in holiness, and cause the church to become complacent. Of course, in our day, churches often allow these men to confess and repent and then be promptly restored back to the pastorate, which is clearly not biblical. You might say, "Not biblical?! What do you mean? Doesn't God forgive all sin?" Of course, He does! But there are some sins which disqualify a man from the pastorate permanently.

As we venture into chapter three of 1 Timothy, we will come to see the qualifications for the job of pastor, according to his Boss, the Lord Jesus Christ! Let's read these qualifications together in 1 Timothy 3:1-7:

1 Timothy 3:1-7

> This is a faithful saying: If a man desires the position of a bishop, he desires a good work. ²A bishop then must be blameless, the husband of one wife, temperate, sober-minded, of good behavior, hospitable, able to teach; ³not given to wine, not violent, not greedy for money, but gentle, not quarrelsome,

not covetous; ⁴one who rules his own house well, having his children in submission with all reverence ⁵(for if a man does not know how to rule his own house, how will he take care of the church of God?); ⁶not a novice, lest being puffed up with pride he fall into the same condemnation as the devil. ⁷Moreover he must have a good testimony among those who are outside, lest he fall into reproach and the snare of the devil.

In this lesson, we will discover sixteen non-negotiable qualifications for an elder in the church. Before we look at the first qualification, let's consider what Paul has to say about this job of the pastor.

> This is a faithful saying: If a man desires the position of a bishop, he desires a good work. (1 Timothy 3:1)

Perhaps you're wondering about this position of *bishop* or elder and how this role began. As you might know, when churches were established in various cities in New Testament times, elders would be appointed for each church. It was imperative that the church have leaders, just as it is imperative that nations have leadership, that schools have leadership, that corporations have leadership, that the family has leadership. There is one thing different about leadership in the local church, however, and that is that its leaders must be qualified according to Scripture, according to what God says.

Paul begins by saying *this is a faithful saying*. In other words, what he is about to say is something that is not to be doubted. What is it that is not to be doubted? *If a man desires the position of a bishop, he desires a good work.* The word *bishop* means overseer, so this would include elders and pastors. Notice that it is the *man* who desires this *position*, not the woman. In our last lesson, we learned that Paul is clear that women are not to teach or to exercise authority over men in the local assembly, but here is another passage that makes it clear that pastors and leaders of the church should be men and not women. If there were any question about this, Paul would have said if any man or woman desires the office of a bishop. To *desire* means to eagerly desire something; it is something that one is passionate about and has their heart set upon. The office of elder or bishop is not something you go into with a half-heartedly lackadaisical mindset; rather, this person should be passionate about wanting to shepherd people. I've met some pastors and elders who probably need to step down because they have no passion for the sheep or for their office as elder. Paul says that those who have this passion *desire a good work*. This is a good thing. My husband and I have met numerous pastors and their wives over the years who've told us that they simply don't care for the pastorate. And we're always shocked by this because we love the pastorate. Is it hard? Absolutely! Do we want to quit sometimes? Sure! But we both love it and we're both passionate about it. What then are the requirements for this good work? Well, there are sixteen to be specific, according to 1 Timothy 3. Let's consider the first seven in verse 2.

> A bishop then must be blameless, the husband of one wife, temperate, sober-minded, of good behavior, hospitable, able to teach; (1 Timothy 3:2)

1. *The first qualification for an elder or pastor is that he must be blameless.* This is a *must*, not an option. This specific requirement is the heading for all of the rest of the qualifications. In other words, this man must be blameless in his social life, his family life, his spiritual life. *Blameless* is defined as "nothing to take hold upon him." It means that no evil can be proved about this man, no charge can legitimately be made against him. You should be able to look at his life and see that he cannot be charged with any blight because no such blight exists. In our day, you should be able to look at his phone records and internet searches and see nothing that is worthy of blame. Does this mean he must be perfect? No. That would be impossible. One man helps us here; he says that there are four reasons why this is so essential:

> First, they are the special targets of Satan, and he will assault them with more severe temptation than others. Those on the front lines of the spiritual battles will bear the brunt of satanic opposition. Second, their fall has a greater potential for harm. Satan knows that when a shepherd falls, the effect on the sheep is devastating. Third, leaders' greater knowledge of the truth, and accountability to live it, brings greater chastening when

they sin. Fourth, elders' sins are more hypocritical than others' because they preach against the very sins they commit.[28]

2. *The second qualification is that he must be the husband of one wife.* Here is another proof text for why woman can't be pastors. It would be hard for her to be the husband of one wife. (Well, in our day, maybe not so much!) Some will say that a pastor has to be married, but you would have a hard time proving that because, according to 1 Corinthians 7:8, Paul wasn't married. Some will also say that a man is disqualified even if his divorce and remarriage were biblical, but Paul doesn't say that either. He also doesn't say that such a man can't be widowed or that his wife can't be an unbeliever. Paul just says that this man must be *the husband of one wife*, literally, a one-woman man. He must be devoted to one woman and one woman alone. He must have *one wife*. This clearly means that a pastor cannot be a polygamist, though there are some examples of men practicing this in the Scriptures. He must not be looking around at other women or be emotionally attached to other women. This is huge for pastors! Truly, it is almost daily that you hear of a pastor stepping down from ministry because of moral failure. Such temptations must be nipped in the bud immediately! Men in leadership must be above reproach in this area. Recent statistics of pastors who have issues with pornography are staggering. In a recent poll, 51% of pastors said that cyber-porn is a possible temptation, while 37% said it is a current struggle. That means those 37% are disqualified; not one of them can be said to be a one-woman man. But this isn't their only disqualifying characteristic; they're also disqualified because they are no longer blameless or above reproach. This is appalling to say the least.

3. *He must be temperate.* This means that he must be vigilant, watchful, awake, and alert. He must be clear-headed. This would include not getting drunk, which is another qualification in itself. He must not have his mind dulled with drugs or any other substance. I don't know about you, but I want a shepherd who is clear-headed as he shepherds me. I want him to be watchful and aware of what is

---

28 John MacArthur, *The MacArthur New Testament Commentary: 1 Timothy* (Chicago: Moody Press, 1995), 103.

going on so that he can feed and tend to the needs of his flock.

4. *An elder or pastor must be sober-minded.* This means to be of healthy or sound mind. An elder must be sensible, having his desires and passions under control. This does not mean he cannot have a sense of humor, but it does mean that he must be serious about the things of the Lord. Paul said some pretty humorous things at times; in Acts 23:3, he called Ananias a whitewashed wall. Of course, that was before Paul knew Ananias was the high priest.

5. *He must be sensible and have good behavior.* Whereas sober-minded is in reference to the mind, the internal, good behavior is in reference to the actions, to the external. This man should have orderly behavior; he should not be rude, self-centered, or insensitive to the needs of others. I've met some pastors over the years who, in my humble opinion, need a great deal of help in this area. They come across as rude, self-centered, and arrogant. It's hard for me to imagine our Lord acting like that! And He doesn't want those who work for Him to act like that either!

6. *Job qualification number six is being hospitable.* For one to be hospitable means that he is a lover of strangers. In biblical times, most inns were few and far between, and were notoriously filthy and unsuitable for travelers. Traveling missionaries or others would need a place to stay, much like Joseph and Mary needed when they arrived in Bethlehem. Pastors, of all people, should be welcoming to those who need a place to stay. We are blessed in our day to have nice accommodations for people traveling through town, but we should still be willing to open our homes to those in need, even strangers. I saw a beautiful example of this not long ago when my husband and several other pastors were having a meeting at our house with a missionary from the Philippines. The meeting adjourned and the missionary's wife, along with their children, came to pick up her husband. As they were leaving, I overheard one of the pastors explain to the missionary's wife that she and her family would be spending the night with him and his wife. The missionary's wife said, "Does your wife know how many kids we have?" to which he

replied, "She won't care." (These missionaries had six children, five of whom were present with them!) This is what Paul means when he says that a pastor must be hospitable.

7. *The seventh on Paul's list of qualifications is being able to teach.* Paul says this again in 2 Timothy 2:24, "And a servant of the Lord must not quarrel but be gentle to all, able to teach, patient." He must have the gift of teaching and he must be able to effectively communicate God's Word. He must be skilled in teaching and he must be a student of the Word. I remember, when our kids were growing up, we were in a church briefly where the pastor could not teach worth a lick. We'd get in the car after church and the kids would tell me how many times that pastor said "um" in his sermons. Needless to say, we were not in that church very long, and that pastor was not in the pastorate very long. The pastor must not only be able to teach, but he must devote his time to study and to prayer. He should first be feeding himself and then feeding the sheep. A good question to ask your pastor is how much time he spends in the Word and in prayer. How much time did he spend preparing his sermon for last Sunday? As we move on to verse 3, we explore more qualifications which Paul mentions for those who serve as an overseer.

> not given to wine, not violent, not greedy for money, but gentle,
> not quarrelsome, not covetous; (1 Timothy 3:3)

8. *Not given to wine is number 8 on the Lord's list of pastoral job qualifications.* We cannot prove a requirement of abstinence from alcohol from the Word of God, but we can prove that drunkenness is a sin. In fact, Paul will tell Timothy later on, in 1 Timothy 5:23, to take a little wine for his stomach problems. But Paul also says in Ephesians 5:18 that we are not to be drunk with wine. Elders are not to tarry long at the wine or to stay near it, as the Greek renders this phrase. Most churches have some kind of statement for their elders and deacons indicating that they are not to engage in drinking of any kind, and I must say that is probably wise, especially since our wine is much different than the diluted wine of biblical times.

Unlike the water most of us have access to today, water in biblical times was not safe to drink, and so wine was used as a purifying drink. I remember, during my husband's first pastorate, coming to pick our children up at the home of one of the church leaders. He met us out in the front yard, drunk and carrying an alcoholic beverage in his hand. We were both shocked. Needless to say, he did not remain in leadership and was even excommunicated. It was a hard introduction to the pastorate for us! Unfortunately, in our day, drinking alcohol is becoming more and more common for pastors and churches! I've even heard of alcohol being offered at Bible studies and Christian conferences.

9. *Not being violent is a necessary characteristic of a pastor.* If you are violent, then you are disqualified from being a shepherd. I guess if you're going to tarry long at the wine, then you might just be violent, since the two seem to go hand in hand. To be violent means to be a striker or someone who is quarrelsome. In that same church, where we had the drunk leader, there was also a man in leadership whom my husband confronted because of behavior he had observed on a leadership trip. A few days after the confrontation, the guy came over to our house with a gun and in anger threated to kill my husband. Needless to say, that man was also out of there pretty quick. (You might be wondering if all the leaders were bad in that first pastorate, but I assure you that wasn't the case. Two of the godliest men I've met were elders in that first church.) Charles Spurgeon told his Pastor's College students, "Don't go about the world with your fist doubled up for fighting, carrying a theological revolver in the leg of your trousers."[29] Just the day before I wrote this lesson, I was having a conversation with several people, including my husband, and the question was asked, "If someone attacked you at a gas station and demanded the keys to your car, would you fight them or give them your keys?" My husband said, "I'd give him my keys," to which someone replied, "I'd expect you to say that!"

10. *The 10th necessary quality for someone who oversees the church is that he must not be greedy for money.* In other words, he is not

---

29 Google E-Read, *The Homiletic Review: Volume 5* (New York: I.K. Funk, 1881), 462.

to earn money in unjust ways. The apostle Peter, when addressing elders in 1 Peter 5:2, says, "Shepherd the flock of God which is among you, serving as overseers, not by compulsion but willingly, not for dishonest gain but eagerly." Jude says in verse 11 of his epistle that being greedy for money is a character of false teachers. "Woe to them! For they have gone in the way of Cain, have run greedily in the error of Balaam for profit, and perished in the rebellion of Korah." The pastor I mentioned in my introduction would definitely be guilty of this, since he was embezzling money from his church.

11. *A pastor must also be gentle.* This means he is to be patient and forbearing even when he is being criticized. He must listen patiently and lovingly.

12. *He must not be quarrelsome.* This means that he is not to be contentious. He should not love an argument. He might not agree with you, but he should not be disagreeable. It is one thing to be firm on truth and debate it, but it is quite another thing to quarrel. Paul says in 2 Timothy 2:24-26 "And a servant of the Lord must not quarrel but be gentle to all, able to teach, patient, in humility correcting those who are in opposition, if God perhaps will grant them repentance, so that they may know the truth, and that they may come to their senses and escape the snare of the devil, having been taken captive by him to do his will."

13. *The number 13 qualification is also one of the 10 commandments: thou shalt not covet.* The meaning here seems to pertain to money, that he should not love money. Paul will write later, in 1 Timothy 6:10-11, "For the love of money is a root of all kinds of evil, for which some have strayed from the faith in their greediness, and pierced themselves through with many sorrows. But you, O man of God, flee these things and pursue righteousness, godliness, faith, love, patience, gentleness." Pastors should be paid, but they should not covet money. Paul mentions in Acts 20:33 that he did not covet anyone's gold or silver or clothes. And 2 Peter 2:3 talks about false teachers making merchandise of others because of their love for money. But true shepherds deplore such evil!

Paul spends more time on the last three qualifications than he does on any of the previous ones, so they must be of great importance. He also explains the reasons behind qualifications 14, 15, and 16 in the next few verses.

> one who rules his own house well, having his children in submission with all reverence (1 Timothy 3:4)

14. *One who rules his house well is qualification number 14. Rules* means to manage, to have authority or preside over. And he must do that *well* or good. He must be the head of his home. Some have taken this verse to prove that a pastor must be married, but I think that might be stretching it a bit. I do think that it would be ideal for him to be married, but to read that into the text is not fair to the text. This man rules his house well by *having his children in submission with all reverence.* He should have his children under control. When I was growing up, I often heard that preacher's kids were the worst-behaved kids, but the opposite should be true. Minister's children should be the best-behaved children. They are a reflection of his leadership. They should respect his leadership and be obedient and honoring. I remember when our daughter was about 13 that she told her father, "No." It was a first in our house, and he gave her three days to abide by the rules of the house or she could move out. I wept and fasted and prayed and got others to do so with me. The third day came, and she was broken and repentant. It was soon after that that she embraced the Lordship of Christ. My husband knew that if her choice was one of rebellion, he would be disqualified and would have to step down as pastor. Now, you might be thinking, "That doesn't seem fair," but Paul gives a valid reason why this would be disqualifying.

> (for if a man does not know how to rule his own house, how will he take care of the church of God?) (1 Timothy 3:5)

If a man can't manage his family, which is far smaller than his church, how could he possibly manage his church? If there is disorder in his home, there will more than likely be disorder in his church. If he neglects his home, he will more than likely neglect his church. Part of his ministry, so to speak, is his family. Failure in his home could mean failure in his church.

> not a novice, lest being puffed up with pride he fall into the same condemnation as the devil. (1 Timothy 3:6)

15. *An elder must not be a new convert.* The word *novice* means newly planted, or a young plant. Paul will say later in 1 Timothy 5:22, "Do not lay hands on anyone hastily, nor share in other people's sins; keep yourself pure." So, there must have been some problem with this in the church at Ephesus. Perhaps the two men mentioned in chapter 1, Hymenaeus and Alexander, had not been Christians very long. Men who lead need to be men who have been in the faith for a while and who are grounded in God's Word. Paul gives a reason why this, too, is necessary; he says that a novice might be *puffed up with pride. Puffed up* means to be inflated with self-conceit. Such a man would think more highly of himself than he ought and would fall into the condemnation of the devil. His pride would get the best of him as it got the best of Satan, who wanted to be like God. In Isaiah 14, we read of Lucifer, who was the son of the morning and yet he wanted to be like God. Isaiah says of Satan, "Yet you shall be brought down to Sheol, to the lowest depths of the Pit." In other words, you are going to hell, Satan. Pride will get the best of any man, but especially a man who is a new convert. He will think more of himself than he should. As Proverbs 16:18 says, "Pride goes before destruction, and a haughty spirit before a fall."

I don't know about you, but I would not want a new convert shepherding my soul; instead, I want a shepherd who is seasoned in the faith, who knows the Word of God and is a man of prayer. Paul ends the list of qualifications much like he began it, as he gives the last qualification.

> Moreover he must have a good testimony among those who are outside, lest he fall into reproach and the snare of the devil. (1 Timothy 3:7)

16. *He must have a good testimony before unbelievers.* *Those who are outside* is a reference to unbelievers, those who are outside the church family. This is similar to the first qualification, being blameless, because both have to do with his testimony before others. *Good testimony* means there must be no reproach on his name. This is an interesting quality, because Acts 16:2 says that Timothy was well reported of, or well-spoken of, by the brethren in Lystra and Iconium. There was no reproach on Timothy's name. Unbelievers should be able to watch a preacher's life and not say, "That preacher at such and such a church is my next door neighbor and you know he is the rudest man," or "I hear him yelling at his wife all the time," or "I've seen him come in late at night drunker than a skunk," or "The bill collectors are after him because he never pays his bills on time." It is such a sad state we are in today, with so many leaders falling into immorality and other sins! We do not have a good testimony to the unbeliever and we are a mockery to a lost world. A friend was telling me recently that her husband, who is lost, was at a restaurant years ago where her pastor was in the booth next to him. Her husband knew it was her pastor, but the pastor didn't know this man. He overheard the pastor say to the people he was eating with that his church was gullible and a bunch of morons. What kind of testimony was that pastor to this lost man?

Paul gives a reason why an elder must have a good testimony toward unbelievers and it has to do with the devil again: *lest he fall into reproach and the snare of the devil.* If this man doesn't have a good report from those around him, he might *fall into reproach,* which means that he might bring disgrace on the name of Christ. But he may also fall into *the snare of the devil,* which means to be trapped by the devil. The devil loves to entrap all of us, but especially those in leadership. Satan wants to trap ministers and to render them ineffective, and he's certainly doing a pretty good job in our day, as pastors seem to be falling like flies.

Summary

You might be thinking, "Well, this was a most interesting lesson, Susan, but what does this have to do with me? I am not an elder and I am not desirous of ever being one." That's a good thing, since as a woman you can't be one anyway. In reality, my friend, this lesson has quite a bit to do with you. Tucked away in Hosea 4:9, we read, "And it shall be: like people, like priest." And in Luke 6:40, "A disciple is not above his teacher, but everyone who is perfectly trained will be like his teacher." A congregation will most often reflect the character of their pastor. I've often found this to be true as I've traveled around to speak. You show me women who love God and are warm and loving, and I will show you a pastor who is the same. You show me women who are cold and dead to the things of God, and I will show you a pastor who is the same. I can't tell you how many churches I have spoken in where you can tell that something is dreadfully wrong and, almost 100 percent of the time, we will hear months or even years later that the pastor has stepped down due to some disqualifying sin, usually infidelity.

Having said all of that, this lesson has a lot to do with you. As we saw in our last lesson, we are to be godly women with good works and one of those good works is prayer. We must be praying for the leaders in our churches. Maybe you'd like to pray that God would give you a different pastor, but maybe God wants you to start praying for the one that you have! Do you pray for your church leadership? Wouldn't it be a wonderful thing if we as women would take these sixteen qualifications and pray them for our leadership?!

We need to pray for our leaders that they would be blameless, that there will never be one blight upon their name that would exempt them from ministry. We need to pray for their marriages, that they would love their wives the way Christ loved the church and be devoted to her and her only. We need to pray that they would be the leaders of their homes, rearing their children in the nurture and admonition of Christ. We need to pray that they would avoid all vices that would muddle their minds and their actions; that they would never be arrogant, hostile, or argumentative, but that they would always be gentle and patient, even with those who might oppose them or criticize them.

We need to pray that they would love people and never show partiality. We must pray that they would be men of the Word and men of prayer, studying hard to come to the intended meaning of the Scriptures, so that they would feed their flocks with the rich nourishment of God's Word. We need to pray they would not covet the things of this world or desire material possessions. We need to pray that they would be wise stewards of the money God gives them. We need to pray that the evil one would not ensnare them and render them useless for God's service and that they would not be ignorant of his devices. We must pray for our spiritual leaders! A.W. Tozer once said, "Until self-effacing men return again to spiritual leadership, we may expect a progressive deterioration in the quality of popular Christianity year after year till we reach the point where the grieved Holy Spirt withdraws—like the Shekinah from the temple."[30]

---

30 Mark Water, *The New Encyclopedia of Christian Quotations* (Grand Rapids: Baker Book House Co., 2000), 600.

Questions to Consider

Is Your Pastor Qualified According to His Boss?
1 Timothy 3:1-7

1. (a) Write down all the qualifications for a leader that you see in 1 Timothy 3:1-7 and Titus 1:5-9. (b) List the similarities as well as the differences you notice between these two passages.

2. Memorize 1 Timothy 3:2.

3. (a) Read 1 Samuel 2:12-4:22. What qualifications of a leader (from 1 Timothy 3:1-7) do you find that are missing from Eli, who was a priest at this time? (b) What were the repercussions of his failed leadership? (c) What can we learn from this passage about leaders who are not qualified according to the Scriptures?

4. (a) Look up the following passages and list the leader that is mentioned as well as the qualification from 1 Timothy 3:1-7 that either qualifies or disqualifies him. You should find one qualification for each passage. Exodus 32:1-5; Judges 13:2-7; 1 Samuel 2:12; 1 Kings 11:1-4; Isaiah 28:7-8; Luke 1:5-6; 7:36; John 12:3-6; Acts 5:34-39; 15:36-41; 16:1-2; 20:27; 23:1-5; 24:16; 1 Thessalonians 2:7 (see 1 Thessalonians 1:1 to identify who this is referring to); 2 Peter 2:1-3; (b) What does this teach you about the importance of leaders being qualified according to the Bible?

5. (a) Do you think a pastor should step down who has disqualified himself according to 1 Timothy 3 and Titus 1? (b) Do you think he should be restored back to the pastorate if he repents? Please support your answer with Scripture.

6. (a) Do you know the elders and deacons in your church? (b) Do you know if they are qualified according to God's Word? (c) How can you better acquaint yourself with your spiritual leaders? (d) What will you do to make sure this happens?

7. Please write out a prayer for your pastor. I would encourage you to pray often for your pastors and elders, if not daily. These are tumultuous times we're living in, with many pastors disqualifying themselves because of their heinous sins.

Chapter 8

The Seven Determining Qualities of a Deacon

1 Timothy 3:8-13

An old deacon who used to pray every Wednesday night at prayer meeting always concluded his prayer the same way: "And, Lord, clean all the cobwebs out of my life." The cobwebs were those things that ought not to have been there, but had gathered during the week. It got too much for one fellow in the prayer meeting, and he heard the old deacon one time too often. So, when the man made that prayer, the fellow jumped to his feet and shouted: "Lord, Lord, don't do it! Kill the spider!" That's what needs to happen.[31]

This comical story emphasizes what Paul says in 1 Timothy 3 as he continues writing about the qualifications for officers in the church, specifically the deacons. They, too, are to have blameless lives. Having outlined the requirements necessary for the elders of the church, Paul moves on to lay out the qualifications of the deacons. Some have thought of deacons as the lesser of the church officers, but nothing could be further from the truth, as we'll see in our lesson. In fact, the elder and deacon qualifications are nearly identical, with only minor exception. Let's look at them together.

1 Timothy 3:8-13

[8]Likewise deacons must be reverent, not double-tongued, not given to much wine, not greedy for money, [9]holding the mystery of the faith with a pure conscience. [10]But let these also first be tested; then let them serve as deacons, being found blameless. [11]Likewise, their wives must be reverent, not slanderers, temperate, faithful in all things. [12]Let deacons

31   Paul Lee Tan, Th.D., *Encyclopedia of 7,700 Illustrations: Signs of The Times* (Rockville: Assurance Publishers, 1979), 1234.

be the husbands of one wife, ruling their children and their own houses well. [13]For those who have served well as deacons obtain for themselves a good standing and great boldness in the faith which is in Christ Jesus.

In our last lesson, we saw sixteen non-negotiable qualifications for an elder. In this lesson, we will consider seven qualifications for deacons and I have put them in an acrostic for you to remember: *DEACONS* (though they will not show up in this order in the text). We might be tempted to think that deacons don't have to be qualified biblically, that they just need to be warm male bodies from within the church, willing to do menial tasks—but this is a faulty assumption. Let's begin by examining the first four qualifications in verse 8.

> Likewise deacons must be reverent, not double-tongued, not given to much wine, not greedy for money (1 Timothy 3:8)

Paul begins by saying *likewise*, which means in the same way. In the same way that elders are to be godly men of integrity, so also are deacons to be men of integrity. Again, let me say that the office of deacon is no less important than the office of elder. They have different functions in the local church, but both are servants of the Most High God, just as you and I are when we use our gifts to His glory. Since we are going to be learning about deacons, we should take the time to define what the word means. The word *deacon* is the Greek word diakonis, and it means a table waiter, attendant, humble servant. The first accounting of deacons is found in Acts 6:1-6:

> Now in those days, when the number of the disciples was multiplying, there arose a complaint against the Hebrews by the Hellenists, because their widows were neglected in the daily distribution. Then the twelve summoned the multitude of the disciples and said, "It is not desirable that we should leave the word of God and serve tables. Therefore, brethren, seek out from among you seven men of good reputation, full of the Holy Spirit and wisdom, whom we may appoint over this business; but we will give ourselves continually to prayer and to the ministry of the word." And the saying pleased the whole multitude. And they chose Stephen, a man full of faith and the Holy Spirit, and Philip, Prochorus, Nicanor, Timon, Parmenas, and Nicolas, a proselyte from Antioch, whom they set before the apostles; and when they had prayed, they laid hands on them.

Evidently, the widows among the Hellenists were being neglected and not receiving the monies they needed to sustain their lives, and naturally, there was some complaining about this. The apostles called the followers of Jesus together and basically said that they needed to appoint men to do this work so that they could devote themselves to the Word and to prayer. They refer to this work as serving tables, which is where the word deacon comes from. But these men couldn't just be riff-raff off the street; these men needed to have wisdom, to be filled with the Holy Spirit, and to have a good reputation. Deacons, in biblical times, looked after the needs of the poor; took care of the physical needs of others; kept the place of worship in order; and collected the contributions. This is pretty similar to what is expected of deacons in our churches today; they look after the physical needs of the church and the people, and they are usually involved in serving the communion elements and taking up the offering.

Paul says the first thing deacons must be is *reverent. This is the D on your acrostic: they must be dignified.* This is what it means to be reverent. Deacons must be respectable; they must be serious. This does not mean, as we saw in our last lesson, that they can't have a sense of humor, but it does mean that they must not use their sense of humor in a godless way.

Secondly, deacons must not be double-tongued. *This would be the C on your acrostic: they must have a controlled tongue.* The word *double-tongued* means to speak one thing to one person and something else to another person; this is nothing more than lying and hypocrisy. This would probably be fitting for deacons in New Testament times, as there would be temptation to use flattery and deception as they ministered to the needs of others and took care of the church of God. But the same is also true in our day, as deacons can be tempted to be man-pleasers rather than God-pleasers. For example, if there was an apparent need in the body and a deacon talked with the person expressing that need, that deacon might be tempted to say, "We see you have a financial need and we will certainly take care of it." Yet, he may not be bold enough to truthfully explain to that person that if they would find a job or stop misusing their money, they would not be in the position they're in. So instead, he reports back to the pastor or talks to another member of the church body, saying, "I know so and so says they have a need, but honestly if they would just stop spending their money foolishly and go and get a decent job, they wouldn't have this problem!" Deacons need to be straightforward as they deal with the needs in the body and not be double-tongued. We had an elder in one of our former churches who was double-tongued like this. I never knew what to believe from him; he would say one thing to one person and another thing to another person. I would often say to my husband that this guy seemed doubled-tongued to me. Eventually he was exposed for his hypocrisy, along with other grievous sins.

Thirdly, Paul says deacons are not to be given to much wine; they are not to be drunkards. *This is the N on your acrostic: not a drunk.* Paul mentions this same quality for elders, only here he adds the word *much*: they are *not* to be *given to much wine.* I'm not sure why Paul adds *much* here, except for the possibility that as they went house to house to tend to people's needs they might have a drink of wine at each person's house and if they visited 5-10 people a day, that could result in drunkenness. The wine in New Testament times was much weaker than ours is, but if you drank enough of it, you could still get drunk. One man helps us here; he says,

> It is extremely difficult for the twentieth-century American to understand and appreciate the society of Paul's day. The fact that deacons were not told to become total abstainers, but rather to be temperate does not mean that Christians today can use liquor in moderate amounts. The wine employed for the common beverage was very largely water. The social stigma and the tremendous social evils that accompany drinking today did not attach themselves to the use of wine as the common beverage in the homes of Paul's day. Nevertheless, as the church grew and the Christian's consciousness and conscience developed, the dangers of drinking came to be more clearly seen. The principle laid down elsewhere by Paul that Christians should not do anything to cause a brother to stumble came to be applied to the use of wine.[32]

32 John MacArthur, *The MacArthur New Testament Commentary: 1 Timothy* (Chicago: Moody Press, 1995), 127.

The next qualification and the E on your acrostic is: eager-for-money-a-no-no. Paul says a deacon is not to be greedy for money. *Not greedy for money* means to not acquire money by greedy or disgraceful ways. This was a qualification for an elder as well. However, in the case of a deacon, it is perhaps even more necessary, because he would be entrusted with the church's monies. Deacons would collect the tithes, and they would distribute to those in need, as we saw in Acts 6. In John 12:1-6, we also have the account of Judas and his dishonest use of the apostles' monies:

> Then, six days before the Passover, Jesus came to Bethany, where Lazarus was who had been dead, whom He had raised from the dead. There they made Him a supper; and Martha served, but Lazarus was one of those who sat at the table with Him. Then Mary took a pound of very costly oil of spikenard, anointed the feet of Jesus, and wiped His feet with her hair. And the house was filled with the fragrance of the oil. But one of His disciples, Judas Iscariot, Simon's son, who would betray Him, said, "Why was this fragrant oil not sold for three hundred denarii and given to the poor?" This he said, not that he cared for the poor, but because he was a thief, and had the money box; and he used to take what was put in it.

Judas was, of course, an unbeliever, but the temptation for some might be to pocket the money in the same way Judas did. If a person has this temptation to be greedy for money, such a desire disqualifies him from the office of deacon. Let's look at verse 9:

> holding the mystery of the faith with a pure conscience.
> (1 Timothy 3:9)

The next quality on your acrostic is the S: stand firm in the faith. Paul says deacons are to be *holding the mystery of the faith.* The word *mystery* means something that was once hidden but now is made known. We know from Scripture that the mystery is the gospel and all that it would entail, which would be the death, burial, resurrection, and ascension of our Lord. As Paul says in Colossians 1:26-28, it is:

> … the mystery which has been hidden from ages and from
> generations, but now has been revealed to His saints. To them
> God willed to make known what are the riches of the glory of
> this mystery among the Gentiles: which is Christ in you, the
> hope of glory. Him we preach, warning every man and teaching
> every man in all wisdom, that we may present every man perfect
> in Christ Jesus.

And later in this very chapter of 1 Timothy, Paul writes in verse 16, "And without controversy great is the mystery of godliness: God was manifested in the flesh, Justified in the Spirit, Seen by angels, Preached among the Gentiles, Believed on in the world, Received up in glory." The word *holding* has the idea of something being held in one's possession. Deacons, and all believers really, should hold firmly to their faith; to do otherwise is nothing but false faith. We already saw 1 Timothy 1 that Hymenaeus and Alexander had made shipwreck of their faith; they did not hold fast to the faith. They also did not have a good conscience, which is what Paul says deacons must do. They most hold fast to their faith *with a pure conscience.* Paul adds this here because deacons, like any of us, can have all the right doctrine, but if they don't have the right conduct and a pure conscience, they will not have the right religion, they will not have genuine Christianity. If your heart is corrupt, your life will be corrupt. Paul continues on with the sixth qualification for a deacon in verse 10.

> But let these also first be tested; then let them serve as deacons,
> being found blameless. (1 Timothy 3:10)

To ensure that their faith and conduct are intact, deacons need to first be tested before they're assigned the title of deacon. The word *tested* refers to the testing of coins, to determine whether they are genuine. As with the office of elder, you would not want to put a new convert in the role of deacon; rather, you ought to wait and see what his life demonstrates. Many churches put someone into the office of deacon and then watch to see if that person is qualified. But that is doing it backwards, according to the Scriptures. They are first to be proved or tested by all these qualifications, and then they are to be put into the office. In our church, the leadership observes a person for at least a year before considering them for the office of elder or deacon. And let me pause and say that both elders and deacons should be continually tested. Just because they're qualified when they're installed in their particular office does not mean that they remain qualified for it. There should be frequent testing of elders and deacons, to make sure they are continually living above reproach. Unfortunately, we don't always find out that an elder or deacon is no longer qualified until it becomes a public scandal and they are forced to resign. Wise churches will have men in leadership who are held accountable and frequently tested. When such testing is over, they should be found blameless. *This is the sixth letter on your acrostic, the letter A: above reproach.* This means the same thing as it did for an elder. Deacons should live in such a way that no credible accusation can be made against them; there cannot be any reproach on their name.

In between the qualifications for deacons, Paul inserts a mysterious verse that has caused much controversy and has more than one possible interpretation. Paul brings women into the picture and says,

> Likewise, their wives must be reverent, not slanderers, temperate, faithful in all things. (1 Timothy 3:11)

The word *their* is not present in the Greek, so it would read *likewise wives*. The question comes to mind, "Who are these wives?" Some think this refers to the wives of the deacons and elders, and others hold that the wives are simply women deacons. But this brings up other questions. If it is the deacons' wives, then why would Paul not have listed qualifications for the elders' wives as well? (That would get me off the hook, since I'm an elder's wife!) Because the word their is not found in the original, it appears that this is pointing to women deacons. This is probably the intended meaning because the word for *wives* simply means women. Now, don't be disturbed by this idea; this is a position within the church which has no authority. These would simply be women servants, women table waiters. Also, it appears by the use of the word *likewise* that this is talking about a different classification of people here, in the same way that likewise is used in verse 8 when Paul begins to talk about the role of deacons. There is mention of women deacons in the word of God; Paul mentions a woman named Phoebe in Romans 16:1-2. He says, "I commend to you Phoebe our sister, who is a servant of the church in Cenchrea, that you may receive her in the Lord in a manner worthy of the saints, and assist her in whatever business she has need of you; for indeed she has been a helper of many and of myself also." Women deacons were simply to help the male deacons with the responsibilities of caring for the needs of the church body.

Regardless of which view you wish to take, Paul says that these women must also have certain qualities about them. It is interesting that these qualities are very similar to the four qualities Paul mentions in Titus 2 when he writes regarding the older women who should be discipling the younger women. There, he says they must have behavior that becomes holiness, not be false accusers, not be given to much wine, and be teachers of good things. Paul writes here in 1 Timothy 3 that these women must be reverent (behavior that is holy), not slanderers (same as false accuser), temperate (sober), and faithful in all things (similar to being a teacher of good things).

The first of these qualities, that these women must be *reverent* in their behavior, means that they must have behavior that is becoming as a priest. She must be a holy woman, or a priestess, we might say. She must have a godly, separated life. She must be dignified, just as Paul has already said that deacons must be dignified or reverent.

Secondly, she must *not* be a *slanderer*. This means that she should not be involved in gossip or slander. John Calvin once said, "Talkativeness is a disease of women and it gets worse with age." He also said there is nothing more slippery or loose than the tongue. This woman must not be loose with her tongue. Not long ago, I heard of a pastor who had to resign because his wife was using her tongue for slander and gossip.

Thirdly, Paul says they must be *temperate*. This means sober-minded. This means she must have her senses about here. She must wise up to her wifely duties. She should be self-controlled with her emotions, her spending habits, her thought life, her physical passions, her sexual passions, and her speech. Included in this would also be the admonition to not be given to wine, just like the elders and the deacons.

Lastly, Paul mentions that she is to be *faithful in all things*. This would include being faithful to the Lord, to her family, to her church, to the use of her spiritual gifts. To anything that she is called to do, she is to be faithful. Having said these things, Paul now shifts back to the qualities of the deacon and finishes up with the seventh and last quality of a deacon.

> Let deacons be the husbands of one wife, ruling their children and their own houses well. (1 Timothy 3:12)

The seventh and final quality of a deacon is the O on your acrostic: he must have an ordered family life. He must be the husband of one wife and must rule his children and his house well. The *husband of one wife* requirement is the same as what we saw in our last lesson regarding elders, so I won't elaborate on it here. He must also rule his children and house well, which is also similar to the qualifications of an elder. Paul finishes his remarks regarding deacons in verse 13 and says,

> For those who have served well as deacons obtain for themselves a good standing and great boldness in the faith which is in Christ Jesus. (1 Timothy 3:13)

Those who have served well as deacons obtain for themselves two things: *a good standing and great boldness in the faith.* The words *good standing* indicate the spiritual growth of the deacon. He is respected by all, having obtained good standing in the eyes of others. Such men receive a good report and are well-respected. The word *standing* is interesting; it includes the idea of a step up, which would mean that he is respected and put on a pedestal. Obviously, it is a respected position, and not an opportunity for a deacon to be puffed up with pride.

Paul says he obtains *great boldness in the faith*, which means that as he serves well and receives a good and respectable reputation for his service, he becomes confident and bold in his service toward God and others. Notice that this boldness and confidence is not in himself but *in the faith which is in Christ Jesus*. In himself, he knows he is nothing, but because of his servant's heart and the gifts which God has given to him, he can be confident.

Summary

What are the seven qualifications for deacons? *Dignified* (v 8); *Eager-for-Money-a-No-No* (v 8); *Above Reproach* (v 10); *Controlled Tongue* (v 8); *Ordered Family Life* (v 12); *Not a Drunk* (v 8); and *Stands Firm in the Faith* (v 9).

Once again, this lesson may not send any spiritual goose bumps up your spine. But, dear sister, we must be concerned about the leaders in our churches, whether they are elders or deacons. They must be qualified according to the standards which God set up for us and not according to what man thinks. We must pray for our leaders; we must encourage them; and we, too, must live our lives as they do.

Regardless of the view you take of verse 11, we women should be blameless in our home lives, blameless in our speech, and blameless in our walk with Christ.

> When Dr. John Watson was a child, he loved to see the procession of deacons at the administration of the Lord's Supper, and one old man with very white hair and a meek reverent face especially interested him. One day he was walking on the road and he passed a man breaking stones. The white hair caught his attention, and he looked back and recognized the deacon who had carried the cup at communion. Full of curiosity and surprise, he told his father the strange tale. His father explained

to him that the reason why the old man held so high a place in the church was that although he was one of the poorest men in all the town, he was one of the holiest. "James," he said, "breaks stones for a living, but he knows more about God than any person I have ever met."[33]

---

33   Paul Lee Tan, Th.D., *Encyclopedia of 7,700 Illustrations: Signs of The Times* (Rockville: Assurance Publishers, 1979), 1630.

Questions to Consider

The Seven Determining Qualities of a Deacon
1 Timothy 3:8-13

1. (a) Read 1 Timothy 3:1-13 and list the qualifications for elders as well as the qualifications for deacons. (b) Which of these qualifications are the same? (c) Which of them are different? (d) Do you think there is a reason for this?

2. Memorize 1 Timothy 3:11.

3. 1 Timothy 3:11 is a verse that is debated within the evangelical church. Some say it is referring to the qualifications of deacons' wives alone; some say it pertains to qualifications for both deacons' and elders' wives; and still others say it is a reference to women deacons. Using Bible study helps, what would be your conclusion? Of course, provide biblical support for your answer!

4. (a) Paul mentions in 1 Timothy 3 that both deacons and elders are not to get drunk with wine. Considering the following passages, why do you think this is essential for the officers of the church? Genesis 9:20-23; Proverbs 20:1; 23:29-35; Isaiah 5:11-12, 22; Habakkuk 2:15-17; Ephesians 5:18. (b) Why do you think more and more churches in our day are tolerating alcohol at church gatherings as well as promoting the attitude that drinking is the expected "norm" for believers?

5. If you knew for a fact that one of your elders or deacons was not qualified, according to the qualifications mentioned in 1 Timothy 3, what would you do?

6. Make an effort this week to reach out to one of the elders and/or deacons in your church by writing them a note of encouragement or inviting them to your home for a meal.

7. How can you be a blessing to the officers in your church? Write a prayer to the Lord asking Him to help you with this.

Chapter 9

Six Non-Negotiable
Fundamentals of the Faith

1 Timothy 3:14-16

Each year in December we celebrate the birth of our Savior, Jesus Christ—God manifest in the flesh. This is a mystery indeed! And perhaps it has become so mysterious that some churches have forgotten to put this truth before our mind's eye. A great many churches have left this fundamental of our faith, along with a number of the other truths Paul mentions as he closes out chapter three of his first letter to Timothy. Thus far, Paul has been writing concerning the church and the importance of sound doctrine. He's been writing about false teachers who have veered from the truth and turned to fables and endless genealogies and other nonsense. And, as he closes chapter three, Paul reminds Timothy of the essentials of the church of Jesus Christ, the pillar and ground of the truth. He makes it clear that the foundation of our faith is built not on fables but upon truth! It is not, as some would sing, "Santa Claus is Coming to Town," but "What Child is This, Christ the King, the Word Made Flesh." Let's consider these precious truths as we bring chapter three to a close.

1 Timothy 3:14-16

These things I write to you, though I hope to come to you shortly; [15]but if I am delayed, I write so that you may know how you ought to conduct yourself in the house of God, which is the church of the living God, the pillar and ground of the truth. [16]And without controversy great is the mystery of godliness: God was manifested in the flesh, justified in the Spirit, seen by angels, preached among the Gentiles, believed on in the world, received up in glory.

In these verses, we will come to see

Saint Paul's Reason for Writing this Epistle (vv 14-15) and *Six Pointed Realities of the Christian Faith* (v 16).

The leadership of the church needs to know what is to be taught in the church—and it's not fables; it is truth! But before he expounds on what is to be taught in the church, Paul begins by explaining his reason for writing this epistle, in verses 14 and 15.

Saint Paul's Reason for Writing this Epistle

1 Timothy 3:14-15

These things I write to you, though I hope to come to you shortly; (1 Timothy 3:14)

Paul begins in verse 14 by saying *these things I write to you*. The question we must ask is: what are *these things*? Some think Paul is referring to what he has just mentioned in chapter three, while others believe he's referring to the whole epistle. I'm inclined to think it is the latter, because Paul has set out to write an entire epistle and, at this point in it, he is not yet finished writing about how things should be conducted in the church. Paul's readers have yet to read what he has to say about doctrines of demons that are in the church, about using our spiritual gifts, about how to confront members in the church, about what qualifies a widow, about the role of young women, and so on. He's far from being finished writing about the way things should go for those who belong to God's church, for those who are members of God's household, the body of Christ! So, Paul says, even though I write these things to you, *I hope to come to you shortly*. This means I hope to come sooner rather than later; I hope to come with speed or quickness.

We know from chapter one of this letter that Paul and Timothy were in Ephesus ministering together, that Paul had to leave for Macedonia, and that he evidently wanted to come back to Ephesus and share with Timothy personally but was hindered at the time. We don't know why he was providentially hindered, but I would imagine, knowing Paul, that it involved ministry demands and not something trivial. I expect Paul's words encouraged Timothy because, as we learned in chapter one of this letter, Timothy was young and struggled with fear. Knowing that Paul would endeavor to come soon would likely give this young man hope, and perhaps, the courage to remain steadfast in the difficulties of ministry in Ephesus. Unfortunately, neither the Scriptures nor church history record for us whether Paul was ever able to make his way back to Ephesus to see young Timothy. But Paul does say in verse 15,

> but if I am delayed, I write so that you may know how you ought to conduct yourself in the house of God, which is the church of the living God, the pillar and ground of the truth. (1 Timothy 3:15)

Paul essentially says, "I do indeed hope to come to you quickly, but if for some reason I'm held back, I'm writing so that you will know how you ought to conduct yourselves in the house of God." The term *conduct* pertains to how people behave themselves. And because the house of God is a reference to all believers, the term *ought* pertains to all the church members; no one is exempt from being obedient to what God has said in His Word. We all have various issues, but our lives should be marked by overall obedience.

Paul says he's writing this letter to let Timothy, the church at Ephesus, and all of God's children know how to conduct themselves in the house of God. So, what does *conduct yourself in the house of God* mean? It means that we should know how we should behave in the house of God. That begs the question, "What is the house of God?" Is it the literal, physical place of worship? No, though I personally think it's a good idea to show respect and reverence in the literal place where we worship and teach our children to do the same! Rather, *the house of God* is a reference to the family of God. The house of God in the Old Testament was a reference to the tabernacle which was the place where God dwelt. We might say that it refers to the householders of God, or the members of the church, or God's family. In the context of this letter, Paul is referring to the church at Ephesus, but in the larger context of God's Word written to all of God's people, it would refer to the church of Christ universal, the body of believers in its entirety. As Paul puts it clearly in Ephesians 2:19-22, "Now, therefore, you are no longer strangers and foreigners, but fellow citizens with the saints and members of the household of God, having been built on the foundation of the apostles and prophets, Jesus Christ Himself being the chief cornerstone, in whom the whole building, being fitted together, grows into a holy temple in the Lord, in whom you also are being built together for a dwelling place of God in the Spirit." Paul is basically saying, as he has in so many other places, that we are to behave like children of God, we are to live out our faith, we are to be holy as He is holy, and we are to conduct ourselves in a manner worthy of our calling.

Paul also reminds us that this is not the church of just any god, but it is *the church of the living God. The living God* is a stark contrast to the Temple of Artemis, or Diana, which was so prominent in Ephesus. There was nothing living about that for sure! It was a dead, dumb idol! But we serve a living God, and in fact, we who are God's children are referred to in 1 Peter 2:4-5 as living stones. And Hebrews 10:31 tells us that it is a fearful thing to fall into the hands of the living God. Some give no thought to the fact He is living and that one day we will stand before Him but, my friend, this is the truth!

This church of the living God is also *the pillar and ground of the truth*. To what exactly does this refer? A *pillar* is a large column that holds something up, usually a roof or a building. The church at Ephesus would understand this terminology because the temple of Diana was held up by 127 pillars, each of which represented a king. In the case of Diana's temple, these pillars supported idolatry. But the house of the living God is supported by the pillar *of the truth*, that is, it holds up the truth. It supports the Word of God, which is the truth. Let me pause here and say that if you are not in a church that upholds the Word of God, then you need to prayerfully consider removing yourself from that church and getting into one that upholds

God's Word. Anything else is nothing more than sinking sand. The church today is a far cry from what Christ intended it to be. In fact, the day I was writing this lesson, I spoke on the phone with a young lady I have never met. I was giving her counsel about a particular problem she was having, and I was giving her the Word of God as the authority. Before I hung up with her, she mentioned that she had spoken to another "Christian" counselor just the day before, and she mentioned to me the counsel she had received. When I asked, "So, what Scripture was used to back up that counsel?" She simply admitted, "None." And I answered, "That's because there is none to support it." My friend, God's Word is the plumb line for our lives.

Paul goes on to say that the church is not only the pillar but also *the ground of the truth*. The *ground* of the truth would indicate that the truth is our foundation; it is fixed and cannot move. It is what Peter says in 1 Peter 2:6-7 about Christ being the chief cornerstone. It is interesting that both Peter and Paul refer to the body of Christ as a building where Christ is the foundation or chief cornerstone. Dear one, Christ is our solid rock, and any other foundation is only sinking sand that will collapse and crumble. Consider the parable Jesus told in Matthew 7 regarding the foolish man and the wise man. The wise man built his house upon the rock; the winds blew and the storms came, but the house stood firm. This man's foundation was solid; he did not waver when the trials of life came. But there was also a foolish man who built his house upon the sand. The same storms came his way, yet his house fell, and Jesus said, "And great was its fall" (Matthew 7:27).

It is interesting that when we start our next lesson, in chapter four, verse 1, Paul will write that some will depart from this truth, from the church of the living God, the pillar and ground of the truth. Some will indeed sink because their foundation is nothing but sinking sand!

As Paul closes his thoughts here on the church being founded upon and upholding the truth, he transitions to some essential truths that should form our confession of faith. So, we turn from Paul's reason for writing, which is so that Timothy, the church at Ephesus, and the church universal should know how to conduct themselves in the house of God, to now consider several realities of the Christian faith.

Six Pointed Realities of the Christian Faith

1 Timothy 3:16

> And without controversy great is the mystery of godliness: God was manifested in the flesh, justified in the Spirit, seen by angels, preached among the Gentiles, believed on in the world, received up in glory.

Right here in this verse are listed the foundations of the Christian faith. If you do not hold to these truths, then you need to rethink what you believe. In my opinion, too many churches have veered far from heralding these doctrines, and I fear we are becoming like the church in the following story:

> There once was an old church in England. A sign on the front of the building read, "We preach Christ crucified." After a time, ivy grew up and obscured the last word. The motto now read, "We preach Christ." The ivy grew some more, and the motto read, "We preach." Finally, ivy covered the entire sign, and the church died. Such is the fate of any church that fails to carry out its mission in the world.[34]

Paul says *without controversy*, which means this cannot be disputed, this is certain. What cannot be disputed? What is certain? That *great is the mystery of godliness*. This is very interesting terminology because we know from Acts 19:34 that when the uproar was happening in Ephesus the crowd cried out for two hours, "Great is Diana of the Ephesians!" But God's people know better; those who are members of His household know that He alone is the pillar and ground of the truth; they know that great is the mystery of godliness, not great is the goddess Diana!

---

34 John MacArthur, *The MacArthur New Testament Commentary: 1 Timothy* (Chicago: Moody Press, 1995), 143.

We have come across this word *mystery* before, and we've learned that it means something that was once hidden but is now revealed, and it is specifically a reference to the gospel—here is the mystery of godliness, the mystery of the gospel. And six clear statements are made about this mystery. The first is this: *God was manifested in the flesh.* This means that God was revealed in the flesh; He came to earth and was born of the Virgin Mary. He had flesh and blood just like you and me. He had parents just like you and me. He felt pain, hunger, and thirst, and He got weary. He had a name, and His name was Jesus. John puts it well in John 1:14, "And the Word became flesh and dwelt among us, and we beheld His glory, the glory as of the only begotten of the Father, full of grace and truth." And, as Paul says in Galatians 4:4-5, "But when the fullness of the time had come, God sent forth His Son, born of a woman, born under the law, to redeem those who were under the law, that we might receive the adoption as sons." Jesus was God in the flesh.

The second mystery of this gospel is a mystery indeed, in that it's a bit difficult to understand: He was *justified in the Spirit.* There are a few thoughts about the meaning of this phrase. The word *justified* means vindicated or declared righteous. So, this phrase could refer to Jesus' human spirit, which would indicate that Jesus was declared righteous in regard to His spiritual nature. This would be validated by Matthew 3:17, which is the account of Jesus' baptism: "And suddenly a voice came from heaven, saying, 'This is My beloved Son, in whom I am well pleased.'" However, it could also refer to the Holy Spirit, which would mean that Jesus was vindicated by the testimony of the Holy Spirit who attested to Jesus' righteousness. This would be much like what is written in Hebrews 9:14, "... how much more shall the blood of Christ, who through the eternal Spirit offered Himself without spot to God, cleanse your conscience from dead works to serve the living God?" Yet another possibility is that Christ was justified by the Spirit through the works He did while on earth. As Christ did works of miracles, healings, signs and wonders, it vindicated who He was. The centurion gazing upon Christ after His death on the cross said it well in Luke 23:47, "So when the centurion saw what had happened, he glorified God, saying, 'Certainly this was a righteous Man!'"

The third mystery of godliness is that He was *seen by angels*. This indeed happened numerous times. He was seen by angels at His birth, as Luke 2:13-14 records: "And suddenly there was with the angel a multitude of the heavenly host praising God and saying: 'Glory to God in the highest, and on earth peace, goodwill toward men!'" There were angels also present when He was tempted in the wilderness. In Matthew 4:11, it states that after Satan was finished with his temptation of Christ, angels came and ministered to Him. Angels were also present in the garden of Gethsemane when He was in deep agony and prayer before the crucifixion. Luke 22:41-44 says, "And He was withdrawn from them about a stone's throw, and He knelt down and prayed, saying, 'Father, if it is Your will, take this cup away from Me; nevertheless not My will, but Yours, be done.' Then an angel appeared to Him from heaven, strengthening Him. And being in agony, He prayed more earnestly. Then His sweat became like great drops of blood falling down to the ground." In John 20:11-13 and Acts 1:10-11, we also see that angels were present at Jesus' empty tomb and at His ascension.

The fourth pointed reality of our Christian faith is that He was *preached among the Gentiles*, or preached among the nations, which would include all the kingdoms of the world. This would be an astonishing point because Christ broke the barrier between Jew and Gentile. He came to save all races; there is no distinction between Jew or Greek. Acts 26:17 clearly states that Paul's charge on the Damascus road was to take the gospel to the Gentiles. Jesus also makes this charge clear—that the gospel should be preached to all nations—just before His ascension into heaven. Matthew 28:18-20 states:

> And Jesus came and spoke to them, saying, "All authority has been given to Me in heaven and on earth. Go therefore and make disciples of all the nations, baptizing them in the name of the Father and of the Son and of the Holy Spirit, teaching them

> to observe all things that I have commanded you; and lo, I am
> with you always, even to the end of the age. Amen."

This is certainly a part of the mystery—that the gospel would be offered to the Gentiles. This preaching of the gospel to all nations, including the Gentiles, would take place after Christ's ascension into heaven, which is the sixth fundamental of our faith.

But before we get to that sixth fundamental truth, let's consider the fifth one. Paul writes that Christ was *believed on in the world*. This is an amazing fact, indeed, that wicked men and women would believe the gospel and be saved. When we consider that the whole world lies under the sway of the evil one (1 John 5:19), it is truly amazing that some would believe the gospel. John 3:16, a verse that most of us can probably quote, is truly profound. "For God so loved the world that He gave His only begotten Son, that whoever believes in Him should not perish but have everlasting life." And even verse 17, "For God did not send His Son into the world to condemn the world, but that the world through Him might be saved." (See also Acts 2:41; 4:4; 9:42; 11:21; 17:4, 34; and 18:8 for great examples of this reality.) This also is a part of this mystery of godliness that the world would believe on Christ, even those who crucified Him. I think of what the centurion said in Mark 15:39 after Jesus breathed His last breath: "Truly this man was the Son of God!"

The final pointed reality of our faith is that Christ was, sixth, *received up in glory*. This is a reference to His ascension, to when He went back into heaven. Acts 1:1-9 says,

> The former account I made, O Theophilus, of all that Jesus
> began both to do and teach, until the day in which He was taken
> up, after He through the Holy Spirit had given commandments
> to the apostles whom He had chosen, to whom He also presented
> Himself alive after His suffering by many infallible proofs,
> being seen by them during forty days and speaking of the
> things pertaining to the kingdom of God. And being assembled
> together with them, He commanded them not to depart from
> Jerusalem, but to wait for the Promise of the Father, "which,"

He said, "you have heard from Me; for John truly baptized with water, but you shall be baptized with the Holy Spirit not many days from now." Therefore, when they had come together, they asked Him, saying, "Lord, will You at this time restore the kingdom to Israel?" And He said to them, "It is not for you to know times or seasons which the Father has put in His own authority. But you shall receive power when the Holy Spirit has come upon you; and you shall be witnesses to Me in Jerusalem, and in all Judea and Samaria, and to the end of the earth." Now when He had spoken these things, while they watched, He was taken up, and a cloud received Him out of their sight.

It is interesting to consider that all three members of the Trinity are referred to in this account.

Summary

As we began our study of these verses, we saw *Saint Paul's Reason for Writing this Epistle* (vs 14-15). The reason Paul writes this epistle is so that they, and we, would know how to conduct ourselves as believers, as members of God's household. Do you know how to conduct yourself as a child of God? Are you so familiar with the 66 books of the sacred library that there is no question in your mind when things arise that you are sure of what you should say, do, or think because it is what God says you should say, do, or think? How have you grown in the past year in your knowledge of God's Word?

Next, we saw *Six Pointed Realities of the Christian Faith* (v 16): God was manifest in the flesh, justified in the Spirit, seen by angels, preached to the nations, believed on in the world, and received up into glory. Do you believe these truths? Do you believe them intellectually, or have you believed them in your heart to the point that they have changed the way you live? Are these truths non-negotiable to you or are you toying around with novel ideas that have crept into the church regarding the validity of these truths?

Each year, as we celebrate the Christmas holiday, we have a wonderful opportunity to make sure that He is who we celebrate— Christ. We have a wonderful opportunity to tell others that Christ was manifest in the flesh, He came to earth as a baby to grow up and to die for our sins. We have the opportunity to tell the lost world that the one who ascended into heaven will come again to judge the living and the dead. We have the opportunity to compel them to repent of their sins and give their lives to His Lordship. This is our charge before God, for it was His Son who commanded us to go into all the world and preach the gospel. This is one of the many ways that His Word says we are to conduct ourselves as members of His household. We are to be his witnesses!

A few weeks before I wrote this lesson, a man shared with our church how the pastor that had married his son had made it his aim in life to share the Lord with one person every day. I found myself pricked in my heart because of my negligence. Around that same time, I was asking a friend of mine who was the last person she knew who had embraced the gospel. We both had a difficult time thinking of anyone. My friend, does the fault lie with you and with me? Are there few conversions in our day because there are few of God's children zealous for the gospel? Will you be obedient to the Lord in this area of your life and will you endeavor along with me to make it your aim to share the glorious gospel, these six non-negotiable fundamentals of the faith, with others?

Questions to Consider
Six Non-Negotiable Fundamentals of the Faith
1 Timothy 3:14-16

1. (a) As you read 1 Timothy 3:14-16, note what you learn about the house of God and about God? (b) Summarize 1 Timothy chapter three in a few sentences.

2. Memorize 1 Timothy 3:16.

3. (a) In 1 Timothy 3:15, what does Paul call the church? (b) Who is the head of the church, according to Ephesians 5:23? (c) What did this Head do for the church, according to Ephesians 5:25-27? (d) According to Ephesians 5:24, what is the church's responsibility to the Head of the church?

4. (a) According to Acts 20:28; Romans 16:16; 1 Corinthians 1:2; 3:16; Ephesians 2:19-22; Colossians 1:13, 24; Hebrews 12:22-23; and 1 Peter 2:4-5, what else is the church called? (b) Based on what you know from God's Word, how would you define the church of God? (c) What does the church mean to you personally?

5. (a) Paul lists six non-negotiable fundamentals of the Christian faith in 1 Timothy 3:16. What other fundamentals of the faith does Scripture speak of? (Please give biblical reference!) (b) What precious truths of your Christian faith stand out as most important to you?

6. One of the non-negotiable fundamentals of our faith is God manifested in the flesh. As you consider the way we celebrate this reality each year at Christmastime, what things can you think of doing to ensure that you are focusing on the true meaning of Christmas each year?

7. Will you endeavor to share with at least one person this week regarding their need to embrace the truth of the gospel? Paul has given six basic truths that will help you get started. Please come with a prayer request for an opportunity to share with someone.

Chapter 10

Are You Being Deceived by Doctrines of Demons, or Do You Believe and Know the Truth?

1 Timothy 4:1-5

The very day I was preparing this lesson, I received a phone call from a woman in another state. She was very troubled and in need of advice, and a friend of hers had given her my name and told her I'd be able to give her some guidance. She proceeded to tell me that the Lord had told her to go off coffee, gluten, and a number of other things, and had called her to eat only fruits and veggies, as well as to fast. She went on to share some other things with me, and then mentioned that she had come across 1 Timothy 4:1-5 and now she was troubled, and that's why she was calling me. What should she do? Was she participating in doctrines of demons? Had Satan deceived her when she thought God was telling her to do these things? After all, the evil one does appear as an angel of light. I spent nearly an hour with her on the phone trying to help her think biblically, and I am certain that it was not "by chance" that I was studying this passage the day she called me for help. So, what does the Scripture say regarding these issues? Well, let's look at what Paul says and discover first-hand!

1 Timothy 4:1-5

Now the Spirit expressly says that in latter times some will depart from the faith, giving heed to deceiving spirits and doctrines of demons, ²speaking lies in hypocrisy, having their own conscience seared with a hot iron, ³forbidding to marry, and commanding to abstain from foods which God created to be received with thanksgiving by those who believe and know the truth. ⁴For every creature of God is good, and nothing is to be refused if it is received with thanksgiving; [5]for it is sanctified by the word of God and prayer.

As we ended chapter three of Paul's letter, we learned that Paul's reason for writing to Timothy was that the church at Ephesus would know how to conduct themselves as believers, as members of God's household. Then, we saw six pointed realities of the Christian faith, that God was manifest in the flesh, justified in the Spirit, seen by angels, preached to the nations, believed on in the world, and received up into glory. In the verses we'll consider in this lesson, we will see

> *Two Causes of Apostasy* (v 1);
> *Two Characteristics of Apostates* (v 2);
> *Two Creeds of Apostates* (v 3); and
> *Two Commands Regarding What God Created* (vv 4-5).

As we begin chapter four of this epistle, we are sobered to immediately learn that there are some who will not conduct themselves as members of God's household but choose, rather, to conduct themselves as members of Satan's house. There were and are some who, unfortunately, choose not to hold to the six non-negotiable fundamentals of the Christian faith but to adopt Satan's seducing doctrines instead. Paul begins by writing regarding those who have and will apostatize and mentions two causes for their departure from the faith, in verse 1.

Two Causes of Apostasy

1 Timothy 4:1

> Now the Spirit expressly says that in latter times some will depart from the faith, giving heed to deceiving spirits and doctrines of demons, (1 Timothy 4:1)

Paul begins with the word *now*, but the Greek term is <u>de</u>, which is better translated as *but*. This makes sense because the word *but* is a word of contrast, and Paul is here contrasting what he has just said in the previous verse about the six non-negotiable fundamentals of the faith. Some obviously do not hold to those fundamental truths; some will depart from them. He explains that *the Spirit expressly says that in latter times some will depart from the faith.* So, we need to ask the question, "When did the Spirit say this?" A number of possibilities exist. Paul could be referring to a direct prophecy the Holy Spirit gave to him personally concerning this matter. Or, he could be referring to the prophecy he himself gave through the Holy Spirit in Acts 20:29 when he was addressing the elders at Ephesus, which is the church Paul is writing to in 1 Timothy. He said to them, "For I know this, that after my departure savage wolves will come in among you, not sparing the flock. Also from among yourselves men will rise up, speaking perverse things, to draw away the disciples after themselves." Or, he could be referring to the reality that everyone knew apostasy would take place because of Christ's teaching in Mark 13:22: "For false christs and false prophets will rise and show signs and wonders to deceive, if possible, even the elect." Whichever it might be, the Holy Spirit said this *expressly*, which means that He said it an outspoken way, or openly.

So, what did the Spirit say? *In the latter times some will depart from the faith.* What are the *latter times?* The latter times, or last days, began with the ascension of Christ and will culminate when the Lord returns. We know from what Paul writes in 2 Thessalonians 2:3 that as we wind up the end of the age there will be a great apostasy, a great falling away from the faith: "Let no one deceive you by any means; for that Day will not come unless the falling away comes first, and the man of sin is revealed, the son of perdition." Here in 1 Timothy, however, Paul speaks of *some* who will depart from the faith. Paul already mentioned two of the some in chapter 1 when he mentioned Hymenaeus and Alexander. So, what will these some do? Paul says they *will depart from the faith,* which means they will desert, they will abandon, they will withdraw, they will apostatize from the faith. This would be like Hymenaeus and Alexander, who Paul says made shipwreck of their faith. These are those who willfully abandon the faith they claim to have. As sad and sobering as this may be, it does happen. And the apostle John tells us why this happens in 1 John 2:19, when he writes, "They went out from us, but they were not of us; for if they had been of us, they would have continued with us; but they went out that they might be made manifest, that none of them were of us."

Here in 1 Timothy, Paul adds two more reasons why they departed from the faith. Not only were they never in the faith, as John says, but they were *giving heed to deceiving spirits* and *giving heed to doctrines of demons*. These are the two causes of apostasy, according to this text. Now, what does it mean to give heed to deceiving spirits? To *give heed* means to cling to something, and the word *deceive* means to wander and it is a term that is related to the English word planet. *Deceiving spirits* would be spirits which cause people to wander from the truth and cling to what is false. These cannot be from the Holy Spirit because the Word tells us in John 16:13 that He leads us into all truth. A deceiving spirit would be any spirit that seduces or misleads, that is an imposter or a fraud. It has been said that "Deception has her spirits, emissaries of every kind, which she employs to darken the hearts and destroy the souls of men."[35] My dear friend, this would include all false teachers and all false teaching. It would include anything that doesn't match up to the truth of God's Word. This was Eve's problem, which we saw when we were in chapter two; she listened to Satan and doing so got her and the whole world into a lot of trouble. As women, we must know the truth, and we must not for one moment accept anything that does not measure up to Scripture, though well-meaning friends might try to convince us otherwise. The wonderful promise of 1 John 4:1-6 assures us that genuine believers will not be led away by false spirits.

Paul mentions another cause of apostasy and that is giving heed to doctrines of demons. What are *doctrines of demons*? They are the teachings, or *doctrines*, that are engineered by Satan. *Demons* are the source of false doctrine; either something is of the Holy Spirit or it is of another spirit, which is demonic. There are so many

---

35 Adam Clarke, PC Study Software, Version 5, 1988-2008

false teachings that would fall into this category that it would be impossible to mention them all, but certainly cults, the prosperity gospel, mysticism, salvation by works, new age teachings, devil worship, and the like would fit the bill. Most of these we are familiar with and we would agree with Paul that they are false and say, "Oh yeah, those *are* awful! I wouldn't be led away by that stuff!" But oh, my friend, when we get into verse 3 in a moment, I'm afraid we will all be pricked in our conscience, because I fear that many have bought into seducing spirits and doctrines of demons. But before we look at verse 3, let's look at verse 2 and notice the two characteristics of apostates.

Two Characteristics of Apostates

1 Timothy 4:2

> speaking lies in hypocrisy, having their own conscience seared
> with a hot iron, (1 Timothy 4:2)

Before we look at the first characteristic of apostates, notice that there is a contrast between what we saw in verse 1, where we're told what the Holy Spirit speaks, and what we see here in verse 2, where it is the false spirits that speak. And Paul says they *speak lies in hypocrisy*. This is the first characteristic of apostates. (Paul only mentions two characteristics of apostates here, but the Scriptures teach many characteristics of apostates. So, what does it mean that they speak lies in hypocrisy? It refers to the fact that they are liars; they are hypocrites; they are actors in a play. The things they say and do have nothing to do with truth but have everything to do with lies. Naturally, the question comes to mind, "Do they know they are lying?" Many of them know indeed that they are lying, but some have even gone so far in their deceptions that lying has become a way of life to them and they know nothing else but to speak lies; their conscience has become so seared that they don't know a lie from the truth. My friend, this is a scary place to be; I've met people like this, and you cannot trust anything they say. Their lives are a sham and everyone around them, except themselves, seems to know it. These people teach doctrines that are made up in their own minds to their own liking and not the doctrines of the Word of God. They are like the prophets of 1 Kings 22:23, in whose mouths the Lord put a lying spirit.

Paul next mentions a second characteristic of apostates, and it is *having their own consciences seared with a hot iron*. There seems to be a progression here, from habitually lying to the point that the *conscience* becomes seared. Paul elaborates on this truth in Romans 1:24-32 when he says,

> Therefore God also gave them up to uncleanness, in the lusts of their hearts, to dishonor their bodies among themselves, who exchanged the truth of God for the lie, and worshiped and served the creature rather than the Creator, who is blessed forever. Amen. For this reason God gave them up to vile passions. For even their women exchanged the natural use for what is against nature. Likewise also the men, leaving the natural use of the woman, burned in their lust for one another, men with men committing what is shameful, and receiving in themselves the penalty of their error which was due. And even as they did not like to retain God in their knowledge, God gave them over to a debased mind, to do those things which are not fitting; being filled with all unrighteousness, sexual immorality, wickedness, covetousness, maliciousness; full of envy, murder, strife, deceit, evil-mindedness; they are whisperers, backbiters, haters of God, violent, proud, boasters, inventors of evil things, disobedient to parents, undiscerning, untrustworthy, unloving, unforgiving, unmerciful; who, knowing the righteous judgment of God, that those who practice such things are deserving of death, not only do the same but also approve of those who practice them.

Did you notice what Paul states in this Romans passage that they exchanged the truth of God for? For lies! They left the truth and embraced and clung to lies! It is for this reason God gives them up to a debased mind, a seared conscience.

What does it mean to have a conscience that is *seared with a hot iron*? For something to be *seared* means that it is cauterized and has become rigid, hard, and insensitive. In biblical times, those who had committed crimes would be marked so that they would bear the stigma of what they had done. So it is with those who are caught up in doctrines of demons; they bear their hypocrisy and others can see what they have done or are doing. They bear the marks of their hypocrisy just like a garment bears the permanent marks of an iron that is too hot. We've all done that, right? We get our iron too hot and the next thing we know we have permanently marked a beautiful garment and most of the time it is not repairable or wearable! In biblical times, a branding iron was used on livestock to indicate ownership; today, farmers and ranchers brand cattle for the same purpose. In this same way, those who have their consciences seared with a hot iron are the property of seducing spirits and doctrines of demons. My friend, it is frightening to think of a conscience being seared, and yet more frightening is what Paul says in the next verse, something which might shake all of us up.

What do these apostates teach? Surely it must be something like "dishonor your parents," "burn your children at the stake," "worship demons," "denial of the virgin birth," "denial of Jesus being the Son of God," or some other horrendous doctrine, right? Even though those are all doctrines of demons, they're not quite as subtle as the two he mentions in verse 3, the two creeds of apostates. And isn't that just what Paul said, that they are seducing spirits? Satan comes as an angel of light to trip us up in subtle and seemingly inoffensive ways.

Two Creeds of Apostates

1 Timothy 4:3

> forbidding to marry, and commanding to abstain from foods which God created to be received with thanksgiving by those who believe and know the truth. (1 Timothy 4:3)

These two specific doctrines or creeds of demons seem to stem from the heresy of Gnosticism. We could take a whole lesson and still not be able to cover all that this heresy teaches, but suffice it to say for now, that Gnostics taught that it was knowledge and not faith that was essential for salvation. They were involved in many of the errors we see in our day: legalism, mysticism, astrology, angel worship, and rigid Asceticism (the doctrine that by abstinence and self-denial a person can train himself to be conformed to God's will; Paul confronts this error in Colossians 2:20-23). This heretical belief fleshed itself out in acts such as abstaining from marriage and adhering to strict dietary restrictions. Some accepted marriage as necessary to preserve the race, but regarded it as evil, and so they would adopt children. Other Gnostics thought that was too extreme because one cannot escape evil, so they cultivated an indifference to the world of sense; they would simply follow their fleshly impulses. This belief led them to an immoral life because they reasoned that the spirit was entirely separate from the body and therefore was not responsible for the acts of the body. Gnostics drank no wine and ate no meat; they lived on bread and vegetables alone. They condemned any natural cravings, believing our bodies to be evil and, because of that, denied themselves marriage and certain types of food.

Having said that, notice that Paul mentions the first condemning doctrine that these apostates taught: forbidding to marry. To forbid means to prevent or hinder. I've already mentioned what the Gnostics taught regarding marriage. In our day, most of us would look at the Roman Catholic Church and find that false teaching is practiced by priests who do not marry, but it seems that this error is a much broader category than that alone. It is true that forbidding to marry could be interpreted as a command to be celibate. But since the word forbid means to hinder or prevent, we could broaden our understanding of this to include what in our day has become the norm, even among professing Christians—not getting married but still living together. I am appalled at the growing number of people who call themselves "believers" and yet are living in fornication themselves or endorsing others who do.

> A study from the National Marriage Project found that more
> and more young adults today are delaying marriage because
> they see it as a capstone that comes after achieving one's life
> goals—professional and otherwise. And younger generations
> aren't the only ones staying single. According to the U.S.
> Census, the number of couples aged 50 and over who simply
> live together but are not married rose from 1.2 million in 2000
> to 2.8 million people in 2010. These people think that whether
> you're young or old, it is OK in some cases, even beneficial, to
> never get married.[36]

Encouraging others to not get married when marriage is a God-
ordained institution is blasphemous. (Unless, of course, that person
has been given the gift of singleness.) Paul will state later in this
very letter, in 1 Timothy 5:14, "Therefore I desire that the younger
widows marry, bear children, manage the house, give no opportunity
to the adversary to speak reproachfully." The writer to the Hebrews
also states in Hebrews 13:4, "Marriage is honorable among all, and
the bed undefiled; but fornicators and adulterers God will judge."
Jesus Himself states in Matthew 19:4-6, "Have you not read that He
who made them at the beginning 'made them male and female,'"
and, "'For this reason a man shall leave his father and mother and
be joined to his wife, and the two shall become one flesh'? So then,
they are no longer two but one flesh. Therefore what God has joined
together, let not man separate." And before we go on, I will also
make clear that the Scriptures clearly articulate that marriage is
between a man and a woman, not a man and a man, a woman and a
woman, or any other abominable combination.

The second thing apostates command is to abstain from foods
which God created to be received with thanksgiving. There were
certain foods, some meats in particular, that both Jew and Gentile
were forbidden to eat in biblical times under the Mosaic Law. But
Christ came to free us from the curse of the law and part of that
was proclaiming that everything He created was good to eat. In Acts
10, Peter is even rebuked for the error of his way regarding certain

---

36   http://www.huffingtonpost.com/2014/05/14/reasons-not-to-get-married_n_5274911.
html

meats he refused to eat. Romans 14:2 even addresses this, calling those weak who are offended with certain foods: "For one believes he may eat all things, but he who is weak eats only vegetables." When Paul uses the word "weak," he is referring to someone who is weak in their faith and needs to educate their conscience about what God says regarding food. Hebrews 13:9 says, "Do not be carried about with various and strange doctrines. For it is good that the heart be established by grace, not with foods which have not profited those who have been occupied with them." My dear sister, these preoccupations we have with diets and foods and what we think we should and should not eat lead us to what Paul says are various and strange doctrines, being seduced by demons. This is serious stuff, and it behooves us all to examine ourselves in this area.

Paul says to us, "Don't forbid marriage and don't forbid certain foods!" Why? Because everything is good if it is received with thanksgiving by those who believe and know the truth. These things are good if they are received with a thankful heart by those who believe and know the truth. This is kind of a scary statement, because it indicates, again, that those who are teaching this stuff do not believe the truth, nor do they know it—in short, they are lost. Those who are in the truth know that food and marriage are created by God, and they are thankful for both! Again, we have this concept of knowing the truth, which is a stark contrast to who in verse 2 are said to be speaking lies. Paul again repeats himself in verse 4, so this must have been a big issue; whenever you find repetition in the Scriptures, it is for the purpose of giving emphasis. And as Paul repeats himself, he also presents us with two certainties about what God has created.

Two Commands Regarding What God Created

1 Timothy 4:4-5

> For every creature of God is good, and nothing is to be refused
> if it is received with thanksgiving; (1 Timothy 4:4)

This is an interesting statement, in light of our reference in Romans 1, because verse 21 of Romans 1 says, "because, although they knew God, they did not glorify Him as God, nor were thankful, but became futile in their thoughts, and their foolish hearts were darkened." Instead of being thankful for what God created, they are unthankful. But God's children know better; they are thankful for whatever God gives them, whether it is marriage, food, or any other thing. Paul says *every creature of God is good.* Notice that he doesn't say everything is good, but that every created thing that *God* has made is good—this would include food and marriage. Listen to how this truth is expounded in Genesis 1:27-31:

> So God created man in His own image; in the image of God He created him; male and female He created them. Then God blessed them, and God said to them, 'Be fruitful and multiply; fill the earth and subdue it; have dominion over the fish of the sea, over the birds of the air, and over every living thing that moves on the earth.' And God said, 'See, I have given you every herb that yields seed which is on the face of all the earth, and every tree whose fruit yields seed; to you it shall be for food. Also, to every beast of the earth, to every bird of the air, and to everything that creeps on the earth, in which there is life, I have given every green herb for food'; and it was so. Then God saw everything that He had made, and indeed it was very good. So the evening and the morning were the sixth day. God saw *everything* He had made and *indeed* it was *very good*! (all emphases mine)

In our text, Paul gives two commands, or charges, regarding what God has created. The first charge is to refuse it not; he says *nothing is to be refused.* This means that *nothing*, not one thing that God has created, is to be *refused*, to be rejected or thrown away. (I don't think that includes throwing out leftovers, but I am for keeping them!) Secondly, Paul commands that we also *receive* what God has created *with thanksgiving.* We should be thankful for what we have to eat, and we should be thankful for the institution of marriage. Genuine believers, who believe and know the truth, know that food and marriage are both created by God and are therefore able to give humble thanks for them. Paul goes on to say, for it is sanctified by the word of God and prayer. (1 Timothy 4:5)

Food and marriage are pure and holy, which is what *sanctified* means. We who know God recognize this truth and are not seduced into forbidding marriage and forbidding foods which God has created for us to be received with thanksgiving. We know that these things are sanctified *by the Word of God*, the Word which God said in Genesis 1, when He declared that all He had created was indeed very good. This is God's Word, and it is not to be tainted with false ideas! We must not twist God's Word as Satan did when he asked Eve, "Has God said …?" making it mean something it did not! God's creation is not only sanctified by His Word, but also by *prayer*, which means that the recipients of these two graces, food and marriage, receive these things with gratitude. As Paul says in 1 Corinthians 10:31, "whether you eat or drink, or *whatever you do*, do all to the glory of God" (emphasis mine). This would encompass eating, drinking, marriage, and a myriad of other things. Both marriage and food are blessings and are sanctioned by God. One man says of this, "Those who thank not God for their food, and pray not for his blessing in the use of it, are unworthy even of a morsel of bread, and of the breath they breathe."[37] And I would add that those who do not thank God for their marriage and don't pray for His blessing on it are unworthy of it! This should challenge each of us to thank the Lord each time we eat a bite of food and to train our children to be thankful for the food they eat, as well as anything that God gives them. This should also challenge us to be more thankful for the marriage God has given us and to train our children and grandchildren that marriage is good and not something to be avoided.

Summary

What are the *Two Causes of Apostasy* (v 1)? Giving heed to deceiving spirits and giving heed to doctrines of demons. Are you guilty of listening to teachers and teaching that you know might be just a little "off," but you find enticing? Do you read things that tickle

---

37   Adam Clarke, PC Study Software; Version 5—1988-2008

your ears but don't challenge you spiritually? Is the Word of God more important to you than food or money? Do you cling to godly teaching and are you growing in your knowledge of God?

What are the *Two Characteristics of Apostates* (v 2)? Speaking lies in hypocrisy and having one's conscience seared. Are you in the habit of examining your words to make sure you are speaking truth and not half lies or flattery? Do you think "white lies" are okay? When you sin, are you convicted of it by the Holy Spirit, or have you minimized sin and rarely find yourself confessing or repenting of it? Is it possible you have quenched or grieved the Spirit of God and that your conscience is on the brink of being seared with a hot iron?

What are the *Two Creeds of Apostates* (v 3)? Forbidding marriage and forbidding certain foods. Do you believe that marriage is good? Have you been accepting of the new norm in our age, which says living together is okay or that same-sex marriage is acceptable? Do you confront professing Christians who you know are fornicating or have ungodly ideas about marriage? What about your diet, the things you eat? Do you make those spiritual issues and think that your way of eating is the only right way? Do you judge others in your heart because they are not convinced that your way of eating is the right and only way? Do you try and push your way of eating on others to the point of being offensive? Obviously, if we eat too much of anything it can be a bad thing; if we eat too much of things like sweets, or if we only eat certain things, like bread, it could result in any number of physical ailments. But what we have to be so careful about is making these concerns an idol and imposing our preferred dietary restrictions on other believers. We cannot make our eating habits a spiritual issue. We must keep in mind that healthy doctrine is of far more eternal value than healthy food.

What are the *Two Commands Regarding What God Created* (v 4-5)? Refuse it not and receive it with thanksgiving. Are you refusing to educate your conscience about what God says regarding food and marriage? Are you willing to study the Word of God so that you will be able to rightly divide the Word of truth, especially the truth regarding what God has created? Do you thank God for the food you eat and are you training your children to be grateful for the food they receive? Do you complain when you don't get to eat the things you like to eat? Do you allow your children to whine about the food they're given? Do you thank God for your marriage and the marriages of others? Are you praying against the attacks of the evil one, who would like nothing better than to destroy your marriage, the marriage that God instituted?

My friend, these are troublesome times in which we live, and these are the latter days. We must be on guard as we see the day approaching, ever alert so that we do not give heed to seducing spirits and doctrines of demons, but that we do as Paul will mention in just a few verses, "Take heed to yourself and to the doctrine. Continue in them, for in doing this you will save both yourself and those who hear you" (1 Timothy 4:16).

Questions to Consider

Are You Being Deceived by Doctrines of Demons, or Do You Believe and Know the Truth?
1 Timothy 4:1-5

1. (a) Read 1 Timothy 4:1-5 and list the things you notice about those who depart from the faith and the things you notice about those who know the truth? (b) What differences are there between these two lists?

2. Memorize 1 Timothy 4:4.

3. (a) Who is behind all seducing spirits, according to Genesis 3:1-5? (b) According to 2 Corinthians 11:13-15, why is it difficult at times to discern false spirits? (c) From what you find in 2 Peter 2:12-22; 1 John 4:1-6; and Jude 1:16-20, how can one discern seducing spirits?

4. (a) According to the Mosaic Law, what kinds of things were forbidden to be eaten? (See Leviticus 11.) (b) What took place in Acts 10:9-48 that changed what you read about in Leviticus 11? (c) How does this help you to better understand 1 Timothy 4:1-5? (d) What principles can you glean from Romans 14 that might help you when you have differences with others regarding what is proper to eat and what is not?

5. Paul says every creature of God is good and nothing is to be refused if it is received with thanksgiving. In context, this would include both food and marriage. Make a list of things that you are particularly thankful for, specifically pertaining to certain foods and the blessings of marriage.

6. (a) What would be some current "doctrines of demons" that you see being promoted within the Christian world today? (b) How do you keep yourself from being led away by seducing spirits and doctrines of demons?

7. Write out a prayer of thanksgiving to God for either food or the institution of marriage, or both.

Chapter 11

Five Things You Must Do to Get in Shape!

1 Timothy 4:6-11

After the feasting and festivities of a holiday season, many of us find ourselves a little thicker around the middle and that gets us contemplating the notion of going on a diet to shed those extra pounds. There are more diet plans than ants at a picnic. In addition to a new diet plan, some of us might also consider incorporating some exercise into our daily routine. Again, there are many options available.

But how many of us have given as much thought to our spiritual fitness as we have to our physical fitness? After the kinds of breaks we take around the holidays or the summer, do we return to things like Bible study only to find that we are in even worse shape spiritually than we are physically? During those seasons, how many of us find ourselves spending less time with God in prayer and in His Word and more time in things that lead to vain pursuits? How many of us vacate worship for the worldly vanities offered to us? Yes, we need to go to boot camp for sure, but it's not the boot camp the world has to offer; it's the boot camp the Word has to offer. In this lesson, we will consider five things we must do to get in shape—and they're not eating less, exercising more, taking vitamins, eliminating stress, and getting more sleep. Paul tells us what they are in 1 Timothy 4:6-11.

1 Timothy 4:6-11

If you instruct the brethren in these things, you will be a good minister of Jesus Christ, nourished in the words of faith and of the good doctrine which you have carefully followed. [7]But reject profane and old wives' fables, and exercise yourself toward godliness. [8]For bodily exercise profits a little, but godliness is profitable for all things, having promise of the life that now is and of that which is to come. [9]This is a faithful saying and worthy of all acceptance. [10]For to this end we both labor and suffer reproach, because we trust in the living God, who is the Savior of all men, especially of those who believe. [11]These things command and teach.

The apostle Paul states very plainly in 1 Corinthians 9:24-27 that the Christian life is like a race and each of us are running that race; he puts it like this:

> Do you not know that those who run in a race all run, but one receives the prize? Run in such a way that you may obtain it. And everyone who competes for the prize is temperate in all things. Now they do it to obtain a perishable crown, but we for an imperishable crown. Therefore I run thus: not with uncertainty. Thus I fight: not as one who beats the air. But I discipline my body and bring it into subjection, lest, when I have preached to others, I myself should become disqualified.

As we consider getting into spiritual shape in this lesson, we'll examine five things we must do as we run this race. Those five things include:

The Proper Diet for the Runner (v 6);
The Prohibited Diet for the Runner (v 7);
The Profitable Discipline for the Runner (v 8);
The Painful Demands of the Runner (vv 9-10); and
The Passionate Directives for the Runner (v 11).

Paul continues his thoughts regarding sound doctrine by reminding Timothy and his readers that we must make sure that we too do not get caught up in false doctrine. And in order to avoid such tragedy, we must run the race properly. The first thing a runner must do is have a proper diet. In the same way that a desire to be physically healthy means we must eat right, spiritual health is only possible if a Christian maintains a proper spiritual diet. What is that diet? Let's read verse 6 and find out.

The Proper Diet for the Runner

1 Timothy 4:6

If you instruct the brethren in these things, you will be a good
minister of Jesus Christ, nourished in the words of faith and
of the good doctrine which you have carefully followed.
(1 Timothy 4:6)

Paul begins by saying *if you instruct the brethren in these things*,
which means if you put in their remembrance these things, or if you
keep these things before their mind's eye. The question naturally
comes to mind, "What are *these things?*" The context tells us that
this is referring to what Paul said in verses 1-5, which we considered
in our previous lesson, specifically the dangers of getting caught up
in false teachings. Dear ones, we are no different than the church at
Ephesus in that we too need to be reminded of these things over and
over because we so easily forget the dangers of false teaching. In
fact, we probably need to be reminded more than they did because
we have more nonsense going on in the church today than they did
(just as Jesus predicted). Paul wrote to the church at Ephesus, in
Ephesians 4:14, warning them "that we should no longer be children,
tossed to and fro and carried about with every wind of doctrine, by
the trickery of men, in the cunning craftiness of deceitful plotting."

Paul goes on to say to Timothy, if you keep instructing them, *you
will be a good minister of Jesus Christ*, which means you will be
a noble or excellent servant. Did you catch what Paul said? "You
will be a good servant, a good minister." In our day, we would say,
"Timothy is putting his nose where it doesn't belong! Who is he
to judge regarding false teachers and false teaching? That young
Timothy is nothing but a legalist!" Many well-meaning Christians
say that we should not confront these things and that we need to show
love by being tolerant and silent. But this verse would certainly do
away with such nonsense. We are to defend the truth, not deny it!
Ministers, of all people, should be able to confront and refute those
who teach false doctrine, and yet, those who do so are often termed

judgmental. Titus 1:9 clearly states that this is the duty of a faithful minister: "holding fast the faithful word as he has been taught, that he may be able, by sound doctrine, both to exhort and convict those who contradict." He is a good minister who aims to please the Lord and not to please men. We must defend truth and we must speak out against error! This is for the glory of our Lord, whose reputation is at stake when false teachers and false doctrines are given a voice. My friend, we must be concerned about pleasing one person only and that is God!

> The failure to think biblically and theologically has cost the church dearly. It has allowed the infiltration of all sorts of error. That, in turn, has led to the church's becoming confused and weak. Convictionless preaching, consisting of watered down teaching, platitudes, and weak theology has replaced doctrinally strong expositional preaching. The resulting legacy has been one of charismatic confusions, psychological encroachment, mysticism, even psychic and occult influence. Much of that chaos can be attributed directly to the failure of pastors to think critically and preach with conviction. So many pastors have failed to draw the line clearly between truth and error and to build their people up in the rich and sound doctrine of God's Word. Such weak preachers are often said to compensate by having what some call a "pastor's heart." A pastor's heart, however, is not measured by how good a man is at petting sheep, but by how well he protects them from wolves and feeds them so they grow to be mature and strong.[38]

Why would instructing these believers regarding doctrines of demons and seducing spirits make Timothy a good minister of Jesus Christ? Because, by doing so, he would *nourish them in the words of faith and of good doctrine*, not the doctrines of demons and seducing spirits. The term *nourish* means to be constantly nourishing yourself. In the physical realm you must eat daily to sustain your physical life. So it is in the spiritual realm. You must constantly feed on God's Word or you will die spiritually; you will be malnourished. What is the proper diet for a runner? The *words of faith and of good doctrine*! And notice that it is *good doctrine*, not the doctrines of demons as

---

38   John MacArthur, *The MacArthur New Testament Commentary: 1 Timothy* (Chicago: Moody Press, 1995), 159-160.

we learned about in our last lesson. *Words of faith* would include the entire body of truth contained in God's Word—all of God's Word. I am shocked at the number of believers I know who admit they've never read their Bible through even once and are satisfied with a dribble of God's Word once a week. How can they be nourished?! How can they survive?! The words *good*, or sound, *doctrine* indicate sound theology that arises out of the proper study and interpretation of God's Word.

Ladies, this takes time; we cannot casually glance at the Word of God and possibly think we know it. In James 1:25, James talks about the man who looks into the perfect law of liberty, and when he speaks of looking into the Word, he is referring to the idea of bending down to study it for long periods of time, not a casual glance. Paul says in 2 Timothy 2:15, "Study to shew thyself approved unto God, a workman that needeth not to be ashamed, rightly dividing the word of truth" (KJV). I know well-meaning women who nourish themselves spiritually in "Christian" romance novels and devotional literature, and I feel sad for them because their strength will undoubtedly fail in the day of adversity because they are not strong in the faith and they have not nourished themselves in the meat of God's Word.

An interesting and yet very pertinent side note is this: Timothy's mother and grandmother taught him the Scriptures from his childhood; they were the ones who began that good spiritual nourishment for him. Wise mothers and grandmothers will realize that the nourishment a child needs is not just physical but spiritual. In fact, the spiritual is far more important because it has one's soul at stake. The body will decay, but the soul will live forever—either in heaven or in hell. This should be an encouragement to moms and grandmas that the influence we have on our children can be of eternal value if we influence them toward godliness, if we spend time instructing them in the ways of the Word and not in the ways of the world. Timothy knew that he must not let the business of life and the distractions of the age keep him from the one thing that is needful, to sit at Jesus' feet. We must do the same as in our age. We have the temptation to get caught up in reading and writing blogs, in various social media platforms, and substituting that for meaningful time with God.

Timothy, being a good minister, not only nourished himself in good doctrine but he also *carefully followed* it, which means he closely followed sound doctrine. He conformed to it like a pattern we would trace on fabric. Oh, that we would carefully follow sound doctrine! So many in our day are carelessly following sound doctrine, and yet curiously following novel ideas. Now we will move from the proper diet for the runner to the prohibited diet for the runner, in verse 7. What should a good servant who is running the spiritual race avoid? Paul tells us in verse 7.

The Prohibited Diet for the Runner

1 Timothy 4:7

> But reject profane and old wives' fables, and exercise yourself toward godliness. (1 Timothy 4:7)

But is a word of contrast; in contrast to words of faith and good doctrine which are proper nourishment, profane and old wives' fables are prohibited nourishment. Paul even uses a strong word, *reject*, which means to refuse, avoid, don't pay attention to, don't waste your time, have nothing to do with. These things we are to reject are *profane and old wives' fables*. Paul mentions something similar in 2 Timothy 2:16: "But shun profane and idle babblings, for they will increase to more ungodliness." *Profane* means that they are wicked or heathen. *Old wives' fables* are fables or tales that are not founded upon fact and which old women think are important. (We looked at this idea in 1 Timothy 1:4.) These silly tales would go back and forth between old women who liked to gossip and especially loved to pass these on to children. The women of Paul's day were not encouraged to be educated or to study, so the result, many times, would be that they'd get caught up in foolish nonsense. My sister, we have so many privileges in our world today and so many resources for Bible study that there is simply no excuse for such silliness. Instead of being involved in such nonsense, Paul says we are to *exercise*, or discipline, ourselves *toward godliness*. The term *exercise* comes the Greek word gumnazo, from which we get our English word gymnastics. This would be strenuous exercise or training. *Godliness* is a word which means piety or right conduct. In biblical times, young athletes would spend most of their days in physical training for the Olympic Games. In fact, in our day it takes 4-8 years of disciplined training to get ready for the Olympics. And such training would require many hours a day, six days a week of grueling training. But just as that training pays off in the privilege of competing in the Olympics, so the hard work of exercising ourselves toward godliness brings great reward—only ours is a much greater reward! As older women, we need to be sure we are not guilty of setting ungodly examples by getting caught up in foolish chatter and the nonsense of our day. Rather, we must work to set godly examples by being disciplined and godly. Paul is clear in 2 Timothy 4:3-4 that a time is going to come when people won't endure sound doctrine but will instead turn their ears away from truth and indulge in fables. Dear sisters, we are there!

Not too long ago while I was speaking at a church I was invited to go out with the leadership wives. I was so excited to be able to spend time with them and pick their brains about ministry and the things of God. Much to my surprise, the whole evening was spent talking about some diet their whole church was on and how much weight they'd collectively lost. They went on to describe the diet in detail. And I remember coming back to the hotel and sharing with my friend, Debbie, how sorely disappointed I was, and how I had wanted to say, "Are you this passionate about the gospel?" Paul tells us in verse 8 why godliness is the thing the good Christian runner pursues.

The Profitable Discipline for the Runner

1 Timothy 4:8

For bodily exercise profits a little, but godliness is profitable for all things, having promise of the life that now is and of that which is to come. (1 Timothy 4:8)

Notice that Paul doesn't condemn *exercise*, but he does want his readers to know that it only *profits a little*. The athletes of his day were just as obsessed with their bodies as we are in our day. Paul doesn't condemn exercising the body. Bodily exercise does have some advantage, some benefit, but Paul says it's only a *little* profit, which means that it is profitable for only a brief period of time and then your body is in the grave! Even the Mayo Clinic tells us that there are benefits to exercise, seven of them to be exact:

1. Controls weight
2. Combats health conditions and diseases
3. Improves Mood
4. Boosts energy
5. Promotes better sleep
6. Puts the spark back into your sex life
7. Exercise is fun![39]

But, ladies, as good as physical exercise is for your body, there is a spiritual exercise that is of eternal value. In contrast to bodily exercise, there is a kind of exercise that is profitable in this life and the life to come, and it's called *godliness*! One man writes,

> Godly people are disciplined people. It has always been so. Call to mind some heroes of church history—Augustine, Martin Luther, John Calvin, John Bunyan, Susanna Wesley, George Whitefield, Lady Huntington, Jonathan and Sarah Edwards, Charles Spurgeon, George Muller—they were all disciplined people. In my own pastoral and personal Christian experience, I can say that I've never known a man or woman who came to spiritual maturity except through discipline. Godliness comes through discipline.[40]

---

39 https://www.mayoclinic.org/healthy-lifestyle/fitness/in-depth/exercise/art-20048389
40 Donald S. Whitney, *Spiritual Disciplines for the Christian Life* (Colorado Springs: NavPress, 1991), 19.

Paul says that godliness *is profitable for all things*, which is exactly what it means; godliness is profitable for everything, things like your home, your work, your play, your church, all the decisions you make—everything! And it's profitable for both *the life that now is and the life which is to come.* The profitable discipline for the runner is not going to the gym to work out but training himself in godliness! Godliness does not come easily, my friend; we do not get it by osmosis. It is painful, and Paul will explain to us the painful demands of the runner, in verses 9 and 10.

The Painful Demands of the Runner

1 Timothy 4:9-10

> This is a faithful saying and worthy of all acceptance. For to this end we both labor and suffer reproach, because we trust in the living God, who is the Savior of all men, especially of those who believe. (1 Timothy 4:9-10)

Just in case there are some who object to what Paul is writing, he says *this is a faithful saying and worthy of all acceptance*—essentially, "Listen up, what I'm saying is true and right, and it needs to be accepted and followed." And then he says *to this end we both labor and suffer reproach*. Runners are always reaching for the goal, for the prize, to win the race. So are we, as believers; we press toward the prize for the high calling in Christ Jesus. Paul puts it like this: *to this end*, for this reason, for this goal, this is why *we both labor and suffer reproach*. These are the painful demands of the runner of Jesus. Both of these are athletic terms. *Labor* means to work hard to the point of feeling fatigued. My friend, a lazy Christian is not a godly Christian. To *suffer* means to agonize, fight, and labor fervently. These two terms are not describing the physical exercise of a believer, but the spiritual exercise, the labor and toil that is involved when we work for the kingdom. It is difficult; it is hard; and many times it incurs persecution and hatred even from people within your own church. Jesus said, "Woe to you when all men speak well of you" (Luke 6:26). Paul said, "We must through many tribulations enter into the kingdom of God" (Acts 14:22). Jesus said, "Strive to enter through the narrow gate" (Luke 13:24). These are not tickle-your-ear phrases. But, my dear sister, the joy of knowing our Lord and the blessing of being His child far outweighs any difficulty in this life. The sufferings of this life are not worthy to be compared to the glory that will be revealed in us.

You might be saying, "This is just a little too nuts for me. Paul must be a masochist! He is sick in the head and needs a psychiatrist if he thinks this is the good life of a runner!" Paul would beg to differ with you; he says we do these things *because we trust in the living God*, because we hope in the living God, *who is the Savior of all men*. The Psalmist says in Psalm 27:13, "I would have lost heart, unless I had believed that I would see the goodness of the LORD in the land of the living." This is our hope, this is our joy—abundant life now and in eternity

When Paul says that the living God is *the Savior of all men*, he is not claiming to be a Universalist, and he doesn't believe that all men will be saved. God is the *Savior*, He is the deliverer, and He is the preserver of *all men*. He sends rain on the just and the unjust, He causes the sun to rise on the evil and the good. He gives common grace to all. But to those who believe He gives special grace. And that grace isn't only the grace of eternal life, which is the runner's prize, and not some trophy that will rot away, but an inheritance that won't fade. It also consists in gifts like the Holy Spirit and the fruit He produces in us—love, joy, peace, longsuffering, goodness, gentleness, meekness, self-control—and a list so long we could take a whole lesson on it alone! So, what should runners do with all of this? Should we store all this information away and refer to it now and then? No, a good runner will not keep these things to himself, but will pass them on to others. Let's close out this lesson by looking at the passionate directives for the runner.

The Passionate Directives for the Runner

1 Timothy 4:11

These things command and teach. (1 Timothy 4:11)

Paul ends this section in a manner similar to how he began it. He says here, *teach and command these things*; in verse 6 he told Timothy to instruct his people in these things. Here, Paul is referring to the things he has just said. We should *command* these things, which means to pound them in, to give notice or regard to something. To *teach* would be to explain these things so that they can be understood. We must not be timid and fearful, as Timothy often was tempted to be, but courageous and bold. We must speak the truth, guard the truth, and defend the truth. We must pass the baton of these truths on to the next runner in the Christian race so that they too can run the race for the eternal prize.

Summary

What is *The Proper Diet for the Runner* (v 6)? The words of faith and good doctrine! Are you nourishing yourself on the junk food the world has to offer, the food that provides no lasting nourishment? My friend, all those things that you waste valuable time on are going to burn up. Or, are you nourishing yourself in the Word of God? How much nourishment have you fed yourself this week; how much time have you spent in the Word? Included in that would be study time so that you can understand sound doctrine.

What is *The Prohibited Diet for the Runner* (v 7)? Profane and old wives' tales. Are you partaking of all the stuff out there that women gravitate toward—Pinterest, Facebook, Twitter, Instagram, shopping, meddling—when you could be feasting on the riches of Christ? How much time do you spend in these trivial pursuits compared to the time you spend in the Word, with other believers, and fulfilling the great commission?

What is *The Profitable Discipline for the Runner* (v 8)? Godliness. My dear friend, God will have no other idols before him, even if it's one's body! How much time do you spend on disciplining your earthly body in comparison to disciplining yourself to godliness? Why do we spend so much time on a body that will turn to ashes, when we could be spending time on our soul that will be with our glorious Lord forever?

What are *The Painful Demands of the Runner* (vs 9-10)? To labor and suffer reproach. Are you running the race avoiding the difficult pain that is involved? Are you laboring to the point of exhaustion for Him? Are you suffering for the gospel's sake? Have you lost family members and good friends because of your stand for truth?

What are *The Passionate Directives for the Runner* (v 11)? To command and teach these things. Are you taking the truths that you know, along with what you are learning in 1 Timothy, and sharing them with others? Who are you pouring your life into? Who will you pass the baton to when you step out of this life into eternal life?

It has been said that Americans have more food to eat than any other people in the world, and yet we have more diets to keep us from eating it. I would add that American Christians have more resources and privileges for study and meaningful time in the Word than any other people in the world, and yet we have more and more distractions to keep us from knowing it! What will it be for you, my friend? Will it be the love of this world and the evil one or the love of the Word and the Holy One?

Questions to Consider

Five Things You Must Do to Get in Shape!
1 Timothy 4:6-11

1. Read 1 Timothy 4:6-11, and as you do, write down at least five observations (things you see) to share with your group. (An observation would be a comment, a thought, or a reflection you might have as you observe what is written in the text. This is a good exercise for Bible study!)

2. Memorize 1 Timothy 4:8.

3. (a) Why is it imperative that we nourish ourselves with God's Word and sound doctrine, according to Psalm 19:7-11; John 7:16-17; 1 Timothy 4:16; 1 Peter 2:2; and 2 John 9? (b) According to 1 Timothy 6:3-5 and 2 Timothy 4:3-4, what happens if we choose not to feed ourselves sound doctrine?

4. (a) Paul describes the Christian life as laborious and suffering reproach. According to 1 Corinthians 4:9-13; 2 Corinthians 4:7-12; 2 Corinthians 6:3-10; and 2 Corinthians 11:22-33, what were some of the difficulties Paul encountered as a believer? (b) Using the same passages mentioned in part (a), as well as 2 Corinthians 12:1-10, what joys and blessings did Paul enjoy during these tumultuous times? (c) How do these passages encourage you to press on amidst suffering for the cross of Christ?

5. (a) What changes do believers need to make in order to labor and suffer reproach joyfully for the sake of the gospel? (b) Why do you think we shrink from these things? (c) What changes do you need to make?

6. (a) How much time do you spend on physical exercise, disciplining your body, each day, in comparison to how much time you spend in disciplining your spiritual life? (For example: reading God's Word, meditation, Scripture memorization, prayer, meeting with God's people for fellowship and discipleship, public and private worship, etc.) (b) After reading 1 Timothy 4:8, are there any changes you need to make in this regard?

7. *Prayerfully* looking over questions 3 and 6, what changes do you need to make in order to be feeding more on God's Word and less on the junk of the world? What changes *will* you make? Please put your need in the form of a prayer request.

Chapter 12

Eight Excellent Mandates for Young Timothy (and You Too!)

1 Timothy 4:12-16

The day I first taught this lesson, I awoke around 1:30 in the morning (which is not usual for me) with the song *Before the Throne of God Above* running through my mind. I attempted to turn over and go back to sleep but was unsuccessful. When I reached for my phone, I noticed an email from my son, who pastors a church in Wichita, Kansas. The email said,

> Just getting back from Wellington, Kansas, where one of my new friends and fellow elders here at Wichita Bible Church breathed his last. Rick and his wife D'Annette were on their way back from Oklahoma City tonight and they pulled over at a rest stop for him because he was feeling sick. He passed out and didn't have a pulse, but the EMT was able to revive him off and on. God eventually changed Rick's address from Wichita, Kansas to 'eternity with God' a few hours ago. Rick was a kindred to me—even though I only knew him for 10 months. I teased him often because he looked like Spurgeon and had a real passion and fervor that I appreciated.

In addition to this email, my morning reading that day just "happened" be in Acts, specifically where Paul's emotional farewell to the elders at Ephesus is mentioned, along with the warning to them that some of them would depart from the faith. All these morning events got me praying for my son and his church and thinking about elders, about those who shepherd God's church. "Rick," said my son, "had a real passion and fervor that I appreciated." The apostle Paul said to the elders at Ephesus, "some of you men will arise speaking perverse things and will drag others along with you" (Acts 20:30, my paraphrase.) What was it that made Rick the shepherd he was?

And what was it that made some of the elders at Ephesus the false shepherds they proved to be? The answer lies in the passage we will cover in our lesson; in it are certain mandates that shepherds must adhere to if they are to be good shepherds. This is Paul's charge to Timothy, who, oddly enough, was also ministering at Ephesus. What is it that would keep Timothy passionate about Christ and His kingdom? In these verses are eight excellent mandates for this young pastor, which he—and we—would do well to pay attention to. Let's read them together.

1 Timothy 4:12-16

> Let no one despise your youth, but be an example to the believers in word, in conduct, in love, in spirit, in faith, in purity. [13]Till I come, give attention to reading, to exhortation, to doctrine. [14]Do not neglect the gift that is in you, which was given to you by prophecy with the laying on of the hands of the eldership. [15]Meditate on these things; give yourself entirely to them, that your progress may be evident to all. [16]Take heed to yourself and to the doctrine. Continue in them, for in doing this you will save both yourself and those who hear you.

As we consider these eight mandates for young pastor Timothy, we will put them in an acrostic for your remembrance: MANDATES (though they will not be presented in that order). These will not only be important for you as you consider your own shepherds and how you might pray for them, but they will also be excellent mandates for you to adhere to as well.

As we began chapter four of 1 Timothy, we learned that there are doctrines of demons that threaten to creep into the church, which we must beware of and avoid at all costs. Having said that, Paul then transitioned to the importance of setting our eyes on the goal of godliness as we run the race of the Christian life. Closing out chapter four, Paul now has a charge to the lead runner, Timothy, as he leads the church. Timothy, and all those who shepherd God's flock, are to lead their people in how to run the race properly, all the while protecting them from seducing spirits and doctrines of demons. Specifically, Paul instructs Timothy regarding eight excellent mandates he must follow. In verse 12, we'll discover the first two mandates.

> Let no one despise your youth, but be an example to the believers in word, in conduct, in love, in spirit, in faith, in purity. (1 Timothy 4:12)

Paul begins by telling Timothy, his son in the faith, that he is to *let no one despise* his *youth*. Timothy was probably in his mid-twenties or early thirties at the time this letter was written, which would have posed some challenges because in that day one would've only been considered a young man until the age of 40. In biblical times, most pastors or shepherds were older in physical age, so Timothy's youth would not have been looked upon favorably by some. Timothy was not to live his life in such a way that others would *despise* his youth, which means to think against or think down upon. This word can actually suggest disgust and hatred. Paul is telling him to act in such a manner that none will despise him because of his age. Some might look at Timothy and say he's too young to be a pastor; by his actions he should prove them wrong. He must be exemplary in character. Timothy's first mandate is this: *Act in such a manner that no one will despise you because of your age. This is the first A on your acrostic.* No matter what age you are, dear one, you should behave yourself in such a way that no one would be disgusted with your behavior. When John writes to the church at Ephesus in 1 John 2:12-14, he writes to all believers, whether they are children, young men or fathers in the faith, and he says to the young and to the old that they know the Father. All of God's children know Him and should therefore act as children of God, no matter their age, young or old.

To avoid the issue of others looking down upon him because of his age, Timothy is to set an example. Paul puts it like this: *but be an example to the believers. This is the last letter on your acrostic, the S. Set an example for other believers.* The word *example* means to be a pattern, be someone that they can trace or follow. It is imperative that a pastor set a good example, because the sheep are watching, and they will follow his example. It is also imperative for the sheep to have someone to follow as they follow Christ. And Paul goes on to tell Timothy that he should set that example in 6 specific ways. Obviously, these aren't all the ways a pastor should set an example, as the 16 qualifications for elders make clear, but these are the six Paul mentions here.

1. Timothy must set an example *in word*. This is referring to his speech. In other words, the words Timothy speaks should be in accordance with those of a child of God. They should not be words that are idle, words that include gossip, slander, or flattery, or words that are improper or crude. His speech should be encouraging and edifying, pointing people to the Lord. Sometimes those words affirm, and sometimes they rebuke. To borrow from a modern phrase, it would be like asking the question, "What would Jesus say?" Timothy's speech should be God-honoring, whether it is public or private.

2. Timothy must be an example *in conduct*. This means he should be exemplary in how he behaves. When Paul writes to the church at Ephesus regarding their conduct, he says, "… that you put off, concerning your former conduct, the old man which grows corrupt according to the deceitful lusts, and be renewed in the spirit of your mind, and that you put on the new man which was created according to God, in true righteousness and holiness" (Ephesians 4:22-24). Certainly, Paul's conduct before Christ was not an example he wanted them to follow, as he mentions in Galatians 1:13, "For you have heard of my former conduct in Judaism, how I persecuted the church of God beyond measure and tried to destroy it."

3. Timothy must set an example *in love*. This would include both love for man and for God. If a pastor doesn't love God foremost, above everything and everyone else, then he should probably think about resigning. If you and I don't love God more than anything and anyone else, we would be wise to examine our faith, since it is the greatest commandment, to love the Lord our

God with all our heart, soul, and mind. But there is something which follows that command: to love our neighbor as ourselves (Matthew 22:37-39). Timothy must love God foremost, but he must also love people. I have often thought it odd that some pastors don't love people and seem to avoid being with them.

4. Timothy must set an example for his church *in spirit*. This is a reference to the manner in which something is done. A pastor must have a humble, mild, forgiving, and meek spirit. This does not mean that he is weak or that he doesn't sharply rebuke opposers. It does mean that he must be a leader, and that his leading must be with strength under control.

5. Timothy must set himself before others *in faith*. This is not a reference to his faith in God, though that is certainly a must; rather, this is a reference to faithfulness. A shepherd must be faithful to his responsibilities, whether it is in the church or in his home; anywhere or anything. He must be known as a faithful man.

6. Timothy must set an example *in purity*. This means he must be chaste. Ephesus was a city given over to sexual immorality, and Timothy was not to succumb to the sexual temptations or pressures around him. He was to keep himself pure. In his second epistle to Timothy, Paul will tell Timothy, in 2 Timothy 2:22, "Flee also youthful lusts; but pursue righteousness, faith, love, peace with those who call on the Lord out of a pure heart." That's why in chapter five of 1 Timothy, Paul will also tell Timothy how to behave around both old women and young women; he must be above board in that regard. Paul also tells Titus, another of his sons in the faith, that older women must teach the younger women (Titus 2:3-5). This is a wise practice for a number of reasons, but especially since being alone with a member of the opposite sex can lead to sexual temptations, which many pastors make no effort to resist, and giving in to those temptations has caused many a pastor their job, in addition to their moral failure. (Thirty percent of pastors recently surveyed said they had

committed adultery with someone in their church.)[41] We have a rule in our home that we will not be alone with a member of the opposite sex; this means that I also don't counsel men alone and my husband doesn't counsel women alone. If there is a couple in need of counseling, we counsel them together. I know of at least two women who have committed adultery with pastors and in both cases it started with each of them going in for counseling! Having made clear to Timothy what is required of him in his personal life, Paul now moves on to exhort him regarding his public life.

> Till I come, give attention to reading, to exhortation, to doctrine. (1 Timothy 4:13)

Paul begins by saying *till I come.* In 1 Timothy 3:14, Paul explained that he hoped to come see Timothy soon, and here again he references the fact that he hopes to come. But until Paul can get there to see how things are going, Timothy must continue in the work of the ministry and he must continue with three things. *Here is the second A on your acrostic. Attention needed to three things: reading, exhortation, and doctrine.*

First, Timothy must give attention to *reading.* Paul is not telling Timothy that he needs to make weekly trips to the library in order to check out books to read. The reading Paul is referring to here is the reading of the Scriptures. In fact, he actually is saying, "Pay attention to reading the Scripture. This is important!" In biblical times, few believers would have had personal copies of the written Word, so they would have been dependent on hearing the public reading of it. This meant that they would have to pay attention to the Word of God being read when they gathered together in the public assembly for worship. You probably noticed some of this when you completed the Questions to Consider for this lesson. In 1 Thessalonians 5:27, Paul says to the church at Thessalonica, "I charge you by the Lord that this epistle be read to all the holy brethren." Such public reading was imperative because church members would have no means of

---

41 http://www.intothyword.org/apps/articles/?articleid=36562

reading 1 Thessalonians on their own in the privacy of their own home. A similar exhortation is made in Colossians 4:16, where Paul says, "Now when this epistle is read among you, see that it is read also in the church of the Laodiceans, and that you likewise read the epistle from Laodicea." Acts 15:21 also refers to the fact that the reading of Moses was done every Sabbath day; this would mean Genesis, Exodus, Leviticus, Numbers and Deuteronomy. Can you imagine what would happen if we did that today? Obviously, Paul intended for Timothy to read the Word in private, but here his exhortation seems to be talking about publicly reading the Scriptures to those in his church.

Secondly, Timothy is to give attention to *exhortation*. Exhortation is similar to the preaching of the Word, which would include explanation, or exposition, of the passage, as well as application of it. Such application might include encouragement, rebuke, or comfort, depending on the text.

Thirdly, Timothy must give attention to *doctrine*. This is a common word in 1 Timothy; Paul uses it eight times in this letter alone. Doctrine pertains to the teachings of the Christian faith. This is such a rebuke to our age, in which most church services typically consist of 30-45 minutes spent on trivialities and the pastor gets 10-15 minutes for his "sermonette for christianettes." Just think what would happen today if someone preached past midnight like Paul did in Acts 20! We'd certainly have more than someone falling asleep and falling out the window like Eutychus did; we'd have people getting up and walking out because they want to make it to the restaurant before noon or get home before their favorite sporting event is on. No wonder Christians are anemic and weak! Still speaking about Timothy's public life, Paul says,

> Do not neglect the gift that is in you, which was given to you
> by prophecy with the laying on of the hands of the eldership.
> (1 Timothy 4:14)

Paul says *do not neglect the gift that is in you. This is the D on your acrostic.* **Don't neglect your spiritual gift.** *Neglect* means to make light of something, to be negligent. A *gift* here is referring to a spiritual, divine endowment. Paul doesn't mention what Timothy's gifts are, but I can imagine they would be speaking gifts like teaching, pastoring, exhortation, and the like. My friend, you should not neglect the gift that is in you, either. Paul says that this gift was given to Timothy by prophecy with the laying on of the hands of the eldership, something which seems to be referenced in 2 Timothy 1:6-7: "Therefore I remind you to stir up the gift of God which is in you through the laying on of my hands. For God has not given us a spirit of fear, but of power and of love and of a sound mind." Timothy received certain gifts from the Holy Spirit, as we all do, and this laying on of the hands was his formal commission to the office of elder. Interestingly, verse 7 of this passage is often used out of context to refer to any number of things, and yet it is really a reference to not being afraid to use one's gifts. Paul goes on to give two more mandates in verse 15. He says,

> Meditate on these things; give yourself entirely to them, that
> your progress may be evident to all. (1 Timothy 4:15)

Paul says *meditate on these things*, so the question naturally comes to mind, "Meditate on what things?" Paul is saying to Timothy, "Give careful thought to the work of the pastorate; don't be negligent; don't be slothful. This is a high calling from God that requires deep consideration and careful thought." Timothy must remember that he will someday give account to the Chief Shepherd (Hebrews 13:17; 1 Peter 5:4). *This is the M on your acrostic.* **Meditate on your calling.**

If all Timothy did was meditate on his calling and not actually do something about it, that would be ludicrous, right? Thought must lead to action, so Paul gives Timothy a mandate, and that is: *give yourself entirely to them.* In this case, that means giving himself *entirely* to the things pertaining to his calling. This means to give yourself completely to them, literally to be in them. This is your life, Timothy! *This is the T on your acrostic.* **Totally give yourself to your calling.** We might say one's life is all wrapped up in their kids, or in some sport, or in work, or some other thing, but a pastor's life should be known for being absorbed in the pastorate. If it isn't, he probably needs to rethink what he is doing. Christianity is not a religion for lazy people; we must do things with excellence.

There's a reason Paul gives these two mandates to Timothy: *that your progress may be evident to all.* The word *progress* is a Greek military term that means "pioneer advance," and it is a description of particular soldiers who would go ahead of the rest of the troops in order to clear away any obstacles or dangers in the way, for the purpose of allowing the soldiers behind them to easily follow. So it is with the pastor; he goes before his congregation, leading the way and clearing away any junk, i.e., false teaching, etc., so that his people can follow behind him. As is most often the case, a pastor's congregation will become like him. They should be able to watch his life over the years and see that he is growing in spiritual things, just like he should be able to watch their lives and see that they are growing in spiritual things. Why is this important? Because it will convince his congregation that he is who he says he is; it will convict them to follow his steps; and it might even convert some of them as they ask themselves why they aren't growing like he is. Paul finishes his exhortation to Timothy with yet two more mandates.

> Take heed to yourself and to the doctrine. Continue in them, for in doing this you will save both yourself and those who hear you. (1 Timothy 4:16)

Paul seems to repeat again the need for Timothy to take heed to his calling, to himself, to what he is doing, and also to his doctrine, which he also mentioned back in verse 13. *This is the N on your acrostic. Notice needed to yourself and to doctrine.* We won't elaborate on this here, since Paul has already mentioned this, but suffice to say that it must be very important for Paul to mention it so many times in such a short space. He's saying: watch yourself and watch what you believe!

But then Paul gives a final mandate and that is to *continue in them,* which means to stick to these things. This is a vital mandate that, again, is not just meant for Timothy but for you and me; my friend, this is imperative, because it could mean your eternal life! Paul says in his second letter to Timothy, in 2 Timothy 3:14, "But you must continue in the things which you have learned and been assured of, knowing from whom you have learned them." Paul says that by continuing in these things, *you will save both yourself and those who hear you.* Obviously, Paul is not speaking of salvation here, as Timothy has no power to save himself or anyone else; we are saved by grace alone through faith alone. What Paul is saying here is similar to what Peter says in 2 Peter 1:10, that we are to make our calling and election sure. In Hebrews, we read several times that we are God's children if we hold fast to the end (Hebrews 3:6; 3:14; 6:11). Yes, our salvation is secure, but our salvation is proved genuine by our perseverance to the end; we must continue in the faith.

This is the E on your acrostic. **Endure to the end.** We already know from this epistle that at least two men, Hymenaeus and Alexander, did not endure to the end. Paul doesn't want Timothy to make shipwreck of his faith like those men did but instead to make his calling and election sure. A minister, of course, cannot save anyone, but his example as a Christian in both his public and private life have such an impact on the church that it could be influential in saving them or in causing them to flee, saying, "If that Timothy is a Christian, then I want nothing to do with it." Oh, dear sister, it is damaging to the cause of Christ when ministers are not living or teaching the truth. Many are fed up with it and have left the church and the faith altogether. We too must be careful of our example. Tragically, I once heard a woman say of another woman, "If she is a Christian, I would rather spend eternity in Hell than be in Heaven with her."

Summary

What are the eight excellent mandates for Timothy and for you? As an acronym, they spell out the word MANDATES.

Meditate on your calling. Timothy was to give careful thought to what God had called him to do. What about you? Do you give careful thought to what God has called you to do? Do you take your calling as a mother and a wife, or whatever else God has called you to, seriously? How much thought do you give to it? Are you upset or bothered by what God has called you to do?

Act in such a manner that no one will despise you because of your age. Timothy was to act in such a way that no one would even consider that he was young. Are you young like Timothy? Are you old like me? It doesn't really matter what our physical age is, but it does matter that we act like children of God! Would others look at you, young or old, and stand in awe at your maturity in Christ Jesus?

Notice needed to yourself and to your doctrine. Timothy needed to pay attention to himself and to what he believed. Do you take time to pay attention to yourself? I'm not talking about narcissism; we have enough of that going around! I'm talking about looking at yourself seriously and making sure you are who you profess to be; that you're growing in the grace and knowledge of the Lord Jesus Christ; that you're different this year than you were last year, becoming more and more like Jesus all the time. This also means taking notice of what you believe. What do you believe? Do you hold to the fundamentals of the faith and are you growing in sound doctrine?

Don't neglect your spiritual gift. Timothy was not to neglect his spiritual gift but to use it. What are your spiritual gifts? How are you sharpening your spiritual gift? How are you using it for God's glory?

Attention needed to three things: reading, exhortation and doctrine. As a pastor, Timothy was to publicly read the word, exposit the word, and teach the word (doctrine). Do you have a steady diet of the Word of God and are you passing it on to others? Are you growing in your understanding of God's Word?

Totally give yourself to your calling. Timothy was to be known as a pastor, not a golfer or a sports fanatic, but a shepherd of people's souls. If I were to ask your closest friends what comes to mind when they think of you, what would they say? Would they tell me that they think of a woman who is faithful to her God-given calling, or would they tell me you're faithful to watch your favorite TV show every night, or faithful to make sure you're wearing the latest fashions? Would they tell me you're passionate about the Word and about your walk with God, or would they tell me you're passionate about the latest hair care product or make-up product or the diet you're currently on?

Endure to the end. Timothy was to be examining himself to make sure he was continuing in the things that were taught to him as a young child by his mother and grandmother. He was to hold fast the faithful Word that he was once taught. What about you? Are you more passionate today about the gospel and about your life as a believer than you were last year? If not, something is amiss. We should be always growing toward Christ and not away from Him.

Set an example for other believers. Timothy was to be exemplary in six things: in word, in conduct, in love, in spirit, in faith, and in purity. We also are to be exemplary in these things. Do you taste your words before you speak them? Is your conduct becoming of a daughter of God? Do you love God and others, even those who are unlovely? Is the manner in which you do things attractive? Are you faithful to all your responsibilities? Are you feeding your mind anything that is tainted with sexual immorality? Would anyone want to follow you as you follow Christ?

Indeed, these are eight excellent mandates for young Timothy. But, my dear sister, they are eight excellent mandates for you too! Let's endeavor to pray for our shepherds using these eight mandates, and let us endeavor to pray for ourselves as we walk alongside our Chief Shepherd as He shepherds His sheep!

Questions to Consider

Eight Excellent Mandates for Young Timothy
(and You Too!)
1 Timothy 4:12-16

1. (a) What word do you notice that is repeated in 1 Timothy 4:12-16? (b) Why do you think Paul emphasizes this often in 1 Timothy? (c) How would you summarize chapter four of 1 Timothy?

2. Memorize 1 Timothy 4:12 *or* 16.

3. (a) Paul instructs Timothy to pay attention to reading in 1 Timothy 4:13. This is a reference to the public reading of the Scriptures in the worship service. In the following passages, what was the result of the public reading of God's Word? Exodus 24:7; Deuteronomy 31:11-13; 2 Kings 23:1-3; Nehemiah 8 and 9; Luke 4:16-22. (b) Why do you think churches in our age do not read large portions of God's Word in our worship services? (c) What do you think would happen if your pastor read an entire book of the bible in your church's worship service?

4. (a) What is the significance of the laying on of the hands, in Numbers 27:15-23; Matthew 19:13-15; Mark 6:4-5; Acts 6:1-6; 8:17; 13:1-3; and 2 Timothy 1:6? (b) With these passages in mind, what do you think Paul is referring to in 1 Timothy 4:14?

5. (a) According to 1 Timothy 4:12, what are the six things that Paul wants Timothy to be an example in for other believers? (b) What six things do you think are imperative for a believer to live out before others?

6. (a) Are you taking heed to yourself and what you believe? (b) Are you doing your part to make sure you continue in the faith? (c) In what ways are you pressing on toward the goal?

7. How can you be a better example to other believers? Please put your answer in the form of a prayer request.

Chapter 13

How to Reprove Those in the Family of God

1 Timothy 5:1-2

Have you ever wondered what makes a family strong? Just what does a good family look like? According to the world, the things that constitute a strong family include: spending time together; communicating effectively; enjoying and appreciating one another; being committed to one another; sharing common values and convictions; being loyal and honest with one another; having respect for each other; following through on your promises to each other; sticking together during tough times; not yelling at each other; being willing to forgive one another; and eating together. As I pondered this list of strong family qualities, I thought, "Those are really pretty good, and most of them are similar to what I would expect in the spiritual family."

But there is one quality I think is sorely lacking from this list. It's the same quality I think is lacking from the spiritual family, as well, and in my humble opinion it is one reason we are not as strong as we should be as God's children. Do you want to know what that quality is? It is reproving, or confronting, one another. Just think with me for a moment: What if a parent never reproved a child, or a spouse never confronted his or her mate, or a sibling never reproved another sibling for something they had done wrong? What if in the physical family we never lovingly helped each other with the blind spots we have that we, perhaps, fail to see?

We can answer these questions by taking a look at the families in our own culture. Many families allow anger and resentment and hatred for one another to build up; many of them even kill each other and we hear about it daily in the news. Instead of loving each other enough to be transparent about issues of disagreement or sins or bad habits, we choose rather to stuff it or to gossip about it, venting our anger and resentment. Without this missing element, the willingness to reprove, we have family members who are shallow, spoiled, and narcissistic, who think they're better than everyone else and constantly need their self-esteem bolstered. They forget, or we have failed to remind them, that they are members of a family that should be loving and serving one another, not striving to be first, but to be last.

My friend, the same thing is true in the spiritual family. As Christians living in the 21st century, we are anemic, and we are anemic for many reasons. We've left our first love and we've left sound doctrine, but so many of us have also extinguished this one command we'll be looking at in this lesson: confronting one another. Not long ago, I had a conversation with a godly woman who told me that I was the only person who ever confronted her! Yet, while she and I were talking, I told her of at least 12 individuals I could name who reprove me. Proverbs 27:5-6 tells us that open rebuke is better than secret love and faithful are the wounds of a friend. A real friend tells you your faults, because a real friend loves you enough to rebuke you. Others only flatter you or gossip about you behind your back. You might be saying, "Susan, I think you're taking this a little too far. I mean, what about loving one another?" I say a hearty "Amen" to that, but part of loving one another is reproving one another when it is needed. And there is a way in which we do that in the spiritual family, just as there is way in which we do that in the physical family. As we begin chapter five of 1 Timothy, Paul instructs young Timothy regarding how he is to reprove those in his congregation. And, of course, these instructions are for you and me, as well. Let's read these two short verses together.

1 Timothy 5:1-2

> Do not rebuke an older man, but exhort him as a father, younger men as brothers, ²older women as mothers, younger women as sisters, with all purity.

Paul continues on in his instructions to Timothy regarding how he is to conduct himself, especially focusing in on how he is to relate to members of God's household who need to be exhorted. We must remember that as members of God's household we are a family. We have mothers, sisters, fathers, and brothers in our spiritual family, just as we do in our physical family. No one is perfect and spiritual family members often do things that are sinful and when they do, they need to be admonished—but there is a proper way to do it. Paul lets Timothy know how this is to be done, whether that confrontation is with an older church member or a younger member. There will be two parts to Paul's instructions in these verses:

> *The Exhortation from Male to Male, Old and Young* (v 1), and
> *The Exhortation from Male to Female, Old and Young* (v 2).

Let's begin first of all with how Timothy is to exhort another male, whether he be old or young.

The Exhortation from Male to Male, Old and Young

1 Timothy 5:1

> Do not rebuke an older man, but exhort him as a father, younger men as brothers (1 Timothy 5:1)

As we begin chapter five Paul reminds Timothy of how he is to treat various members of his flock. He starts with the older and younger men and the older and younger women, then the widows, including the young widows, then fellow elders and, finally, servants. Paul has just told Timothy in chapter 4 that no one should despise him because of his youth. One of the ways to keep his congregation from despising him because he is young is to treat them all in the ways that Paul explains here in 1 Timothy 5:1-2. As Timothy is faithful to do these things, he will gain their respect rather than losing it. There is a way in which he must conduct himself as he does this: he must remember that they are family. As Wayne Mack has said, "When I counsel, I deliberately try to imagine how I would treat one of my close relatives. I ask myself, how would I talk to them? How would I proceed if this were my mother or father, or my brother or sister sitting across the desk from me? In reality, our counselees are our spiritual brothers and sisters and our heavenly Father demands that they be treated as such."[42]

Paul starts out by saying *do not rebuke an older man but exhort him as a father*. This past summer, my daughter and I were talking about various things and she asked me what I thought should be done with church members who are older and are stagnant in their walk with Christ; specifically, how do you approach them and exhort them about their lack of spiritual growth? The answer to her question is found right here in these two verses. Don't rebuke them but exhort them. *Rebuke* means to reprimand sharply, to strike hard upon; it's the idea of admonishing another with your words. *An older man* would be someone who is an aged man, one whom we might call a senior citizen. I believe anyone who is older than we are in age should be treated with the utmost respect. I am appalled at the youth of our day and the lack of respect they show to anyone who is older than they are. (Not long ago, I was walking with a friend, and we passed by a couple of teenage girls and said, "Hello," to them, and they completely ignored our greeting.) Timothy is to remember that when older people need admonishment, he is not to do it sharply or attack them with his words. Rather, he would be wise to remember his brother Peter's admonition in 1 Peter 5:1-4 about not lording over his flock:

> The elders who are among you I exhort, I who am a fellow elder and a witness of the sufferings of Christ, and also a partaker of the glory that will be revealed: Shepherd the flock of God which is among you, serving as overseers, not by compulsion but willingly, not for dishonest gain but eagerly; nor as being lords over those entrusted to you, but being examples to the flock; and when the Chief Shepherd appears, you will receive the crown of glory that does not fade away.

---

42   John F. MacArthur, Jr. and Wayne A. Mack, *Introduction to Biblical Counseling* (Dallas: Word Publishing, 1994), 178.

Timothy is to remember that he is not to be lord over his flock but set an example for them. He must also remember, and so should we, that we should reprove all ages in a spirit of meekness, as Galatians 6:1 says.

Instead of rebuking an older man, Timothy is to exhort him and to do so as if that man were his own father. To *exhort* would be to encourage, comfort, admonish, entreat, and come alongside one who is weak. And this is to be done in the manner in which one should address *a father*. How would you exhort your father? Personally, I would exhort my father with the utmost respect and caution and in no way would I be harsh with him. Instead of Timothy saying something like, "You know, I can't believe I even have to tell you this, but are you aware that you continually fall asleep in church and snore so loud that others can't listen to my sermon that I've spent hours preparing each week? How can you be so insensitive?!" Instead of harshly rebuking, Timothy is to exhort; perhaps it would sound something like this: "I've noticed that you have a difficult time staying awake in church and I wondered if perhaps you're not getting the rest you need? Is there anything I can do to help you? Perhaps you could consider sitting near the back of the church, so that when you do fall asleep you won't disturb those in front of you with your head bobbing and sometimes loud snoring." Timothy must remember that, yes, he is the pastor, but there are men in his church that deserve his respect simply because they are older than he is in age. As he shepherds them, he must speak and act respectively toward them. In American culture, we don't do this well, but many other nations treat their aged with respect. Even in biblical times, the aged were treated respectfully. I think of the account in Job where Job's 3 miserable comforters tried to help him by giving him advice. In Job 32, there's an interesting account in which a young man named Elihu chimes in. Consider what he says but also how he says it.

> So these three men ceased answering Job, because he was righteous in his own eyes. Then the wrath of Elihu, the son of Barachel the Buzite, of the family of Ram, was aroused against Job; his wrath was aroused because he justified himself rather

than God. Also against his three friends his wrath was aroused, because they had found no answer, and yet had condemned Job. Now because they were years older than he, Elihu had waited to speak to Job. When Elihu saw that there was no answer in the mouth of these three men, his wrath was aroused. So Elihu, the son of Barachel the Buzite, answered and said: "I am young in years, and you are very old; therefore I was afraid, and dared not declare my opinion to you. I said, 'Age should speak, and multitude of years should teach wisdom.' But there is a spirit in man, and the breath of the Almighty gives him understanding. Great men are not always wise, nor do the aged always understand justice. Therefore I say, 'Listen to me, I also will declare my opinion.' Indeed I waited for your words, I listened to your reasonings, while you searched out what to say. I paid close attention to you; and surely not one of you convinced Job, or answered his words — Lest you say, 'We have found wisdom'; God will vanquish him, not man. Now he has not directed his words against me; so I will not answer him with your words. They are dismayed and answer no more; words escape them. And I have waited, because they did not speak, because they stood still and answered no more. I also will answer my part, I too will declare my opinion. For I am full of words; the spirit within me compels me. Indeed my belly is like wine that has no vent; it is ready to burst like new wineskins. I will speak, that I may find relief; I must open my lips and answer. Let me not, I pray, show partiality to anyone; nor let me flatter any man. For I do not know how to flatter, else my Maker would soon take me away."

Did you notice that Elihu waited until the aged men had spoken? He realized that with age comes wisdom (or should come wisdom) and so he respectfully waited until they had all given their advice to Job. He then proceeds in chapter 33 to give his advice. Interestingly enough, at the end of Job (Job 42:7), the Lord says He is angry with Job's three friends because they had not given Job sound advice, but He mentions nothing about being angry with Elihu, the youngest one who spoke. (Let no one despise your youth!)

Having told Timothy how to address older men, Paul then tells him how to treat younger men who need admonishment. He says, *younger men* are to be exhorted *as brothers*. Timothy must treat them as being on the same level with him, remembering that young men are not inferior to him. The very day I was writing this lesson, I received an email from someone who is probably just a bit younger than me but not by much. The person was manipulative and used extremes and unnecessary sarcasm to get a point across that quite frankly did not need to be made at all. It did not motivate me in the least. I quickly deleted it from my inbox and thought, "How sad! This person is either is having a bad day or needs some serious help." This person would have probably accomplished a lot more with an attitude of humility, speaking the truth in love. How would one exhort a brother or a sister in a physical family? Hopefully, with respect, but also in the same manner as they would like to be exhorted. So instead of saying, "I really wish you'd take a good look at yourself and see that your ongoing smoking habit is a nuisance to everyone and that it's going to give you lung cancer, and then how's that going to fare for your family?! Honestly! Do you ever think of anyone other than yourself?!" That would not motivate me in the least, but it would certainly anger me! Something more in line with Paul's exhortation would be, "You know, brother, I sure love you in the Lord, and I get concerned about your health, since it has been proven that smoking can cause lung cancer. Have you ever considered trying to quit? I sure would like to help you and pray for you. How could I be the most helpful to you?" I remember probably 30 plus years ago, I had a peer who was a smoker and I remember deciding that I would stay up all night and pray for her because I was that burdened for her. Do you know she hasn't smoked a cigarette since?! Now, I'm not so smug as to think that it was my prayers that did the trick, but I do believe it was God's mercy in using my prayers and love for her that gave her the victory. So, we move from how males are to address males, whether they are young or old, to how males are to confront females, whether they be old or young.

The Exhortation from Male to Female, Old and Young

1 Timothy 5:2

> older women as mothers, younger women as sisters, with all purity. (1 Timothy 5:2)

In the same way that Timothy needed to know how to properly exhort the men in his church, he would also need to know how to address the women of God's family in a way that pleases the Lord. So Paul tells him first that he is to exhort the *older women as mothers*. While it is clear from Titus 2 that older women are to teach younger women, there are times when pastors and other men must confront or exhort ladies in their church. This is as much a part of a pastor's charge as is confronting and exhorting the men in the church, since women are a part of the pastor's flock as much as the men are. But this is also the responsibility of all males in the church, since females are, like them, members of the church. In Christ, there is no male or female; all are equally members of God's church. So as a young man, Timothy must exhort *older women* as he would exhort his own *mother*. This means doing so with the utmost respect and gentleness.

When my mother was living, there were several occasions in which I had to speak to her about particular issues; it was difficult and didn't always go as I had hoped, but I knew it was my responsibility. My own daughter has also done this on many occasions with me, and I appreciate her willingness to love me enough to do so. I specifically remember one incident when she was in college and had come home on a break. I had been on the phone with someone, and when I hung up, she said, "Mom, do you think what you just said to the lady was necessary?" She was not disrespectful in the least, but she did give me a gentle reminder of my responsibility to guard my tongue. This came from a daughter who loves me enough to reprove me. If she had said, "Mother, I think you are about as wicked as they come, and I wish you were not my mother, and I hope that person you were talking to finds it in their heart to forgive you because I know I never would," that would have been a harsh and unnecessary rebuke.

There is yet another category of women that need exhorting from time to time and that is *younger women*. How is Timothy to exhort them? Paul says you approach them *as sisters*. Treat them as you would treat your own sister when you speak to her. (Again, this is a foreign concept to many of us because in our age we often allow children to speak to their siblings inappropriately.) But Paul adds something he doesn't say regarding the older women and that is *with all purity*. Ephesus was a city given over to sexual immorality and Timothy must make every effort to be above board when it comes to young women. (Of course, there's nothing new under the sun, as our culture is sexually perverse as well!) Timothy must remember that the young women of the church are his sisters in Christ and should be treated as such. Just as he would not be impure with his sister, so he should not entertain that thought with his sisters in Christ. He must remember that if he looks on a woman to lust after her he will have committed adultery with her in his heart (Matthew 5:28). This should be a reminder to all pastors to never counsel any women alone but to always make sure the pastor's wife or perhaps even another elder is present. This serves as vital protection for the shepherd. John Macarthur helps us here by giving six practical ways that pastors (or all men, for that matter) can maintain purity with younger women:

1. Avoid the look. Proverbs 6:25 says, "Do not ... let her catch you with her eyelids." Our commitment must be that of Job: "I have made a covenant with my eyes; how then could I gaze at a virgin?" (Job 31:1).

2. Avoid the flattery. Proverbs 5:3 warns, "For the lips of an adulteress drip honey, and smoother than oil is her speech" (cf.2:16; 6:24; 22:14).

3. Avoid the thoughts. Proverbs 6:25 says, "Do not desire her beauty in your heart."

4. Avoid the rendezvous. Proverbs 7 gives the following account of the naïve youth: "I saw among the naïve, I discerned among the youths, a young man lacking sense, passing through the street near her corner; and he takes the way to her house, in the twilight, in the evening, in the middle of the night and in the darkness. And behold, a woman comes to meet him, dressed as a

harlot and cunning of heart. She is boisterous and rebellious: her feet do not remain at home: she is now in the streets, now in the squares; and lurks by every corner" (vs 7-12). Great care must be taken when meeting with younger women.

5. Avoid the house. Proverbs 7:25-27 warns, "Do not let your heart turn aside to her ways, do not stray into her paths. For many are the victims she has cast down, and numerous are all her slain. Her house is the way to Sheol, descending to the chambers of death" (cf. Proverbs 5:8).

6. Avoid the touch. Proverbs 7:13 records the result of the naïve youth's failure to avoid the rendezvous: "So she seizes him and kisses him." That was the next step in a process that culminated in immorality.[43]

Summary

Young men must exhort older men with respect and younger men as brothers, exhorting them as they would like to be exhorted. Regarding the women, they are to admonish the older women as they would their mothers, and the younger women as they would their sisters, with all purity. We can certainly apply these commands to us as women, as well. As women, we must exhort older men as we would our own father and young men as brothers, with all purity. As women exhorting women, we ought to exhort older women as we would our mothers and younger women as sisters.

As I opened this lesson, I mentioned that confrontation is sorely lacking in our churches today. So, as I close this lesson, I want to leave you with some helps in this vital practice. Confronting someone about their sin is never a fun thing to do, and if you ever start liking it you might want to examine yourself as to why. It is not fun, but it is necessary, and it is being obedient to what God repeatedly tells us in His Word that we must do. Often, we don't

---

43 John MacArthur, *The MacArthur New Testament Commentary: 1 Timothy* (Chicago: Moody Press, 1995), 190.

want to do this because we are afraid—afraid of how we might be perceived, or afraid we might mess it up, or afraid we might come across as judgmental. But I would like to close by giving you some helps and thoughts, and they will come in the form of an acrostic: ADMONISH.

Always go in private first. Matthew 18:15 says that if your brother offends you, you are to go to him in private. The Greek rendering of that command indicates that you might have to go several times, over and over. But you go to him in private. You don't tell others about it but go to him personally. If he refuses to repent, then you follow the steps given in Matthew 18:15-17.

Direct them to God's Word. When you admonish someone, it is essential that it is because of an offense against God and not something that is a personal preference. Show them in Scripture where it says that what they are doing is sin. Let them read the passages out loud to you. I've done this numerous times, and it is profoundly effective. If they are involved in sexual immorality, take them to passages that speak to the danger they're in. If they're not submitting to their husbands, show them the passages in the New Testament that address that command and the reasons God gives as to why they are to be submissive.

Make sure you hear the whole story. If it involves more than one person, this means making sure you hear both sides of the story. I've had to learn this the hard way in counseling when a woman has told me things about her husband, making him out to be the antichrist or the big bad wolf. And then the husband comes in and I hear an entirely different story. Or I go to someone to admonish them, only to find out there is a reason why they are doing what they are doing, and that knowledge sheds helpful light on their situation. Proverbs 18:13 says it is a fool who answers a matter before he hears the whole story.

Offer hope. Give biblical examples of those who were helped in this area. For example, David repented of his adultery with Bathsheba;

Peter repented of his denial of Christ; the prodigal son repented of his waywardness. Give homework to those you are exhorting so that they can study these biblical examples and meet with them again to see what they have learned. Also, give them personal examples of how you have been helped with sin in your own life.

Never give up on them. Be persistent. Paul says he warned the elders at Ephesus for three years day and night with tears about false teachers coming into the church. The very day I was writing this lesson, there was an individual I'd been dealing with for six months, and I found myself saying, "I'm done!" But then, unexpectedly, some new facts were made known to me, so I said to myself, "No, you're not done with this person, and you are not going to give up on them."

Involve yourself. Don't just admonish someone and then never check up on them. Call them or get face to face with them and see how they are doing. Let them know you are praying and that you care for them and you want to see them get victory in this area of sin.

Speak the truth in love. Don't beat around the bush. Don't say something like, "You need to repent of your affair"; say, "You need to repent of your adultery." Don't say, "You need to stop telling white lies"; say, "You need to stop lying." Speak God's truth, not watered-down, psychologized terms.

Humility is a must. Galatians 6:1 states that when we admonish others we are to have a spirit of meekness or gentleness. "You know this is really hard for me and I do love you dearly. It may be that next week you'll be coming to me, and I certainly hope you do if I am in sin." Or "I used to struggle with this same sin, but God helped me, and this is how He did ...."

Can you imagine how healthy our churches would be today if we would take the principles here in 1 Timothy 5:1-2 and those I just gave you? We would have strong spiritual families mentioned at the beginning of this lesson that:

- spend time together

- have effective communication

- enjoy each other

- appreciate one another

- are committed to one another

- have values and convictions

- are loyal to each other

- are honest with one another

- have respect for each other

- follow through on promises that are made

- stick together during tough times

- don't yell at each other

- are willing to forgive one another and eat together

We would have strong spiritual families because we love one another enough to help others get the speck out of their own eye while we work on the beam in our own eye! As we do this, we will have spiritual family members who become strong, humble servants with hearts that are free from bitterness and thus freed up to serve our Master!

Questions to Consider

How to Reprove Those in the Family of God
1 Timothy 5:1-2

1. (a) Summarize 1 Timothy 5:1-2 in one sentence. (b) What thoughts might Timothy have as he reads these words from Paul, his spiritual father?

2. Memorize 1 Timothy 5:1-2.

3. (a) Paul is very clear about how we are to exhort those who are older than us, in 1 Timothy 5:1-2. With that in mind, what do Leviticus 19:32 and Job 32:4 teach you about how we are to treat the aged? (b) According to Job 12:12; Proverbs 16:31; and Ecclesiastes 12:1-7, what are the reasons you should treat the older generation with respect? (c) What happens to those who dishonor the aged or their parents, according to Proverbs 20:20 and Proverbs 30:17? (d) What did you do (or are you doing) to train your children or grandchildren in regard to respecting those who are older, especially in how they speak to them?

4. (a) What principles can you glean from the following verses regarding how to admonish those in the family of God? Matthew 18:15-20; Romans 15:14; Galatians 6:1-5; 1 Thessalonians 5:14; James 5:16. (b) Are you faithful to love others enough to admonish them when they need admonishment? (c) What happens to you and what happens to them if you resist being obedient to God in this area?

5. (a) Share a time when you were admonished and how the Lord used that in your life to conform you more into His image. (b) What are proper responses for Christians to have when being admonished by others?

6. (a) Is there anyone, young or old or even the same age, that you need to admonish? (No names please!) (b) Will you be obedient to do so in a spirit of love?

7. Please write a prayer request for yourself and other believers to be obedient in this area of admonishment, as it is truly the loving thing to do (when it is needed!).

Chapter 14

Destitute, Defended, and Dead Widows

1 Timothy 5:3-10

According to the latest census taken in the United States, there are more than 13 million widows in the US alone. Other countries have numbers that are even more staggering, like China with 43 million and India with 42 million widows. Each year in the United States, about 700-800 thousand women become widows. Of those who are widowed each year, 7 out of 10 will go on to live alone. These are concerning statistics that should move our hearts with compassion. Unfortunately, somewhere along the way the church has forgotten what Holy Scripture says about caring for widows. We have forgotten James 1:27, which says, "Pure and undefiled religion before God and the Father is this: to visit orphans and widows in their trouble, and to keep oneself unspotted from the world." Many of us have rewritten this verse to say that true religion is going to church every Sunday, reading the Bible every day, praying, or memorizing Scripture. And while all of those are indeed important and part of a genuine believer's life, we have substituted those means of grace for true religion, which is to take care of those who are destitute, orphans and widows. Let's see what the sacred Scriptures say in 1 Timothy 5:3-10.

1 Timothy 5:3-10

[3]Honor widows who are really widows. [4]But if any widow has children or grandchildren, let them first learn to show piety at home and to repay their parents; for this is good and acceptable before God. [5]Now she who is really a widow, and left alone, trusts in God and continues in supplications and prayers night and day. [6]But she who lives in pleasure is dead while she lives. [7]And these things command, that they may be blameless. [8]But if anyone does not provide for his own, and especially for those of his household, he has denied the faith and is worse than an unbeliever. [9]Do not let a widow under sixty years old be

taken into the number, and not unless she has been the wife of one man, [10]well reported for good works: if she has brought up children, if she has lodged strangers, if she has washed the saints' feet, if she has relieved the afflicted, if she has diligently followed every good work.

Paul began chapter five writing to Timothy about how to exhort a younger man and an older man, as well as an older woman and a younger woman. He continues with his instructions to Timothy and the church by addressing the treatment of the women among them, specifically the treatment of widows. In this lesson, we will focus on the older widows, and then we will address the needs of the younger widows in our next lesson. As we consider the text before us, we will see three types of widows:

A Destitute Widow (vs 3, 5, 9-10);
A Defended Widow (vs 4, 8); and
A Dead Widow (v 6).

Let's begin this important section on widows by defining what a widow is as we read verse 3.

A Destitute Widow

1 Timothy 5:3, 5, 9-10

Honor widows who are really widows. (1 Timothy 5:3)

Paul begins this section on widows with a command to *honor widows*. What does it mean to *honor*? It means that we value or revere them. This is not only shown by respect, but also by financial support, as will be evidenced by the text. This is a far cry from our culture, which disdains, drugs, and disposes of the elderly. How God must be grieved with us!

Next, Paul says we honor widows *who are really widows*. This phrase might be puzzling to you at first, but let's define what a widow is. The word *widow* simply means someone who is without; she is without a husband, and she is without family. She might be widowed in the sense that her husband has died; she might be without a husband because he has divorced her or deserted her, as Paul mentions in 1 Corinthians 7:15. Because of these factors, she has no means of support. She might be old, or she might be young, as seen in verse 11. But all widows who are real widows are to be honored. A real widow is one who is truly destitute and has no one to help her, not even family. In the biblical world, when a woman's husband died, she could either remain in her husband's house, she could move back in with her parents, or she could move in with her in-laws, as Ruth did when she followed her mother-in-law Naomi. If there was a brother-in-law who was available, he was to marry her; if not, the nearest male relative who was available was to marry her. It would have been very rare for widows in the biblical world to have any means of earning income. It might be difficult for us to understand this because in our culture widows often have life insurance, social security, or the ability to go out and find a job. In the time Paul was writing, however, women were not prominent in the workplace as we see today, and because of that a widow would often need financial support. But even in our world, where we are blessed to have some of these advantages, we still have biblical responsibilities as a church and as families to care for the widows among us. It might be financial support, emotional support, spiritual support, but we are to provide for them. This is the church's responsibility for widows who are indeed widows. This is the first thing we see about a widow who is destitute, that the church should provide for her.

Now, there are some widows who are truly widows, but they are to be provided for by their families because they are not destitute, they are not without help. Paul addresses the defended widow in the next verse.

A Defended Widow

1 Timothy 5:4, 8

> But if any widow has children or grandchildren, let them first
> learn to show piety at home and to repay their parents; for this

is good and acceptable before God. (1 Timothy 5:4)

But is a word of contrast. In contrast to those who have no one to care for them, there are widows who have family, and that family is responsible to take care of her. *If any widow has children or grandchildren*, then they are to *first learn to show piety at home*. In other words, they are to show their holy duty at home by taking care of their parents and grandparents. This is where their religion fleshes itself out. In the time Paul was writing, it was legally binding for family to care for and support their parents. To do otherwise was unthinkable! We would do well to remind ourselves of what Charles Spurgeon once said, "What you are at home is what you are." Real religion begins at home. This holiness, this godliness, is shown in how children and grandchildren *repay their parents*. The idea is that we pay them back for all they did for us when we were growing up. Think about it: Our parents made sure we had food and clothing and shelter. They took us to endless sporting events and practices, piano lessons, school events, church services, and doctor appointments. They were up in the night with us when we were sick. They nursed our wounds, both physically and emotionally. They disciplined us when we needed it. They instructed us and raised us to be decent human beings. We can never, ever pay back the debt we owe our parents, just as we can never, ever pay back the debt we owe to our Lord for our salvation. But, as children with parents, we are to endeavor to pay them back in their old age. Our mothers took care of us when we were young; now, it is our turn to take care of them when they are old. This is our God-given responsibility to care for our parents.

I remember a particular visit with my dad when he was at the veteran's home. I was pushing him in his wheelchair, and he told me he wished I didn't have to do that and that he knew it was hard work. I remember telling him that I was sure he pushed me around in a stroller and carried me often when I was a little girl and that it was hard work too; he replied that it was indeed hard work! Perhaps we need to remind ourselves that one of the Ten Commandments in Exodus 20:12 is, "Honor your father and your mother, that your days may be long upon the land which the Lord your God is giving you." And in Ephesians 6:2-3, that commandment is reiterated: "'Honor your father and mother,' which is the first commandment with promise: 'that it may be well with you and you may live long on the earth.'" This is a commandment that comes with the wonderful promise of blessings—long life and a life that goes well. That's a pretty good deal!

Paul goes on to say that this is a good deal because it *is good and acceptable before God.* We also had this very same phrase in 1 Timothy 2:1-3, where we learned that is was good and acceptable to pray for our governing leaders so that we might lead a quiet and peaceable life. It means the same thing here as it did back in chapter 2; God considers it *good*—He considers it excellent, beautiful, and admirable—to care for the widows in our family. It is also *acceptable* in His sight, which means that it is received gladly and with satisfaction. Our care for our widowed family members is well-pleasing to God and viewed by Him as a good thing. This verse is a rebuke to our culture, which does little to care for its widows. I've known people who have taken an aged parent into their home and have been criticized for it. I've known people who have moved from one state to another to care for aged parents and they're criticized for it. But, my friend, this is a righteous thing to do! Too many are like the Pharisees in Mark 7:9-13, who gave money to the temple in lieu of helping their parents. They excused their neglect of their parents by giving to the temple, and Jesus tells them the Word of God has no effect on them. Remember, James 1:27 says, "Pure and undefiled religion before God and the Father is this: to visit orphans and widows in their trouble, and to keep oneself unspotted from the world." First Timothy 5:16, which we'll get to in another lesson, emphasizes this responsibility again: "If any believing man or woman has widows, let them relieve them, and do not let the church be burdened, that it may relieve those who are really widows." The defended widow is provided for by her family, but Paul goes back to the destitute widow in verse 5 and states:

A Destitute Widow

1 Timothy 5:3, 5, 9-10

Now she who is really a widow, and left alone, trusts in God and continues in supplications and prayers night and day. (1 Timothy 5:5)

Now she who is really a widow is the same wording Paul used in verse 3; he's referring to a real widow. But here he defines that a bit by saying that she is *left alone*, which is the Greek word monos, which means only or alone. A widow is one who is left alone, that is, she doesn't have any family, she is without a husband, either by death, divorce, or having never married. But, she's not alone in the sense that she has God. This reminds me of what Jesus said to the disciples in the upper room in John 16:32, "Indeed the hour is coming, yes, has now come, that you will be scattered, each to his own, and will leave Me alone. And yet I am not alone, because the Father is with Me." A widow is alone, but she is not really alone if she has God, and she manifests her complete reliance upon Him for everything by praying night and day. Paul says she *trusts in God and continues in supplications and prayers night and day*. A great example of this is seen in Anna, in Luke 2:36-37, "Now there was one, Anna, a prophetess, the daughter of Phanuel, of the tribe of Asher. She was of a great age, and had lived with a husband seven years from her virginity; and this woman was a widow of about eighty-four years, who did not depart from the temple, but served God with fastings and prayers night and day." Widows like Anna, who are truly destitute, have an attitude, whether its day or night, of being dependent on God for everything. God is to her a husband and she depends on Him alone. During the day, when anxious thoughts arise, she takes them to God; in the night, when she is awake and troubled, she cries out to her heavenly husband.

There is one widow in Mark 12 who most assuredly trusted in God, though she was desolate. While Jesus was watching people give money at the temple, He commended her. The rich had put in money from their abundance, but this poor widow put in all she had, and

Jesus says her small gift was more than the rich people had given (Mark 12:38-44). A destitute widow not only needs to be provided for by the church, but she also trusts in God and prays about her needs. There is another kind of widow that Paul describes next, and, thankfully, he only gives her one verse; she is a dead widow.

A Dead Widow

1 Timothy 5:6

> But she who lives in pleasure is dead while she lives.
> (1 Timothy 5:6)

Again, *but* is a word of contrast. Instead of depending on God night and day and being in prayer, this widow takes matters in her own hands and lives immorally as a means of supporting herself. She "plunges into dissipation," as it were. *She who lives in pleasure is dead while she lives.* It's interesting that Paul doesn't even refer to this woman as a widow but only *she*. The phrase *lives in pleasure* comes from a root word that means to weave at a fast rate, which indicates lavish excess; it has a slight sense of sexual immorality. It is similar to what James says in James 5:5, where he rebukes the rich for their oppression, and says, "You have lived on the earth in pleasure and luxury; you have fattened your hearts as in a day of slaughter." This woman pampers herself; she indulges herself in food and drink and luxurious and voluptuous living. It might be that she engages in prostitution in order to support herself. Widows who live for pleasure and worldliness are not to be put on the widows' list. With her husband now dead, she is living it up; she is not living for God. In fact, Paul says *she is dead*, which means that she is dead spiritually; she's never been born again to new life. But honestly, she might as well be dead physically, too, because those things do not bring true happiness. "There have been two deaths, two funerals: her husband died, and the spiritual life in her died. He is a corpse, she a living one, her state is far worse than his."[44] The dead widow

---

44 R.C.H. Lenski, *Commentary on the New Testament* (Peabody: Hendrickson Publishers, 1937), 661.

is obviously not provided for by her family or by the church; rather, by her own choice, pleasure is her provision (at least in this life, but certainly not in the life to come)! Paul now writes a sentence that could mean a number of different things.

> And these things command, that they may be blameless.
> (1 Timothy 5:7)

Some questions that come to mind concerning this verse's meaning are: What are the *things* that Timothy is to command? And, who are the ones who are to *be blameless*? One possible meaning is that Timothy is to make sure the church understands their responsibility to take care of widows, so that they will be blameless in this matter. Another meaning is that family members are to understand their responsibility in taking care of their widowed parents, so that they will be blameless. Yet another possibility is that Timothy is to command the widows to not be involved in the things mentioned in verse 6, so that they can be blameless and be put on the list for support. I can't say that I'd be dogmatic about any one of these three possible interpretations, because they all have some validity and certainly all of these groups could benefit from the command, the church, the family, and the dead widow. Perhaps Paul intends to address them all. He continues on with the defended widow, the one who has family to provide for her and says,

A Defended Widow

1 Timothy 5:4, 8

> But if anyone does not provide for his own, and especially for those of his household, he has denied the faith and is worse than an unbeliever.
> (1 Timothy 5:8)

Paul reminds families of their responsibility to *provide for their own*, and this would mean financial provisions. In fact, the word *provide* means to plan before. It indicates that family members are think ahead as to what they will do when a parent becomes widowed.

One of the first conversations my husband and I had after we got married was regarding the care of our parents and even grandparents in their old age. Decades later, things did not turn out as we had hoped but our desire was always to do what was right before God. Oddly enough, many times we were hindered from doing the right thing by other family members. As you will see in the Questions to Consider, Joseph is a great example of providing for those of his own household; of course, in his case, it wasn't only his widowed dad, but his brothers and their families as well. Joseph's conduct is a stark contrast to our world in regard to loving and caring for our parents.

Paul goes on to tell us how bad this is if we don't provide for our widows. He says the one who does so has *denied the faith and is worse than an unbeliever*. We might proclaim to be Christians, like the Pharisees who cried, "Corban," but we don't live it if we don't provide for our own. (The term "corban" refers to a gift or offering that is consecrated to God. Anything one pronounced as "corban" was irrevocably dedicated to the temple. Jesus condemned the Pharisees for this false teaching, because by this tradition they essentially did away with the commandment for children to honor their fathers and mothers. In doing so, they were excusing themselves from taking care of their parents by using "corban" as a tool for their own selfish use.) How can we say we belong to God and not live like we belong to God? True religion is to visit the fatherless and widows in their affliction. Anything else, as James would say, is dead faith. And Paul says, the one who does this is not just an *unbeliever* but *worse* than one. Unbelievers often provide for their parents, so why wouldn't a believer? That's awful! I have an unbelieving family member who put most "Christians" to shame by her care and generosity toward my Mom and Dad while they were living. But, my friend, it should be the "Christian" who shames the world by her care for her parents. "The Christian who falls below the best heathen standard of family affection is the more blameworthy, since he has what the heathen has not, the supreme example of love in Jesus Christ."[45]

---

45 Frank E. Gaebelein, *The Expositor's Bible Commentary* (Grand Rapids: Zondervan, 1981), 377.

Paul has reminded family members again of their need to provide for the widows in their family. But now he turns to those who are truly destitute and are to be provided for by the church. As he does, he lists three things that must be present in a widow's life in order for her to qualify for such support.

A Destitute Widow

1 Timothy 5:3, 5, 9-10

> Do not let a widow under sixty years old be taken into the number, and not unless she has been the wife of one man, (1 Timothy 5:9)

In order for us to understand this verse, let's consider Acts 6:1: "Now in those days, when the number of the disciples was multiplying, there arose a complaint against the Hebrews by the Hellenists, because their widows were neglected in the daily distribution." We have this account in Acts, shortly after the early church started, in which the widows needed to be taken care of. Evidently, there was a list of widows to be taken care of, as well as certain requirements that a widow had to meet in order to be put on that list. The words *taken into the number* seem to indicate being enrolled, or put on that list.

The first requirement of a widow who is on the list is that she must not be *under sixty years old*; she has to be 60 or older. You might think this odd, but in the biblical world 60 would have been the age when one was considered old. People did not generally live as long then as we do now. Paul will address the needs of younger widows in the coming verses, and when he does, he will indicate their need to remarry.

The second requirement of a widow is that she must have been *the wife of one man*. This does not mean she can't have been married more than once but that she has been loyal to one man at a time, just as we saw when we were studying the qualifications of the elders.

Also, it can't mean that this woman can't be put on the list if she has always been single; rather, the idea is that if she has been married, she has remained devoted to that man. Paul goes on with one more qualifying factor for these destitute widows if they are to be put on the list.

> well reported for good works: if she has brought up children, if she has lodged strangers, if she has washed the saints' feet, if she has relieved the afflicted, if she has diligently followed every good work. (1 Timothy 5:10)

The third qualifying factor for a widow to be supported by the church is that she is *well reported for good works*. In other words, she has a reputation for doing good. One example of this is found in Acts 9 with a widow by the name of Dorcas, who had recently died. When Peter comes to raise her from the dead, all the widows were weeping and showing Peter what she had made for them. In fact, Acts 9:36 says, "This woman was full of good works and charitable deeds which she did." Supported widows are to be known for good works, and Paul lists five of those good works for us.

1. She must have *brought up children*. These could be the widow's own children, or they could be orphans whom she has raised.

2. She is to have *lodged strangers*; she should be given to hospitality. In biblical times, there were not very many places for travelers to stay and so people would open their homes to complete strangers. A widow who is put on the list must have done this.

3. Paul mentions that she is to have *washed the saints' feet*. Now, maybe you're thinking, "Well, I'll never be put on a widow's list because I'm not washing anyone's feet!" Again, it was common for people as they welcomed travelers into their homes to relieve those travelers by washing their feet. No one had tennis shoes in those days and most travel was by foot, and the average traveler would walk 20 miles a day. You can imagine the tired feet and the dirt that would have accumulated during the day. Today we

might equate this with offering a guest a cold drink or a place to rest. Of course, if you wanted to wash your guests' feet, I suppose you could.

4.   Paul says a widow should have participated in *relieving the afflicted*. This means she would minister to the sick, encourage those who need encouragement, take meals to those in need, or perhaps feed those who are hungry.

5.   Paul says she qualifies if *she has diligently followed every good work*. This means she would go about doing good; she would look for opportunities to be a blessing and to serve others. In biblical times, in the days of the early church, widows were known for being very active in the church. They would counsel young women, as Titus 2 commands; they would prepare women for baptism; they were known for prayer and fasting; they visited the sick; they helped with the orphans; they often were known as the intercessors for the church—they followed after every good work. So the destitute widow, Paul says, is not only provided for by the church, but she trusts in God, prays continually, is sixty-plus years old, is a one-man woman, and is known for doing good works.

Summary

A Destitute Widow (vs 3, 5, 9-10): The church provides for her; she trusts in God, prays, is over sixty, is a one-man woman, and is involved in good works. *A Defended Widow* (vs 4, 8): Her family provides for her. *A Dead Widow* (v 6): She lives in pleasure and yet is dead; pleasure is her provision. Or, if you prefer a simpler summary: The destitute widow—the church is her provision. The defended widow—her family is her provision. The dead widow—pleasure is her provision.

A Destitute Widow: Do you know who the widows are in your church who are truly destitute? Do you know any widows in your neighborhood that are destitute? Do you know any widows who are destitute? Do you know their financial needs, their emotional needs, and their spiritual needs? How are you caring for them? Are you now preparing yourself to be put on that list if the times comes that you need to be put on it? Are you devoted to your husband? Do you trust in God and pray often? I'll say this: If you don't trust God now and pray to Him now, it might not come so naturally after your husband's death. But if you are already depending on Him, it will be natural to you when that day comes. Are you involved in good works? What good works are you involved in? Are you relieving the afflicted, washing the saints' feet, being hospitable?

A Defended Widow: Do you have family members who are widows? If so, are you doing your part to care for them? How are you caring for them? Remember, dear one, your children are watching how you treat your parents, and they are learning from you how to treat you when you are old. My husband used to say to me, when things were difficult in the care of our parents, "Remember, Susan, our children are watching us!" That was a mild rebuke for me to adjust my attitude.

A Dead Widow: Do you know any who would be categorized this way? Have you compelled them to go to the cross, to give up their sinful lifestyle while there is time, and to embrace God alone? What about your life now? Are you living it up and finding pleasure in the things of this world? Those things certainly do bring pleasure for a season, but payday will come and sin does have its consequences.

We have repeatedly reminded ourselves of James 1:27, which says, "Pure and undefiled religion before God and the Father is this: to visit orphans and widows in their trouble, and to keep oneself unspotted from the world." But James also says in James 2:14-17,

> What does it profit, my brethren, if someone says he has faith but does not have works? Can faith save him? If a brother or sister is naked and destitute of daily food, and one of you says to them, "Depart in peace, be warmed and filled," but you do not give them the things which are needed for the body, what does it profit? Thus also faith by itself, if it does not have works, is dead.

Perhaps you are wondering, "How do I visit or relieve widows?" The best thing to do is ask them, which is what I did. I asked several widows two questions. The first question was this: What are some of the hardest things about being a widow? Here are the answers I received: "Nights are lonely"; "I don't have a man to bounce ideas off of"; "It's hard not having a guy in my life to fix things and maintain things"; "I don't have enough money to fix things"; "I wish someone would do my yard work"; "Things that were new to me, like how to take care of my finances"; and "The friends that were 'our' friends over time were no longer 'my' friends." The second question I asked was: How can you be best ministered to as a widow? The answers I received were: "to be included in nighttime activities"; "to give a phone call now and then"; "to receive help when help is asked for" (I got this answer twice, so it must be a problem!); "knowing that others are praying for me"; and "maintaining fellowship with other believers." One woman told me that she really never has any needs because the Lord takes care of all of them and she is ministered to by His presence.

My friend, let's remember those who are widows indeed, and let's relieve them in their affliction. Statistics tell us that men usually die first, which means that those of us who are married will likely find ourselves without a husband at some point, and we too will want to be remembered in our affliction. Let's do unto others as we would have them do unto us!

Questions to Consider
Destitute, Defended, and Dead Widows
1 Timothy 5:3-10

1. According to 1 Timothy 5:3-10, what constitutes a real widow?

2. Memorize 1 Timothy 5:5 *or* 5:8.

3. (a) As you read the following passages, look for the Lord's attitudes toward widows, as well as what He expects our attitudes to be toward widows (if it is mentioned in the text). Exodus 22:22-24; Deuteronomy 10:18-19; 14:29; 24:17-18; 26:12-13; 27:19; Psalm 68:4-5; Psalm 146:9; Proverbs 15:25; Isaiah 1:17; Malachi 3:5; Luke 7:11-15; 21:1-4; John 19:26-27. (b) Do you think these are the attitudes that the church expresses toward widows today?

4. (a) As you read Genesis 45:3, 9-13; 46:28-34; 47:7, 27-31; and 50:1-14, what things do you notice about Joseph's care for his father Jacob? (b) How does this compare with those in our world and their care for their widowed parents?

5. (a) In what ways do you see God provide for the widows mentioned in 1 Kings 17:8-16 and in the Book of Ruth (skim the book of Ruth)? (b) How does this give you hope that God will provide (and does provide) for you should you become widowed? (c) How has God provided for you thus far (whether you are widowed, married, or have never married)?

6. (a) Do you know who the widows are in your church? (b) How do you think a church can best minister to widows? (c) How do you minister to widows?

7. As we think about the importance of ministering to widows, we must remember that we reap what we sow (Galatians 6:7). What are you sowing in regard to caring for the widows? Please come with a prayer request for how you might better minister to those who are widows indeed!

Chapter 15

What's a Young Girl to Do? Get Married!

1 Timothy 5:11-16

As we begin our second lesson focusing on widows, I want to remind you of a statistic I gave in our last lesson: There are more than 13 million widows in the United States. With each passing year, in the US alone, 700-800 thousand women become widows. But, did you also know that one third of all those widows are widowed before the age of 60? That's a pretty alarming statistic, especially when you consider that most of those widows lose 75% of their income immediately upon their husband's death! For a young widow, this would mean that she would need to secure immediate financial help to support herself and her children. And, as you'll remember from our previous lesson, widows in biblical times did not have the advantages that we have today with social security, life insurance, and opportunities for a vocation. What were these young, vulnerable widows to do? Paul writes to Timothy, the church at Ephesus, and the church universal as to what young widows are to do, in 1 Timothy 5:11-16. Let's consider this passage together.

1 Timothy 5:11-16

> But refuse the younger widows; for when they have begun to grow wanton against Christ, they desire to marry, [12]having condemnation because they have cast off their first faith. [13]And besides they learn to be idle, wandering about from house to house, and not only idle but also gossips and busybodies, saying things which they ought not. [14]Therefore I desire that the younger widows marry, bear children, manage the house, give no opportunity to the adversary to speak reproachfully. [15]For some have already turned aside after Satan. [16]If any believing man or woman has widows, let them relieve them, and do not let the church be burdened, that it may relieve those who are really widows.

We started our study regarding widows in our last lesson, and we specifically focused in on Paul's instructions concerning the older widows. Paul now writes regarding the younger widows. As we consider these verses, our outline will include:

> *The Duties of the Church to Young Widows* (vv 11, 16);
> *The Dangers of Young Widows* (vv 12-13, 15); and
> *The Desires for Young Widows* (v 14).

Paul begins this section by writing to the church about their responsibility to the younger widows.

The Duties of the Church to Young Widows

1 Timothy 5:11, 16

But refuse the younger widows; for when they have begun to grow wanton against Christ, they desire to marry, (1 Timothy 5:11)

Again, the word *but* is a word of contrast. In contrast to the older widows who are to be put on the list, we have the younger widows who are not to be put on the list, as evidenced by the word *refuse*. Paul says *refuse the younger widows*, which means don't put them on the list like the older ones he has mentioned in verse 9. A *younger widow* would be any woman under the age of 60. Paul says don't put them on the list for a reason, and that reason is because *they grow wanton against Christ* and want to get married. Now maybe you're wondering, "What does this mean? What is wanton?" This is certainly a word we don't use in our age, but *wanton* means to act in a luxurious way. The word comes from a metaphor which describes a pampered horse who is unbridled. Nothing confines the horse so he runs wild or, in this case, the widow runs wild. Instead of being content with widowhood and finding something productive to do, these widows run wild. Isaiah 3:16-17 uses this word wanton when describing the wayward daughters of Zion: "Moreover the Lord says: 'Because the daughters of Zion are haughty, and walk with outstretched necks and wanton eyes, walking and mincing as they go, making a jingling with their feet, therefore the Lord will strike with a scab the crown of the head of the daughters of Zion, and the Lord will uncover their secret parts.'" These young women are unable to control their passions, which are natural to have, but their inability to control themselves leads these women to behave against the dictates of Christ and what He commands for them.

Because of these unbridled passions, Paul says, they *desire to marry*. This is indeed a desire of young women. In fact, not too long ago, I was having coffee with a friend at a coffee shop. Sitting next to us were four young women, and I noticed that every time a young man walked by, up went their eyes. My friend and I were actually talking about widowhood, saying that we thought we would be just fine with the Lord as our husband. Older women, for the most part, don't have the same desire as young women to get married. Paul mentions this passion in 1 Corinthians 7:8, "But I say to the unmarried and to the widows: It is good for them if they remain even as I am; but if they cannot exercise self-control, let them marry. For it is better to marry than to burn with passion." If young widows can't control themselves, then they need to get married. I know some people teach that you can only be married once, even if your husband dies, but Scripture is clear that remarriage is biblically permissible if a widow so desires. Paul says in 1 Corinthians 7:39-40, "A wife is bound by law as long as her husband lives; but if her husband dies, she is at liberty to be married to whom she wishes, only in the Lord. But she is happier if she remains as she is, according to my judgment—and I think I also have the Spirit of God." Instead of wanting to be married to her heavenly husband alone, who has promised to take care of her, these widows want to be married to earthly husbands, and there is nothing wrong with that desire.

So, the responsibility of the church is not to put these younger widows on the widows list, but to refuse them. If a young widow is truly destitute, the church should provide for her financially until she is able to get married again. This would be the duty of the church, in such a case, if she indeed has no family to help her. Paul moves from the duty of the church and these young widows to some of the dangers for these young women.

The Dangers of Young Widows

1 Timothy 5:12-13, 15

> having condemnation because they have cast off their first faith.
> (1 Timothy 5:12)

This is a difficult verse to understand, but we will endeavor to unpack it as best we can. Some believe that this refers to women who were never in the faith and so the trial of widowhood proves who they really are. Such a woman is condemned and has cast off her first faith, perhaps a nominal commitment she once made to Christ. This would be likened to the parable of the soils, specifically when tribulations or trials come, and they become offended and apostatize from the faith. The difficulties of widowhood aren't what these widows bargained for when they signed up for Christianity. That is a possible interpretation and has some good weight to it, especially with verse 15 referring to some being turned aside to Satan. With this interpretation, these widows can be likened to the older widows mentioned in verse 6, who live for pleasure and who are dead while they live.

Another possible interpretation of this verse is this: In biblical times, when the widows were put on the widows list, they were pledging not to get married again. The words *their first faith* could be translated as *their first pledge*. Doing so would mean that they had determined that they would remain as widows, and because of that choice they were put on the list. According to Numbers 30:9, a widow must keep her vows: "Also any vow of a widow or a divorced woman, by which she has bound herself, shall stand against her." It's possible that some of the younger widows had chosen to be put on the list because of being destitute but had later decided they didn't want to be on the list anymore because they wanted to remarry. In doing this, a widow breaks her vow to widowhood and is condemned, having cast off her first pledge, her vow she made when she was put on the list. So, the first danger for these young widows would be the possibility of breaking their vows. It could be a vow to widowhood, effectively putting her on the widows list, or a salvation vow to God that she had once made. Paul goes on to list more dangers of being a young widow in verse 13.

> And besides they learn to be idle, wandering about from house to house, and not only idle but also gossips and busybodies, saying things which they ought not. (1 Timothy 5:13)

Besides breaking their vows, young widows can also *learn to be idle*. This would be the second danger a young widow may fall into: becoming useless and lazy. She's free, because she doesn't have a husband, and if the church or family is providing for her financially, what should she do with her time? The temptation will be for her to quit being useful, and instead to become useless by being *idle*. Someone once said that idle hands are the devil's workshop. In the case of young widows, that's true, not only because of what Paul has just said but also because of what he says in the next verse, that some have turned aside to Satan. Or, as another man has said,

> See how the little busy bee improves each shining hour, and gathers honey all the day from every opening flower! In works of labour or of skill, we should be busy too; For Satan finds some mischief, still, for idle hands to do.[46]

Not having work to do makes widows prone to *wandering about from house to house*. The word here for *wandering* means vagabond. She is not content to be at home and so she wanders about visiting all her friends. In today's world, we might say she spends idle hours on the internet with her Facebook buddies, or some other kind of social networking, talking about things she should not be talking about; that would certainly be a current application of wandering *from house to house*. I remember visiting with a young girl recently about how peaceful her home was and asking her what her secret was. She said that she and her husband had learned that her being out all the time and running here and there led to the kids being out of control and a lot of chaos in their home. Things were better and more peaceful when she limited their outings and the things in which they were involved.

---

46 Dr. Watt,-http://www.victorianweb.org/authors/rands/ajrbion1.html

This wandering from house to house also leads to gossip. This is the third danger of young widows. (It is also a danger of all women, I might add.) This is a temptation for idle women who have nothing better to do than to write idle things on social media. I remember my son telling me once that I would be shocked to see what some of the ladies I disciple write about on their Facebook pages. How quickly we can spread gossip and be a listener and reader of gossip with all that is available to us on the internet! My friend, we must be careful because Satan would like nothing better than to trap us all in his web. The word *gossip* is an interesting Greek word; it means to boil up, throw up bubbles, and blow up soap bubbles. That is an interesting description of a tongue that cannot be tamed and is always on the loose. Gossip was a common sin among the young women in Paul's day, just as it is today. There is nothing new under the sun.

Paul mentions a fourth danger of young widows and that is that they can become *busybodies*. This is the idea of meddling in other people's affairs. Paul mentions this word in 2 Thessalonians 3:10-12, where he says, "For even when we were with you, we commanded you this: If anyone will not work, neither shall he eat. For we hear that there are some who walk among you in a disorderly manner, not working at all, but are busybodies. Now those who are such we command and exhort through our Lord Jesus Christ that they work in quietness and eat their own bread." It is God's will for those He created to work; it was His will for us even before the curse of Genesis 3.

Of course, because of Adam and Eve's sin, that work became difficult and unpleasant, but nonetheless it is expected of us, and when we don't work, we become lazy, and laziness promotes ungodliness. It is also a great contributor to depression; when we become idle and don't do what God has created us to do, we get depressed and many times that depression leads to suicide. Paul says that being a busybody promotes *saying things* that we *ought not* say. This goes right along with gossip, which is saying things about others that are hurtful and harmful and, quite frankly, unnecessary. Having said these things, Paul now contrasts the dangers of these young widows with the desires for young widows. These should be not only Paul's desires but also the desires of widows, as well. Note what he says in verse 14.

The Desires for Young Widows

1 Timothy 5:14

> Therefore I desire that the younger widows marry, bear children, manage the house, give no opportunity to the adversary to speak reproachfully. (1 Timothy 5:14)

Instead of being involved in all the wrongdoing in verse 13, these young widows should be involved in all the right doing in verse 14. Paul says *I desire*, which really means I want or I will. What does Paul desire? *That the younger widows marry*. This should be the first desire of all young widows. Remember, Paul has already mentioned that were some that were teaching doctrines of demons and forbidding others to marry (1 Timothy 4:1-3). This might have been another reminder to them that this should be the desire of all women, unless God has called them to be single. All women should want to marry. (And, just to be clear, the Bible clearly teaches that marriage is between a woman and a man. You have to clarify that in this age!)

Secondly, she should desire to *bear children*. Remember, this is one of the stipulations for the older widows to be put on the list, that is, that she must have brought up children (1 Timothy 5:10). This should be the desire of all women, as God has made that part of our makeup as women. I know there are some young women who don't want children, and sometimes the reasons they give are totally contrary to God's Word and the reasons He gives as to why we should have children. I know some young women are unable to have children and that is a different story. But even then, there are many orphans that need good homes, and caring for them is a sign of true religion, as James says in James 1:27.

The third desire of all women should be to manage their house. Notice that it is *manage her house*, not manage her husband, as some women might like to do. She is to manage her house like the Proverbs 31 woman. When you look at that woman, you notice that she is a far cry from being idle. I usually struggle when women share with me how their husbands don't do this and don't do that, things like, "they don't help with the dishes or the cooking," "they don't take out the trash," "they don't diaper or bathe the kids," etc. I have difficulty with that because the Scriptures are clear that women are to take care of those things. Men have full time jobs for the most part and they don't need to come home and work all evening to satisfy a lazy wife. Now, if you have some sort of agreement with your husband regarding these issues, that is fine, or if he volunteers or likes to help out, that too is fine. If you both work full time and you have agreed upon some of these issues, that is fine. But if not, you need to reread the Word of God and remind yourself of what your role is as a homemaker. In fact, it is rare to find a man that can do the things a wife can do in the home and do them with excellence. God has not wired men that way, but he has wired women that way. My husband often jokes that if I die before him, he'll have to get seven wives to do what I do. When I was younger I would leave the kids with him for some amount of time, and when I'd get home, he would usually say something like, "How do you do all of this?" Ladies, we need to get back to what our God-given role is. If you find yourself not having time to do what you are supposed to do in your home, you need to keep a daily journal of what you are doing. You might be surprised how much of your time is spent being idle or even doing good things, but not doing the most important and excellent things.

Why are young widows to do these things? Why are all women to do these things? Paul says so that *we give no opportunity to the adversary to speak reproachfully. Opportunity* is a military term that communicates the idea of a base of operation. Satan is always trying to destroy us and that is why we must wear our armor, and part of that armor is living right. If we don't, we are open for attack. Now even though our adversary is Satan, the word *adversary* here seems to be more the idea of anyone who is opposed to the gospel and finds fault with those who live it. Oh, my friend, we must live the gospel; otherwise, others will look at us and see that we are not living what we profess, that we blaspheme the Word of God and make it unattractive. The same principle is spelled out in Titus 2:3-5, where Paul writes:

> the older women likewise, that they be reverent in behavior, not slanderers, not given to much wine, teachers of good things— that they admonish the young women to love their husbands, to love their children, to be discreet, chaste, homemakers, good, obedient to their own husbands, that the word of God may not be blasphemed.

The ungodly world, the adversaries, are watching us and when we fail to live out Titus 2 by loving our husbands and children, being pure, homemakers, good, and obedient to our husbands, they have cause to *speak reproachfully* or accusatorily against us. It blasphemes the Word of God and makes it unattractive. Who wants Christianity if it's no different from the world? But when we live out Titus 2, along with 1 Timothy 5:14, we adorn the doctrine of God and make it attractive and the world takes notice that we live out what we profess. I was pondering this around Christmastime and I was thinking about Mary, who told the angel of the Lord, "Be it unto me according to your will." Today, we plan our marriage and we plan our children, and yet too many of us are replacing, "Be it unto me according to your will" with "Lord, I don't have time to manage the house, bear children, or any of that other stuff. I must have a career and go to the spa and go the gym. I don't have time to be obedient to your Word. I will not be a homemaker." But Paul warns us in the next verse about those who fail to follow these godly desires. He says,

The Dangers of Young Widows

1 Timothy 5:12-13, 15

For some have already turned aside after Satan. (1 Timothy 5:15)

This is terminology Paul has used already in 1 Timothy, specifically in 1 Timothy 1:3; 1:6; 1:19 and 4:1. In all these verses, he is speaking of those who have apostatized, who have turned aside to Satan. Here, he is saying that these widows choose to follow Satan rather than the Savior. They are like the widows who are dead while they live; they follow after worldly pleasures and are doomed to damnation. And, my dear friend, you don't have to be a widow to have this happen to you. I hear of women almost daily now who are unwilling to do what they should be doing from verse 14 but are doing plenty of the things mentioned in verse 13, and I tremble and shudder at what their doom will be. Paul now sums up this section on widows and ends with these words in verse 16.

The Duties of the Church to Young Widows

1 Timothy 5:11, 16

> If any believing man or woman has widows, let them relieve them, and do not let the church be burdened, that it may relieve those who are really widows. (1 Timothy 5:16)

The bottom line is this: If there are widows who have family, those family members are to *relieve* their widows, or take care of them, so that the church is not *burdened* to do so. Why? So that the church can *relieve those who are really widows*, those who are truly destitute.

Summary

What are the duties of the church to young widows (vs 11, 16)? Refuse to put them on the list. However, according to verse 16, if those widows do not have any means of help from family, the church should take care of them. What are the dangers of young widows (vs 12-13, 15)? The dangers are breaking their vows to God and man, being idle, being gossips, and being busybodies. What are the desires for young widows (v 14)? To get married, bear children, and manage the house.

This lesson is certainly not just for widows. I fear many young women, and old too, have bought into an ungodly mentality of what their role is. Many are living out verse 13 instead of verse 14. What about you? Do you desire to get married, or do you desire to indulge in gossip? Do you desire to fulfill God's command to bear children, or do you desire to be a busybody? Do you desire to stay active by working in your house, or do you desire to be inactive by wandering from house to house? Again, I remind you that we have many more means of doing this in our age than in Paul's age. Have you stopped to examine how your time is spent? When you read this passage along with Titus 2 and Proverbs 31, does it describe your life, or does it look more like 1 Timothy 5:13? My friend, it is a privilege and a joy to be a wife and a mother and to fulfill the role that God has designed for us.

The story is told of a man named John, who served as a minister in England and whose pastoral duties often called him away from home. He had a large family, and he feared that sometimes he was paying them too little attention because of his many obligations outside the home. One day he was about to start on a journey, and standing near the door, half-way downstairs, he heard a voice in prayer; it was the voice of his wife. He listened as she was praying for the children by name, and when she came to the name, Charles, she said, "Lord, he has a daring spirit; whether for good or for evil, make it Thine own." And the minister wiped away a tear and said to himself, "It is all right; I can go and serve the Lord; it is right with the children." That Charles was Charles Spurgeon.[47]

Who will say that the work of a wife and mother is not valuable? She works in her home, she prays day and night, and she ministers endlessly for those in need. And with that I say, "Go, and do likewise."

---

47   https://biblehub.com/sermons/1_timothy/5-14.htm

Questions to Consider

What's a Young Girl to Do? Get Married!
1 Timothy 5:11-16

1. (a) According to 1 Timothy 5:11-15, what is God's role for young women? (b) What happens to young women who don't follow what God has designed for them, according to this passage? (c) How do you reconcile 1 Timothy 5:11-15 with 1 Corinthians 7:25-40?

2. Memorize 1 Timothy 5:14.

3. (a) What are the dangers of being idle, being a gossip, and being a busybody, according to Proverbs 10:18; 14:23; 19:15; and 1 Peter 4:15? (b) Why do you think these things might be a greater temptation for young women who are not married or who are widowed?

4. (a) Paul says women should manage their houses. According to the description found in Proverbs 31:10-31, what would this include? (b) What would be some things that women should not manage in their homes?

5. (a) Skimming over the book of Ruth, how do you see her as an example of what Paul admonishes the young widows to do in 1 Timothy 5:14? (b) How is she a rebuke to the young widows Paul mentions in 1 Timothy 5:13?

6. (a) How would you counsel a young woman (or any age women) whose life is characterized by gossip, being a busybody, and being idle? (b) What scriptural help could you give her?

7. These two lessons we've had on the role of women are rich with admonition for us. How has the Spirit convicted you or encouraged you through these lessons? Write a prayer request for yourself as you ponder that question.

Chapter 16

What to Do About the Pastor's Salary and the Pastor's Sins!

1 Timothy 5:17-25

Several years ago, I was chatting with one of the ladies who disciples me, a woman who is now in her 80's. She made a statement that was odd to me at the time, but I've since discovered is in fact not odd but true. In her sweet, Georgia accent, she said, "Susan, churches like to keep their pastors poor." Now, I was brought up in a minister's home and I certainly remember us not having much, but we always had what we needed, so I never really gave it much thought. (I do remember one evening when all we had for dinner was apples, but we had something!) In recent years, however, as I've spoken with women whose husbands are in full time ministry and I've learned what their husbands' incomes are, I have been truly shocked by their answers. Many of us would consider their salaries poverty level, and many of them have large families. When we consider the passage before us in this lesson, we will see that this is not the way it should be for those who shepherd God's people well. In my humble opinion, these verses are an indictment on the church today. Of course, Paul makes it clear that the pastor must rule well to be deserving of such a salary. Some don't lead their churches well, and Paul guides us in what to do with a pastor who isn't ruling well but is sinning. Let's consider this important but all too neglected passage on what to do about your pastor's salary and what to do about your pastor's sins.

1 Timothy 5:17-25

> [17]Let the elders who rule well be counted worthy of double honor, especially those who labor in the word and doctrine. [18]For the Scripture says, "You shall not muzzle an ox while it treads out the grain," and, "The laborer is worthy of his wages." [19]Do not receive an accusation against an elder except from

two or three witnesses. [20]Those who are sinning rebuke in the presence of all, that the rest also may fear. [21]I charge you before God and the Lord Jesus Christ and the elect angels that you observe these things without prejudice, doing nothing with partiality. [22]Do not lay hands on anyone hastily, nor share in other people's sins; keep yourself pure. [23]No longer drink only water, but use a little wine for your stomach's sake and your frequent infirmities. [24]Some men's sins are clearly evident, preceding them to judgment, but those of some men follow later. [25]Likewise, the good works of some are clearly evident, and those that are otherwise cannot be hidden.

Our outline for this lesson will include:

The Pastors' Salary (vs 17-18);
The Pastor's Sin (vs 19-21);
The Pastor's Sanctification (v 22);
The Pastor's Sickness (v 23);
and *The Pastor's Selection* (vs 24-25).

Let's first consider the pastor's salary in verses 17 and 18.

The Pastor's Salary

1 Timothy 5:17-18

Let the elders who rule well be counted worthy of double honor, especially those who labor in the word and doctrine. (1 Timothy 5:17)

Paul begins this section by writing about elders, those who are tasked with the leadership of the local church. An *elder* is one who is an overseer or a shepherd in a local assembly of believers. We discussed the role of elder, specifically their list of qualifications, when we were studying chapter 3 of 1 Timothy. Here, Paul says that *elders who rule well* are to *be counted worthy of double honor*. The words *double honor* mean double pay or a generous pay. Interestingly, the word *honor* comes from a word that means honorarium. (Some think that this could also be a reference to not only financial honor but also giving of honor to the office of elder.) Paul clarifies that they are to receive double honor if they *rule well*, which means they must be doing a good job, a job done with excellence. That's why I think it is a wise church that knows what their pastor does with his time, how much time he spends in studying, shepherding, and the various other calls of the pastorate. I am 59 years old now and all but one year of my life has been lived in a pastor's home. In my dad and in my husband, I have had wonderful examples of men who took their calling seriously. My dad would work long hours as a minister, and my husband does the same. I've often teased that I'm going to bury my husband with a yellow marker and a book. (Even now as I'm writing, he is in his office reading his Bible.) A minister who rules well is on call 24 hours a day, in addition to tenacious study of God's Word. Paul says those elders *who labor in the word and doctrine* should be compensated. There are some elders who are not teaching elders and don't spend the hours laboring in the Word; these elders do not necessarily need to be paid. But those who labor in long hours of study of the Word and theology are to be honored; they *labor* to the point of exhaustion, which is what this word means. This is what a true shepherd does.

My husband studies day and night, sometimes to the point that he'll tell me he just can't study anymore because his eyes are tired or burning. Not only does he labor in the Word and doctrine, but he also visits the sick, counsels the weary, rebukes the sinners, and performs weddings and funerals. The day I was writing this lesson, my husband told me of two people in our church who needed our time and attention, not even mentioning another person that he spent time counseling the night before in our home. We like to say that a woman's work is never done, and while there is certainly truth in that statement, my friend, I can say from experience that a pastor's work is never done, either.

Maybe you're thinking that elders shouldn't be paid for all this work; Paul would disagree with you. In fact, in the very next verse, he writes otherwise, and he gives the reasons why such an elder should be paid, and it has to do with what the Bible says. Imagine that!

> For the Scripture says, "You shall not muzzle an ox while it treads out the grain," and, "The laborer is worthy of his wages." (1 Timothy 5:18)

Paul gives two reasons why pastors should be paid. The first reason is because the Scripture says, *"You shall not muzzle an ox while it treads out the grain."* Naturally, we should ask: Where is this quote from, and what does it mean when Deuteronomy 25:4 says, "You shall not muzzle an ox while it treads out the grain." One man helps us with the meaning here and says,

> The Old Testament law provided that the oxen who threshed the grain were entitled to eat of it. They were not to be muzzled to prevent them from doing that. Paul's point is obvious. God required that animals who labored to provide physical food for others were to be fed. How much more would he want faithful pastors, who provide spiritual food to their needy flocks, to be provided for?[48]

In fact, when Paul writes to the church at Corinth, he uses the same quote; he says, in 1 Corinthians 9:1-14,

> Am I not an apostle? Am I not free? Have I not seen Jesus Christ our Lord? Are you not my work in the Lord? If I am not an apostle to others, yet doubtless I am to you. For you are the seal of my apostleship in the Lord. My defense to those who examine me is this: Do we have no right to eat and drink? Do we have no right to take along a believing wife, as do also the other apostles, the brothers of the Lord, and Cephas? Or is it only Barnabas and I who have no right to refrain from working? Who ever goes to war at his own expense? Who plants a vineyard and does not eat of its fruit? Or who tends a flock and does not drink of the milk of the flock? Do I say these things as a mere man? Or does not the law say the same also? For it is written in the law of Moses, "You shall not muzzle an ox while it treads out the grain." Is it oxen God is concerned about? Or does He say it altogether for our sakes? For our sakes, no doubt, this is written, that he who plows should plow in hope, and he who threshes in hope should be partaker of his hope. If we

---

48   John MacArthur, *MacArthur New Testament Commentary: 1 Timothy* (Chicago: Moody Press, 1995), 220.

have sown spiritual things for you, is it a great thing if we reap your material things? If others are partakers of this right over you, are we not even more? Nevertheless we have not used this right, but endure all things lest we hinder the gospel of Christ. Do you not know that those who minister the holy things eat of the things of the temple, and those who serve at the altar partake of the offerings of the altar? Even so the Lord has commanded that those who preach the gospel should live from the gospel.

There is a second reason that elders should be paid. Paul says that *"The laborer is worthy of his wages."* This quote comes from Luke 10, where we read of Christ sending out the 70 to minister. It says in Luke 10:1-7,

After these things the Lord appointed seventy others also, and sent them two by two before His face into every city and place where He Himself was about to go. Then He said to them, "The harvest truly is great, but the laborers are few; therefore pray the Lord of the harvest to send out laborers into His harvest. Go your way; behold, I send you out as lambs among wolves. Carry neither money bag, knapsack, nor sandals; and greet no one along the road. But whatever house you enter, first say, 'Peace to this house.' And if a son of peace is there, your peace will rest on it; if not, it will return to you. And remain in the same house, eating and drinking such things as they give, for the laborer is worthy of his wages. Do not go from house to house."

The idea is that as they go out and minister and receive temporal blessings, they are to receive these and not reject them. As they minister in spiritual things, they are to reap in material things. I remember when I began traveling and speaking that I did not know what to do about honorariums. I chose to leave that up to each church, and still do, but I will admit that it seems like there are some churches that need to consider carefully these passages. My husband often reminds me of the hours I spend for these conferences: 2-3 days away from home; time to pack and unpack; time spent in travel; time spent in study; time spent counseling while I'm there; time spent actually teaching, anywhere from 1 to as many as 12 sessions. In many instances, it is a grueling schedule. As difficult as it was for me, initially, to take an honorarium, I knew that I worked hard and that it was a biblical principle. Just like some of you work very hard at your job and you are compensated for it, so it is with the pastor in your church. What should a pastor's salary be? It should be generous, and it should be given because the Bible commands it for elders who rule well and who labor in the Word and in doctrine.

Paul now moves from writing about a pastor's salary to writing about a pastor's sinning. We know that some elders rule well, yet they are still criticized and falsely accused. On the other hand, some elders don't rule well, and they need to be confronted. What do we do with a sinning pastor? Paul tells us what to do about that in verses 19-21.

The Pastor's Sin

1 Timothy 5:19-21

> Do not receive an accusation against an elder except from two or three witnesses. (1 Timothy 5:19)

What should be done if someone comes to you with *an accusation against an elder* in your church? Paul says you *do not receive* it *except from two or three witnesses*. Now, before we get into what this verse means, let me first say that the word *accusation* means a complaint. With that definition in mind, we all would be wise to be careful about listening to any fellow church member's complaints about an elder. Pastors are on the front line for criticism, and we must guard their testimony for the sake of the gospel and the church. Slander can easily destroy a pastor's reputation and it can just as easily destroy a church. My husband has been a pastor now for about 40 years and hardly a week goes by that either he or myself is not criticized for something. Some of those criticisms are more severe than others, and often those criticisms are unfounded.

People accuse elders just as they accuse all men. Pastors are not exempt from accusations and they're not exempt from sinning, either; they are human beings with human frailties. So, Paul is clear that you don't *receive* those accusations, you don't accept them as truth, until there are *two or three witnesses*. Can you listen to what they are saying? Sure! But from there you need to investigate it and bring in witnesses; this is in line with the teaching of Matthew 18. The individual who has come to you with an accusation against an elder should go to that elder and take care of the offense, following the steps outlined in Mathew 18:15-17, which says,

> Moreover if your brother sins against you, go and tell him his fault between you and him alone. If he hears you, you have gained your brother. But if he will not hear, take with you one or two more, that "by the mouth of two or three witnesses every word may be established." And if he refuses to hear them, tell it to the church. But if he refuses even to hear the church, let him be to you like a heathen and a tax collector.

This principle of two or three witnesses is mentioned a number of times throughout the Scriptures, beginning as far back as the Mosaic Law.

There are a lot of people out there who would like nothing better than to destroy good men's testimonies, and because of that it is imperative that we don't take one person's word for something. But ladies, this principle is true for anyone who shares another person's sins with you. Proverbs 18:13 tells us that "He who answers a matter before he hears it, it is folly and shame to him." This is illustrated to me over and over again when I counsel women regarding marital issues. By the time we finish our first session you'd think their husband was the antichrist! But when and if I am able to get him to come in and meet for counseling with my husband and I both present, I find that there is another side to this story and in many cases the wife comes out looking like Mrs. Antichrist!

There will, however, be occasions in which, after investigating the accusation against an elder, you discover that the accusation is true. What are you to do then? Paul makes it clear that a shepherd is no different than any other of God's children; he must be confronted and disciplined.

> Those who are sinning rebuke in the presence of all, that the rest
> also may fear. (1 Timothy 5:20)

If you have investigated the accusation and have discovered that it is indeed true, then the church has a biblical responsibility to rebuke that elder before all of the church, if he is unwilling to repent. I always find it odd when churches say they do church discipline, but no one ever hears anything about the sin or the sinner. According to Mathew 18, you are to tell the sin and the sinner to the church, and, according to this verse, you are to do the same thing even if that sinner is the pastor! Oh, how I wish churches would get back to the Bible! If they did, we might see a great deal more holy living, which is Paul's point in this verse! Sinning elders should not only not be allowed to remain in the office of elder, but they must be rebuked before all just as any other sinning member would be. Elders are not exempt from church discipline just because they are elders, just as the president is not exempt from obeying the laws of the land and from being sent to prison if he does not.

Paul says that unrepentant, sinning elders must be *rebuked in the presence of all*, which means they must be exposed before the entire congregation. Why? Isn't this embarrassing? Why don't we just ask them to leave and keep it quiet? Well, humanly speaking, what happens when things are not exposed? Gossip! Pretty soon, the gossip mill is up and running and people are imagining all sorts of things. The main reason we do this, however, is simply because God commands it. Yet Paul provides us with even another reason we do this, and that is so *the rest also may fear*. *The rest* is referring to the rest of the elders and also to the rest of the congregation. The other elders would, hopefully, examine themselves to be sure they are not soon going to disqualify themselves by some ongoing sin, and the congregation as a whole would, hopefully, wake up as they see that this body of believers is serious about sin, willing even to expose one of its leaders when necessary. I often think of the account in Acts 5, where Ananias and his wife Sapphira agreed together to lie and both were struck dead for doing so; it says there that fear came upon all who heard about it (Acts 5:5). I would guess so! Whenever we have had to exercise church discipline in our church, and I see that person given over to Satan for the destruction of the flesh, it causes me to pause and soberly examine my life! And, as I mentioned, it is unfortunate in our day that we don't see more churches disciplining sinning members and that we allow those sinning members to either remain in the church or we ask them to leave, but we don't follow the steps given in Matthew 18 where they are publicly exposed. I often hear visitors in our church say to me that our church is the first church they have ever attended that practices church discipline! That, my friend, is tragic and it's an indictment on the church and blight on our Lord's name! Perhaps, though, you think that Paul is being a bit extreme. It would be hard to think that when we consider the next verse.

> I charge you before God and the Lord Jesus Christ and the elect angels that you observe these things without prejudice, doing nothing with partiality. (1 Timothy 5:21)

I charge you are strong words that mean I protest earnestly. And Paul says he does this in the sight of *God, the Lord Jesus Christ,* and *the elect angels.* In other words, God and Jesus and the angels are watching this and we are doing this in their presence. This is very similar to what Jesus says in Matthew 18, where He makes it clear that church discipline is a binding thing that Jesus and God are watching with agreement. We too often just look at verses 15-17 and forget verses 18-20, which are very often taken out of context:

> Moreover if your brother sins against you, go and tell him his fault between you and him alone. If he hears you, you have gained your brother. But if he will not hear, take with you one or two more, that "by the mouth of two or three witnesses every word may be established." And if he refuses to hear them, tell it to the church. But if he refuses even to hear the church, let him be to you like a heathen and a tax collector. Assuredly, I say to you, whatever you bind on earth will be bound in heaven, and whatever you loose on earth will be loosed in heaven. Again I say to you that if two of you agree on earth concerning anything that they ask, it will be done for them by My Father in heaven. For where two or three are gathered together in My name, I am there in the midst of them.

Verse 18 is simply a continuation of Jesus' teaching regarding the church discipline process, and He is saying that whatever you do in that process on earth is approved by God and bound in heaven. And then, in verses 19 and 20, still talking about the church discipline process, He says that if two or three are gathered in His name He is there in the midst of them; He means that He is with them during the church discipline process. I have never understood why people think this is a promise from God to answer prayer if there are two or three people present. Does that mean God doesn't answer prayer when only one person is praying? Is He not present with one person? Ladies, context is always so important! Even in the following verse, Peter asks Jesus about forgiveness and how often we need to forgive one another. The context is sin and forgiveness!

When Paul charges Timothy and the church with this important responsibility of dealing with an elder's sin, he says that he does so in the presence of God and the Lord Jesus Christ and even *the elect angels*. This is a bit mysterious, since angels are not elect to salvation as humans are. However, 2 Peter 2:4 and Jude 6 are helpful to us in understanding what Paul means. Second Peter 2:4 says, "God did not spare the angels who sinned, but cast them down to hell and delivered them into chains of darkness, to be reserved for judgment." And Jude 6 says, "And the angels who did not keep their proper domain, but left their own abode, He has reserved in everlasting chains under darkness for the judgment of the great day." These verses seem to indicate that there are angels who are fallen and are no longer in Heaven. So, the elect angels whom Paul is referring to appear to be those still in glory.

Paul goes on to say that the discipline of sinning elders must be done *without prejudice, doing nothing with partiality*. Perhaps you don't like a certain elder because of his social rank or his race or some other reason. Your heart is filled with *prejudice*, and so you think, "I hope he gets what's coming to him," without really looking at the charges objectively. Or, you could go the other way, showing *partiality*. You might really love a certain pastor because you idolize him, or because he's your closest friend, and because of that you don't see things objectively and you can't even imagine that he is capable of such a charge! Paul says put aside all prejudice and all partiality when you are disciplining a sinning elder. You must not allow someone's money, friendship, or the fact that they might even be a relative, to sway you in your obedience in this area. Two of the hardest church disciplines my husband has had to perform in his 40 years of ministry were in regard to a sibling and a best friend. In both of these we wept, but we knew we could not be partial. God is watching, and the church is watching. What do you do with a sinning elder? You investigate the charge; if it is true and he doesn't repent, you begin the church discipline process, not showing any prejudice or partiality. Well, enough about sinning elders, let's now turn to the pastor's sanctification.

The Pastor's Sanctification

1 Timothy 5:22

> Do not lay hands on anyone hastily, nor share in other people's sins; keep yourself pure. (1 Timothy 5:22)

We have already learned that one of the qualifications for a man serving in church leadership is that he is not to be a novice or a new convert (1 Timothy 3:6). If you put a new Christian into a position of leadership, there is a great probability that you'll later encounter sin issues in his life because he has not been a believer long enough to determine the genuineness of his faith and to allow him to mature. That's why Paul says, first, *do not lay hands on anyone hastily*; (this does not mean physically aggressive, but instead, do not put people into leadership quickly). I know I've made this mistake in women's ministries; on a number of occasions, I've been disappointed by not waiting on the Lord and watching the lives of those women to see if they are indeed faithful.

Secondly, Paul says to Timothy that he is not to *share in other people's sins*. This would include not appointing a man to the office of elder if you know he is sinning; otherwise, you partake of his sins.

It is always wise to interview a prospective elder and sometimes even family members to make sure that there are no hidden sins in his life. Our church usually allows two weeks for people in the church to come forward with biblical reasons why a man should not be an officer in the church once he has been selected for ordination by the elder board.

Lastly, Paul tells Timothy: *keep yourself pure*. Given the context, this would be referring to keeping oneself pure by not partaking in others' sins; otherwise, you're just as guilty as the sinner. This would certainly be reason for some wives—those who cover up their husband's sins—to pause in self-examination. A wife who covers up her husband's sin is partaking in his sin by being silent about it. She is just as guilty as he is. But this keeping pure would also include any other sins Timothy might consider committing. The seriousness of sinning elders should sober him up to make sure he is pure in conduct and in heart. How does an elder make sure he is growing in sanctification? He makes sure he doesn't lay hands suddenly on anyone, because if he does, he will be partaking of their sins. He also strives to be pure in body and in soul. And, speaking of the body, Paul briefly addresses what Timothy should do about his sickness. Yes, pastors are human and get sick just like the rest of us do.

The Pastor's Sickness

1 Timothy 5:23

> No longer drink only water, but use a little wine for your stomach's sake and your frequent infirmities. (1 Timothy 5:23)

Perhaps you're wondering why Paul puts this statement in here at this juncture, when he has been addressing pastors' salaries and pastors' sinning. He's just told Timothy to keep himself pure, and it is possible that Timothy was becoming legalistic about not drinking wine and was drinking water only, which was not purified in those days. Poor quality water, coupled with, perhaps, Timothy's common timidity and fears, may have been causing him to have frequent stomach issues. Wine in biblical times was used for medicinal purposes, and so Paul says drink a *little*—not a lot, but a little. We've already seen that elders are not to tarry long at the wine (1 Timothy 3:3). So, what is a pastor to do when he's sick? It's okay if he takes some medication, if he so desires. He should not be looked down upon for that. My husband is diabetic, which contributes to other health issues, and he has to take insulin along with a number of other medications. Others choose not to do this, and that's okay as well, but we must all remember that pastors are human beings with frail bodies, just like you and me. Of course, as James says in his epistle, pastors are also free to call for the elders of the church to come and pray over them (James 5:14). Well, enough about sickness, let's now close this section regarding pastors by considering their selection, in verses 24 and 25.

The Pastor's Selection

1 Timothy 5:24-25

> Some men's sins are clearly evident, preceding them to judgment, but those of some men follow later. (1 Timothy 5:24)

What Paul is saying is that some men don't even need to be considered for the office of elder because their sins *are clearly evident*. The church doesn't need to judge if these men are qualified; it's obvious they are not. The sins of others, however, don't show up till *later*. It may be that this happens as these men go through the process of determining whether they are qualified for the office of elder or not. Unfortunately, though, some hide their sin well and those hidden sins don't become known until years later. Regardless, none of us can hide our sin from God, and one day, my friend, we will be judged for everything we have done, whether good or bad. Paul goes on to say,

> Likewise, the good works of some are clearly evident, and those that are otherwise cannot be hidden. (1 Timothy 5:25)

Paul says *likewise*, in the same way, *the good works of some are clearly evident*, just like the sins. Some men you don't even have to wonder about, because it is clearly seen that they are godly and involved in *good works*. However, *those that are otherwise cannot be hidden*. Some pastors may be able to hide their sins now, but on judgment day all will be revealed, including the hidden things of the heart. My friend, the same is true for us. You might be able to hide your sins now, but when judgment comes it will be revealed. Wouldn't it be better to forsake those things now? In considering the selection of elders, we want to examine them carefully, making sure there are no outstanding sin issues, along with examining their lives for good works.

Summary

We have considered the pastors' salary, the pastor's sin, the pastor's sanctification, the pastor's sickness, and the pastor's selection. You might be wondering what you should do with all this information? Or, perhaps, what should you do with your pastor? The following was a great idea that was posted years ago in a Christian magazine, and with this I'll close. Here's what to do with your pastor:

> Make him a minister of the Word! Fling him into his office, tear the office sign from the door and nail on the sign: Study. Take him off the mailing list, lock him up with his books and his typewriter and his Bible. Slam him down on his knees before texts, broken hearts, the flippant lives of superficial flock, and the Holy God. Force him to be the one man in our surfeited communities who knows about God. Throw him into the ring to box with God until he learns how short his arms are. Let him come out only when he is bruised and beaten into being a blessing. Set a time clock on him that will imprison him with thought and writing about God for 40 hours a week. Shut his garrulous mouth forever spouting "remarks" and stop his tongue always tripping lightly over everything nonessential. Require him to have something to say before he dare break silence. Bend his knees in the lonesome valley, fire him from the PTA, and cancel his country club membership; burn his eyes with weary study, wreck his emotional poise with worry for God, and make him exchange his pious stance for a humble walk before God and man. Make him spend and be spent for the

glory of God. Rip out his telephone, burn up his ecclesiastical success sheets, refuse his glad hand, and put water in the gas tank of his community buggy. Give him a Bible and tie him in his pulpit and make him preach the Word of the living God. Test him, quiz him and examine him; humiliate him for his ignorance of things divine, and shame him for his glib comprehension of finances, batting averages, and political in-fighting.

Laugh at his frustrated effort to play psychiatrist, scorn his insipid morality, refuse his supine intelligence, and compel him to be a minister of the Word. If he dotes on being pleasing, demand that he please God and not man. Form a choir and raise a chant and haunt him with it night and day: "Sir, we wish to see Jesus." When at long last, he dares assay the pulpit, ask him if he has a Word from God; if he does not, then dismiss him and tell him you can read the morning paper, digest the television commentaries, think through the day's superficial problems, manage the community's myriad drives, and bless assorted baked potatoes and green beans ad infinitum better than he can. Command him not to come back until he has read and re-read, written and re-written, until he can stand up, worn and forlorn, and say, "Thus saith the Lord." And when he is burned out by the flaming Word that coursed through him, when he is consumed at last by the fiery Grace blazing through him, and when he who was privileged to translate the truth of God to man is finally translated from earth to heaven, then bear him away gently, blow a muted trumpet and lay him down softly, and place a two-edged sword on his coffin and raise a tune triumphant, for he was a brave solider of the Word and e'er he died he had become a spokesman for his God.[49]

---

49 Quoted by Floyd Doud Shafer in "And Preach As You Go!" *Christianity Today*, March 27, 1961.

Questions to Consider

What to Do About a Pastor's Salary and a Pastor's Sins!
1 Timothy 5:17-25

1. Read 1 Timothy chapter five and summarize it in a few sentences.

2. Memorize 1 Timothy 5:19.

3. (a) What are our biblical responsibilities to our elders, according to 1 Thessalonians 5:12-13; 1 Timothy 5:17-25; Hebrews 13:7; and Hebrews 13:17? (b) How do you think the collective church is doing in following the admonitions from these verses? (c) How are you doing personally in following these admonitions?

4. (a) What do the following verses have in common? Deuteronomy 17:6; Deuteronomy 19:15; Matthew 18:16; John 8:17-18; 2 Corinthians 13:1; 1 Timothy 5:19; Hebrews 10:28. (b) After considering these verses, why do you think it's essential that an accusation against an elder not be received unless there are 2 or 3 witnesses?

5. (a) How does 1 Timothy 5:20 go against the trend of our day? (b) Why do you think it's imperative that we expose sinning members as well as sinning elders? Use Scripture to support your answer.

6. (a) After studying this lesson, what would you do if someone came to you with an accusation about your pastor? (b) What would you do if you knew your pastor was in sin? (c) What would you do if you knew your pastor was not being paid properly?

7. (a) Do you know if your pastor is receiving a salary that meets his needs and is equivalent to the living wage of the day? (b) Do you know your pastor well enough to know if there are any overt sins in his life? (c) After studying this passage, how do you think you might better pray for your pastor? (d) Please come with a prayer request for him.

Chapter 17

The Proper Disposition for Your Position

1 Timothy 6:1-2

A number of years ago, I was at a Chinese buffet having a birthday lunch with my 9-year-old grandson and my husband. I'm not a big fan of Chinese food, but I do love those fortune cookies! When the meal was over, I eagerly unwrapped my cookie and popped it into my mouth. And of course, the next thing I did was read the fortune. Most of the time, those fortunes are pretty odd, and I've often wondered what those numbers are for on the other side of the fortune. (Is it your wanna-be figure? Is it numbers for the lottery?) As I read my fortune that day, I thought it was really pretty good. It said: "It isn't our position, but our disposition, that makes us happy." (I actually kept that fortune, along with one another one from a past Chinese food eating experience that was pretty comical; it said something like, "You like words. You should write a book!")

It truly isn't our position but our disposition that makes us happy. In a way, that is what the apostle Paul is saying to us concerning the slave and master relationship (or, as our context might dictate, the employee and employer relationship) in the verses we'll be considering in this lesson. It's not the job, the occupation, the position, we have as we work as much as it is the disposition we have that God is looking at—that's what's important to Him. Our disposition is what will make us a good employee or a good wife and mom. It is our disposition that will please not only our earthly master but also our heavenly Master. This is a much-needed lesson in our culture; a recent gallop poll indicated that 70 percent of Americans do not like their job and go to work disengaged. So, what is this disposition, what is this attitude that we should have as a slave or as an employee? Let's read 1 Timothy 6:1-2 to discover it.

1 Timothy 6:1-2

> Let as many bondservants as are under the yoke count their own masters worthy of all honor, so that the name of God and His doctrine may not be blasphemed. ²And those who have believing masters, let them not despise them because they are brethren, but rather serve them because those who are benefited are believers and beloved. Teach and exhort these things.

Before we begin explaining the meaning of these verses, we need to gain some understanding of the times in which they were written. At the time this epistle was written, there were about 60 million slaves in the Roman Empire, which would have been about half its population. Many slaves were educated; among them were doctors, bakers, bankers, craftsmen, and numerous other occupations. Slaves often became close to the family for whom they worked and by whom they were owned. Within the church context, slaves were also accepted. But even with all their skills and their close family and church ties, slaves were still slaves. The gospel of freedom in Christ was often very appealing to a slave, and because of that many embraced the gospel. But, evidently, some Christian slaves thought that with their new freedom in Christ, they were also free from their earthy authorities. They took their liberties too far and forgot, as we often do, that they still had to be submissive to authority. Yet, it's always been that way and it should remain that way. A child is to be submissive to his parents; wives are to be submissive to their husbands; citizens are to be submissive to kings; Christians are to be submissive to their church leaders; and, yes, slaves are to be submissive to their masters—or, as we might say in our context, employees are to be submissive to employers. Being a Christian does not negate that we must all respect and serve those in authority over us. Even Jesus was submissive to His Father, as John 6:38 makes clear, "For I have come down from heaven, not to do My own will, but the will of Him who sent Me."

In this lesson, we will learn

> *The Proper Disposition for the Slave to the Unsaved Master* (v 1) and
>
> *The Proper Disposition for the Slave to the Saved Master* (v 2).

Paul will also give a reason for each of these points. Having just mentioned the importance of honoring elders, Paul now addresses the slaves and the importance of them honoring their masters. Let's consider, first, the disposition a slave should have toward their masters who are not redeemed.

The Proper Disposition for the Slave to the Unsaved Master

1 Timothy 6:1

> Let as many bondservants as are under the yoke count their own masters worthy of all honor, so that the name of God and His doctrine may not be blasphemed. (1 Timothy 6:1)

It is interesting that Paul uses the word bondservant here, because the implication is that the slave, or bondservant, he is referring to is also a slave, or bondservant, of Christ. *Bondservant* comes from the Greek word doulos, which means someone who is under absolute submission to his master and never has the right to say no to that master. Paul is addressing a believing slave in these two verses. The words *under the yoke* also mean slavery. The terminology here is appropriate because masters often treated their slaves the same way they treated their animals that were yoked, or under the yoke. Slaves often were considered to be nothing more than tools. Masters could beat them; they could be forced to do hard labor. The Old Testament gives us a glimpse of this when the Israelites were slaves of the Egyptians; it says in Exodus 1:13-14: "So the Egyptians made the children of Israel serve with rigor. And they made their lives bitter with hard bondage—in mortar, in brick, and in all manner of service in the field. All their service in which they made them serve was with rigor." Such labor certainly wasn't easy, like sitting behind a desk in an office answering the phone from 9-5. It was hard labor; it was rigorous; it was severe and harsh.

What is the Christian slave's attitude to be toward an unbelieving master? Paul says they are to *count their own masters worthy of all honor*. The word *master* simply means someone who has absolute authority. We find a glimpse of this in the New Testament, in Matthew 8, where we read of a centurion who begged Jesus to heal his ailing servant. Jesus assured the centurion that He would come to the centurion's house and heal the servant. "The centurion answered and said, 'Lord, I am not worthy that You should come under my roof. But only speak a word, and my servant will be healed. For I also am a man under authority, having soldiers under me. And I say to this one, 'Go,' and he goes; and to another, 'Come, and he comes; and to my servant, 'Do this,' and he does it" (Matthew 8:8-9). The centurion understood—and we would do well to remember—that Jesus is our Master; He has absolute authority over us. We are His slaves, and we must remember that as we go about our daily living.

What does it mean to count one's master worthy of honor? To *count* means to be conscious, to weigh the facts, to consider. It is indicative of something that we should give careful attention and thought to. *Worthy of all honor* indicates respect. Paul has already mentioned in this epistle that we are to give honor to widows and to elders and now he mentions that slaves are to give honor to *their own* masters. When you think about it, all Christians should be giving honor to all people. Romans 12:10 says, "Be kindly affectionate to one another with brotherly love, in honor giving preference to one another." First Peter 2:17 states, "Honor all people. Love the brotherhood. Fear God. Honor the king." Because of this obligation, slaves are not off the hook in honoring their masters, even if those masters are not redeemed. It's possible that a believing slave might be tempted to look down upon his or her master because of that master's lost condition, making it all the more difficult to work for them. Peter would have a word for these slaves also, as he writes in 1 Peter 2:18, "Servants, be submissive to your masters with all fear, not only to the good and gentle, but also to the harsh." Christians, of all people, should treat their bosses with honor, and there is a reason for this. Paul says, *so that the name of God and His doctrine may not be blasphemed.* To *blaspheme* God's name means that God's name will be spoken evil of or defamed. One man helps us here; he says,

> If a Christian slave dishonored his master in any way by disobedience, by acting disrespectfully, by speaking shamefully of his master, the worst consequence would not be the beating he would receive but the curses he would cause his master to hurl at this miserable slave's God, his religion, and the teaching he had embraced: "So that is what his new religion teaches its converts!" Instead of bringing honor to the true God and the gospel of his high and holy Name, as every Christian should be anxious to do, this slave would bring about the very opposite, to the devil's delight.[50]

My friend, can you imagine the impact this would have, not only back in Paul's day but also now, if we took this verse seriously? We might actually impact the world for the gospel, because unbelievers would see that Christians indeed make the best employees, even under the most difficult of work situations! Who knows how many bosses might take notice and ask about the hope that is within these employees?

Blaspheming the name of God is serious, and this is not the only place Paul mentions it. In Romans 2:24, he says, "For 'the name of God is blasphemed among the Gentiles because of you,' as it is written." As women, we would do well to consider one of the chief ways we blaspheme the Word of God. Paul tells women in Titus 2:3-5,

> the older women likewise, that they be reverent in behavior, not slanderers, not given to much wine, teachers of good things— that they admonish the young women to love their husbands, to love their children, to be discreet, chaste, homemakers, good, obedient to their own husbands, that the word of God may not be blasphemed.

---

50   R.C.H. Lenski, *Commentary on the New Testament: The Interpretation of St. Paul's Epistles to the Colossians, to the Thessalonians, to Timothy, to Titus, and to Philemon* (Peabody: Hendrickson Publishers, 1998), 694-695.

One of the main ways we blaspheme God and His Word is by not fulfilling these admonitions to love our husbands and children, to be pure, sober, keepers at home, good, and obedient to our husbands. When we fail to heed these admonitions, the world looks at us and wonders why we say we are Christians and yet don't live like Christians. And yet we can be such a huge example of the gospel when we live out Titus 2! The world takes notice and sees that we not only say we believe the gospel, but we also adorn it and make it attractive by how we live. We have already seen in 1 Timothy 5:14 that young widows are to "marry, bear children, manage the house, give no opportunity to the adversary to speak reproachfully." The idea is the same here; to do otherwise is to blaspheme the Word of God and make it unattractive.

What is the disposition a slave should have toward an unbelieving master? Her disposition should be one of honor. And the reason for this attitude is that as she does this, she will adorn the doctrine of God and make it attractive. To dishonor one's master is to blaspheme the Word of God and make it unattractive. The temptation for some slaves, however, might be to think, "Well, I certainly can understand why I need to watch my testimony with an unbelieving master or boss, but my boss is a Christian and I can treat him as an equal. Why, we're best buds! And since we are one and the same, equal in Christ, he has no right to tell me what to do and I certainly don't have to obey him." To such a slave, Paul has something a tad bit different to say. In verse 2, he writes about the disposition a slave should have toward a believing master.

The Proper Disposition for the Slave to the Saved Master

1 Timothy 6:2

> And those who have believing masters, let them not despise them because they are brethren, but rather serve them because those who are benefited are believers and beloved. Teach and exhort these things. (1 Timothy 6:2)

In this verse we consider Christian slaves of Christian masters. What should be the disposition of believing slaves toward believing masters? Paul says such slaves should *not despise* these masters. This means the slave should not look down upon his master; he should not neglect or have a careless attitude toward him. We shouldn't despise our earthly, believing masters because they are *brethren*, because they are our brothers or sisters in Christ. Because both slave and master, employee and employer, are equal in Christ, a slave might be tempted to think there is no such thing as a superior and an inferior. But this is not true. Someone has to be the boss. Even our Lord in the Upper Room told His disciples, in John 15:15, "No longer do I call you servants, for a servant does not know what his master is doing; but I have called you friends, for all things that I heard from My Father I have made known to you." Even though their new relationship included friendship, Christ was still the disciples' Master. In fact, after Jesus' resurrection He tells Peter in John 21 to follow Him. There is absolutely no indication that Jesus would ever follow Peter, but there is every indication that Peter is to follow Jesus. Jesus was still Peter's Lord even though He was also Peter's friend. If we find ourselves with believing bosses, we must not get so comfortable with them that we forget that they are our superiors and we are working for them. As believers working for other believers, we should not have the mindset of taking advantage of our superiors but of seeking to please them more than we please ourselves and of considering them as better than ourselves. But, my sister, this applies to all of our relationships—this is the attitude we all should have toward one another! Paul says in Philippians 2:3-4, "Let nothing be done through selfish ambition or conceit, but in lowliness of mind let each esteem others better than himself. Let each of you look out not only for his own interests, but also for the interests of others."

Paul goes on to say that instead of slaves despising their masters, slaves are to *serve them*. What does it mean to *serve*? It means to obey cheerfully. And we do this, Paul says, because those masters are *benefited*, which means they are partakers of the benefit. We are actually to serve those masters more because they are believers.

Paul writes this same thing to the church at Galatia, in Galatians 6:10; he says, "Therefore, as we have opportunity, let us do good to all, *especially* to those who are of the household of faith" (emphasis mine). By serving our believing, earthly masters, we are benefiting them, which is honoring to the Lord. We are benefiting those who belong to the Lord and are related to us in Christ and are *beloved* by Him. The master or boss you are working for who belongs to Christ reaps the benefits of your hard work. Yes, God sends rain on the just and the unjust, the unsaved boss and the saved boss, but there are special benefits for those who belong to God, and by serving a saved master you are being used by God to deliver those benefits. The saved master or boss is loved by God just as the saved slave or employee is loved by God. We must remember that no matter what role we have, slave or master, employee or employer, we are God's children made in His image.

This very truth was illustrated to me not long ago. I had decided that year to read through the first Bible my dad ever owned. The date written in it is 1944, which means that he would have been about 26 years of age at the time he received it. Each page is replete with personal notes and cross references, and it was—and still is—a delight to visit my dad in the pages of this Bible. Even at his young age, he was quite insightful. One of the first personal notes I read was from Genesis 9:6, where it is written that we are not to shed man's blood because he is made in the image of God. In the margin, my dad had written, "Man is made in the image and likeness of God. To murder a man is to strike at God Himself." As I thought about this, it occurred to me that it very much related to this text: To despise a man is to despise God Himself. To hate a man is to hate God Himself. To be bitter toward a man is to be bitter toward God Himself. And to despise one's master or employer is to despise God Himself!

Paul ends this brief section of his letter by saying that Timothy should *teach and exhort these things*. These principles regarding slaves and masters must be *taught*, must be brought to bear upon the minds of others. The word *exhort* means to urge or persuade, to motivate. "Timothy," Paul is saying, "keep on teaching them, keep on exhorting." We, too, must also keep on teaching and exhorting these principles, especially when we consider the statistic that 70 percent of us don't like our jobs! That is an awful indictment on us! (I sure hope the other 30 percent are believers!) One man has illustrated the necessity of this teaching; he says,

> I recall counseling a young lady who resigned from a secular job to go to work in a Christian organization. She had been there about a month and was completely disillusioned. "I thought it was going to be heaven on earth," she complained. "Instead, there are nothing but problems." "Are you working just as hard for your Christian boss as you did for your other boss?" I asked. The look on her face gave me the answer. "Try working harder," I advised, "and show him real respect. Just because all of you in the office are saved doesn't mean you can do less than your best." She took my advice and her problems cleared up.[51]

The disposition a believing slave is to have toward her believing master is not to despise him but to serve him. And the reason Paul gives for maintaining such a disposition is that those masters are fellow believers and loved by God.

Summary

Perhaps you are wondering what you are to do with this lesson. How does one apply the commandments taught in this lesson to the 21st century, where our work is a tad bit different from the day in which Paul wrote this first epistle to Timothy. John MacArthur helps us out with 9 principles of work that I would like to share with you as we close this chapter.[52] All of these principles are derived from this passage and from the slave/master passages in Ephesians and Colossians that you will study in the Questions to Consider.

---

51 PC Study Bible (V5); The Bible Exposition Commentary; New Testament.
52 John MacArthur, *The MacArthur New Testament Commentary: 1 Timothy* (Chicago: Moody Press, 1995), paraphrase of points found on pages 234-235.

1. *Christians should serve their employers obediently.* What about you? When your boss asks you to do something, do you bristle? Do you do it the way you want to do it, or the way your boss would want you to do it? When your husband asks you to do something, do you bristle or make excuses as to why you can't do it? Or, when someone in any position of authority over you asks you to do something, do you cheerfully obey without questioning their authority?

2. *Christians are to serve their employers completely.* Do you finish the task that is asked of you? When you are at home working, do you start a million things and never complete any of them? Can your employer count on you to finish what you start, or does he have to remind you often to complete your task? (Even Jesus completed His tasks; in John 17:4, He prays to the Father and says, "I have glorified you on the earth. I have finished the work which You have given me to do.")

3. *Christians should serve their employers respectfully.* How do you honor your employer? Do you gossip behind his or her back? Do you look for ways to honor and promote him or her? As you work around the home, do you do it with an attitude of respect for the material things that God has given you? Are you teaching your children to take care of their material things with respect?

4. *Christians are to serve their employers eagerly.* Are you one of the 70 percent who go to work disengaged? Do you hate your job? Do you eagerly tackle your tasks, even the difficult ones? Do you eagerly do your duties around the house, like grocery shopping, cooking, cleaning, and taking care of the home and the children, or do you find idle things to do, putting off the things you know you should be doing?

5. *Christians should serve their employers excellently.* Are you half-hearted with your work? Do you only perform with excellence when your boss is watching? What about at home? Do you work

at home with excellence, all the while realizing that the Lord is watching you as you work?

6. *Christians should serve their employers diligently.* Do you serve your employer with persistence? Are you meticulous about your work or sloppy? What about in your home? Will you rise up early and stay up late in order to get something done that you are working on?

7. *Christians should serve their employers humbly.* Do you think you are better than your boss? Do you inwardly despise him? Do you really see yourself as a servant, a slave, of his? What about at home? Do you inwardly wish you could be the one out working, instead of caring for your home and children? Do you secretly wish God hadn't made you a woman? Do you despise the work He has given you to do or do you serve humbly at home?

8. *Christians should serve their employers spiritually.* In other words, they should do so for the glory of God. For those of you who work outside of the home, how would you say your work this week has glorified God? Was God's name exalted by your actions and your words? For those of you working in the home, how was God glorified in your work? Did you set a godly example for those who come in and out of your home and for your family? Would they say God was glorified in your life this week and especially in your work? How have you adorned the doctrine of God and made it attractive this week as you worked?

9. *Christians should serve their employers eschatologically.* This means doing it with a view that one day Christ is coming, and when He does you will receive from the Lord your inheritance. As you have worked this past week, has it been in your mind's eye that God is watching you and that one day you will be judged for every deed done in your body, whether it is good or evil? For those of you who have difficult bosses or difficult home situations, do you work knowing that it really doesn't matter if

you suffer in this life because one day the Judge of all the earth will do what is right and one day you will be in glory with Him, and that's all that really matters?

Remember, dear one, it is not your position in life but your disposition in life that matters! A disposition of honor, respect, and service is what pleases not only our earthly masters but, more importantly, our heavenly Master!

Questions to Consider

The Proper Disposition for your Position
1 Timothy 6:1-2

1. (a) Read 1 Timothy 6:1-2, along with Ephesians 6:5-9; Colossians 3:22-4:1; Titus 2:9-10; and 1 Peter 2:18-20. According to these verses, what are the responsibilities of slaves, and what are the responsibilities of masters? (b) Why do you think more space is given to the role of the slave than the role of the master?

2. Memorize either 1 Timothy 6:1 or 6:2.

3. Read Genesis 24 and answer the following questions. (a) What did Abraham ask his servant to do? (b) Did the servant obey him? (c) What attitudes did the servant have as he carried out this task? (d) In what ways does this story go along with what Paul says in 1 Timothy 6:2?

4. (a) The book of Philemon was written by Paul to encourage Philemon in forgiving his runaway slave, Onesimus. As you read Philemon, what do you glean regarding Onesimus and his failure to be a good slave? (b) How does Paul encourage Philemon in forgiving Onesimus? (c) What encouragement does this offer you for times when those who are under your authority don't obey you? (d) How do you think a Christian employer should handle a disobedient employee?

5. (a) How do you encourage yourself to have a proper attitude when you are working (regardless of whether you work in the home or outside of the home)? (b) What tasks do you find especially difficult and what do you do to make them more enjoyable?

6. (a) How would you use these passages we have looked at to encourage your husband, yourself, or others who are having difficulty maintaining a good attitude about their job? (b) How have you trained your children to work with a proper attitude?

7. After you prayerfully evaluate question 5, write down a prayer request to share with your group.

Chapter 18

Eleven Evil Characteristics
of False Teachers!

1 Timothy 6:3-5

Not long ago, there was some "chatter" on our church's email discussion group regarding what should be done with those who teach false doctrine. Specifically, it was asked, should these teachers be rebuked, should they be tolerated, should they be dealt with gently or sharply, should they be rebuked privately or publicly? These are all good questions that demand biblical answers. Thankfully, our Lord gives us answers to these questions all throughout His Word, so we're not left guessing about how to deal with those who misrepresent His Word, His doctrine, His wholesome words. The text we find ourselves studying in this lesson, 1 Timothy 6:3-5, not only deals briefly with this question but also provides us with eleven things to look for in those who are not teaching sound doctrine, but false doctrine. Let's read these three short but alarming verses.

1 Timothy 6:3-5

> If anyone teaches otherwise and does not consent to wholesome words, even the words of our Lord Jesus Christ, and to the doctrine which accords with godliness, [4]he is proud, knowing nothing, but is obsessed with disputes and arguments over words, from which come envy, strife, reviling, evil suspicions, [5]useless wranglings of men of corrupt minds and destitute of the truth, who suppose that godliness is a means of gain. From such withdraw yourself.

As we began chapter six of 1 Timothy in our last lesson, we learned that slaves are to maintain a specific attitude toward their unbelieving masters and that attitude is one of honor. Evidently, there were some who did not receive this teaching, along with the rest of the teaching of this epistle, and Paul now turns to address this issue. As you know, Paul has something to say about those who don't consent to our Lord's words. Paul is not a coward when it comes to addressing those who are not in line with God's Word, like some in our day are! In the verses we'll study in this lesson, Paul will outline for us eleven evil characteristics of those who teach false doctrine. Each of these evil characteristics I want to contrast with the characteristics of our Lord, because Paul says that false teachers don't consent to wholesome words, even the words of our Lord Jesus Christ. So, with each of these eleven evil characteristics of the false teachers who teach false doctrine, I want to make a contrast with eleven encouraging characteristics of Christ, our true Teacher, who teaches true doctrine. Let's begin with verse 3 as we read Paul's introductory remarks concerning those who deny truth.

> If anyone teaches otherwise and does not consent to wholesome words, even the words of our Lord Jesus Christ, and to the doctrine which accords with godliness, (1 Timothy 6:3)

Paul begins by saying *if anyone teaches otherwise*; in other words, if anyone teaches anything different. Different than what? Different is described in the next few words: different in that it is not wholesome words, different in that it is not the words of our Lord Jesus Christ, different in that it is not doctrine that is in accord with godliness. This would include not only teachers who might be saying that slaves don't have to be submissive to their masters, as we saw in our last lesson but also any teaching that Paul has written, or any teaching that does not line with up God's Word. Paul will make it clear in verse 5 that we are to get away from that person. In fact, when Paul comes to the end of his second letter to the Thessalonians he writes similar words, in 2 Thessalonians 3:14-15, "And if anyone does not obey our word in this epistle, note that person and do not keep company with him, that he may be ashamed. Yet do not count him as an enemy, but admonish him as a brother."

Paul describes the *otherwise* by saying that such a teacher *does not consent to wholesome words*. The word *wholesome* is a word that we don't use much these days, but it means healthy or sound. Paul tells Timothy, in 2 Timothy 1:13, "Hold fast the pattern of sound words which you have heard from me, in faith and love which are in Christ Jesus." We certainly see a dearth today of men and women holding fast to wholesome words. He further describes wholesome words by saying *even the words of our Lord Jesus Christ*. The words in this epistle we are studying are not Paul's but God's; they are the words of the Lord Jesus Christ. They were inspired by the Holy Spirit and written down by the apostle Paul, just as 2 Peter 1:21 teaches. (The Holy Spirit is part of the Godhead, even though we don't speak as much of Him as we do the other members of the Godhead, God the Father and His Son Jesus Christ.)

These words also have results, as Paul says next, when he writes *the doctrine which accords with godliness*. In other words, God's words, which are sound *doctrine*, lead to holy living. If what is being taught in the pulpit isn't backed up by a holy life, then it does not *accord with godliness*. A person can even have all the right doctrine, but if his or her life doesn't back up that doctrine then that person's doctrine is of little value. When Paul wrote to Titus, another son in the faith, he said, "Paul, a bondservant of God and an apostle of Jesus Christ, according to the faith of God's elect and the acknowledgment of the truth which accords with godliness." (Titus 1:1). The words that false teachers endorse do not lead to godly lifestyles, which is Paul's point as he describes for us eleven evil characteristics of such teachers.

> he is proud, knowing nothing, but is obsessed with disputes and arguments over words, from which come envy, strife, reviling, evil suspicions, (1 Timothy 6:4)

The first thing Paul says about those who don't hold to sound teaching is that they are proud. It is interesting that Paul starts with pride because at the root of all sin is pride. Every sin we ever commit is because we are proud, and we think we have better ideas and better ways of doing things—we think our way is better than God's way! *Proud* is an interesting word; it means to be inflated with self-conceit. It's like an envelope filled with smoke. And it is not by chance that pride is at the top of the list of things the Lord hates; listen to Proverbs 6:16-19: "These six things the Lord hates, yes, seven are an abomination to Him: a proud look, a lying tongue, hands that shed innocent blood, a heart that devises wicked plans, feet that are swift in running to evil, a false witness who speaks lies, and one who sows discord among brethren." People who hold to false teaching and unwholesome words are proud because they do not submit themselves to God's words, which are wholesome.

In contrast to these proud, false teachers, we have Him of whom it is said in Philippians 2:5-8, "Let this mind be in you which was also in Christ Jesus, who, being in the form of God, did not consider it robbery to be equal with God, but made Himself of no reputation, taking the form of a bondservant, and coming in the likeness of men. And being found in appearance as a man, He humbled Himself and became obedient to the point of death, even the death of the cross." There certainly was not a hint of pride in our Lord! Humility was not a virtue that the ancients sought after, and it certainly is not a virtue that false teachers seek after. I would strongly encourage you to listen to what they say, and you'll see that this is true! Pride just reeks from their lips! But from this first description of false teachers as proud, it seems that there is a progression from bad to worse in the next characteristic Paul gives.

The second evil characteristic of false teachers is that they know nothing. A false teacher thinks he knows everything, but what he actually knows is dust in the wind or a puff of smoke. He doesn't understand real godliness; he's made up his own religion in his head. He's not dumb, but he certainly has chosen fables over truth! One televangelist said, "You don't have to believe to get to Heaven." What?! My Bible says, "No one comes to the Father but through Him," and "Believe on the Lord Jesus Christ and you will be saved." *Knowing nothing* is certainly not a characteristic of our Savior, as it says about Him in 1 John 3:20, "For if our heart condemns us, God is greater than our heart, and knows all things." First Corinthians 2:16 says "For 'who has known the mind of the Lord that he may instruct

Him?' But we have the mind of Christ." God knows everything, including the motives of our hearts, but false teachers know nothing, even though they think they know everything.

A third evil and concerning characteristic of those who consent to wrong teaching is that they are obsessed with disputes and arguments over words. Such a person likes to argue over silly stuff, like "splitting hairs," we might say. The word *obsessed* means that he is sick in his mind; he has a morbid desire to dispute and argue over this stuff.

False teachers don't have an obsession with sound doctrine, but they sure have an obsession with false doctrine. I've met women like this, and it seems like every new thing they hear tickles their ears and they just can't wait to share about it. What a contrast to Jesus, who was—yes—willing to confront the false teachers and hypocrites of the day but was not obsessed with disputes and arguments. He was obsessed with coming to do the will of the Father. He said in John 5:30, "I do not seek My own will but the will of the Father who sent Me."

From these things come envy, which is the fourth thing we can note about false teachers. Envy is pain one feels because of someone else's success. Envy is poisonous spite. Those that are not consenting to the words of our Lord have a spirit of envy. But, as with all the other characteristics of false teachers, envy is not something that possesses our Lord! The interesting account of Mark 9:38-41 demonstrates this poignantly:

> Now John answered Him, saying, "Teacher, we saw someone who does not follow us casting out demons in Your name, and we forbade him because he does not follow us." But Jesus said, "Do not forbid him, for no one who works a miracle in My name can soon afterward speak evil of Me. For he who is not against us is on our side. For whoever gives you a cup of water to drink in My name, because you belong to Christ, assuredly, I say to you, he will by no means lose his reward."

Christ had no poisonous spite against others and neither should we.

Fifth in the description of false teachers is strife. Strife has to do with being contentious or quarrelling. It's hard to imagine, but Paul speaks of this in Philippians 1:15: "Some indeed preach Christ even from envy and strife, and some also from goodwill." Strife is not something that characterizes our Savior. Right before Christ was crucified, He was being falsely accused by the chief priests and elders. It's recorded in Matthew 27:13-14: "Then Pilate said to Him, 'Do You not hear how many things they testify against You?' But He answered him not one word, so that the governor marveled greatly." Our Lord did not involve Himself in such nonsense.

Reviling is the sixth characteristic Paul mentions of these false teachers. Reviling involves using harsh and abusive speech. Also included in this would be insults, blasphemous speech, and slander, which are all used against another person. Yet, we have some contrasting, precious, and convicting words in 1 Peter 2:21-23 about our Lord that we would do well to heed: "For to this you were called, because Christ also suffered for us, leaving us an example, that you should follow His steps: 'Who committed no sin, Nor was deceit found in His mouth'; who, when He was reviled, did not revile in return; when He suffered, He did not threaten, but committed Himself to Him who judges righteously."

The seventh characteristic in this verse is evil suspicions, or evil surmising. This describes someone who judges other people's actions, words, and gestures. In response to those who don't agree with their wrong teaching, these false teachers react with evil. Another televangelist responded this way, "Those who put us down are a bunch of morons…" This sounds just like James 3, which you will look at in the Questions to Consider, regarding the wisdom from the earth that is sensual and demonic. This is not the wisdom and behavior that comes from God but from the devil. But we have a contrasting example in our Lord in several of the gospel accounts. When the people were crying out to have Christ crucified, Pilate responded, "Why? What evil has He done?" Our Lord was blameless.

In addition to all these evil characteristics of false teachers, Paul now gives four more characteristics that are far more sobering, in my humble opinion, in verse 5.

> useless wranglings of men of corrupt minds and destitute of the truth, who suppose that godliness is a means of gain. From such withdraw yourself. (1 Timothy 6:5)

The eighth characteristic of those who don't consent to the words of our Lord is that they are involved in useless wranglings. What are *useless wranglings*? They're useless and perverse disputes, discussions that would have no value but only waste people's time. In fact, the Greek term comes from two words which mean to rub away, to wear in pieces. So, the idea is that these disputes can never be settled but only cause people to be endlessly involved in idle conversation.

I recently had this illustrated to me when I was visiting with someone and it was evident we were not in agreement on doctrine. I thought, "This is a waste of my time and her time!" and I went on to change the subject. I think of the gospel accounts and how when the religious rulers of the day would try to get Jesus involved in discussions of no value, and He would speak pointed truth to them. Many times they would be so enraged they would try to kill Him.

Men of corrupt minds is the ninth description of these individuals. I think this description is heartbreaking, because it indicates that what has come out of these false teachers' mouths is really what is in their hearts. It means they have wicked hearts. Isn't it interesting that Jesus Himself said to the false teachers of His day, in Matthew 12:34, "Brood of vipers! How can you, being evil, speak good things? For out of the abundance of the heart the mouth speaks." The heart of a false teacher is wicked. Jesus also makes it clear in Matthew 5:8 that it is only the pure in heart who will see God. In contrast, our Lord obviously has no evil in His heart, not even an iota. John says in his first epistle, in 1 John 3:5, "And you know that He was manifested to take away our sins, and in Him there is no sin."

Number ten on the list of characteristics of false teachers is that they are destitute of the truth. They don't know the truth, they are deprived of the truth, they have been robbed of the truth, and they have put the truth away from themselves. This is both alarming and grieving at the same time. One TV preacher said, "Jesus did not come to earth to be the Messiah." Another has said, "Gays go to Heaven. Being gay is a gift from God." What?! Do these men read the Word of God?! Sometimes I am so dumbstruck at why people cannot see the truth! And then I take myself back to what I know is true from God's Word. John 12:39-40 says, "Therefore they could not believe, because Isaiah said again: 'He has blinded their eyes and hardened their hearts, lest they should see with their eyes, lest they should understand with their hearts and turn, so that I should heal them.'" Of course, it goes without saying, but I'll say it anyway, that our Lord is not destitute of the truth. Jesus Himself says in John 14:6, "I am the way, the truth, and the life. No one comes to the Father except through Me."

The succession of these evil characteristics culminates in these men (and women) using all of these things to get money, which is appalling. *Paul ends these eleven evil characteristics with number eleven: supposing that godliness is a means of gain.* The Jews often viewed financial prosperity as a sign of God's blessing. Many of them taught that the more you served God, the richer you got. There's nothing new under the sun, right? The motivation of false teachers is to make money; to make profit off the people who listen to them. There truly is nothing new under the sun; we have this going on in our day as much as Paul did in his day. Second Peter 2:3 warns of this characteristic of false teachers: "By covetousness they will exploit you with deceptive words; for a long time their judgment has not been idle, and their destruction does not slumber." These people look at religion as a business to make money. But what does the Scripture say about our Lord?

Dear sister, these eleven characteristics are evil and alarming, and they describe those who oppose our Lord. Perhaps you are wondering, as some in my church were wondering, "What do I do with these people?" Well, as I mentioned before, the Word of God has a lot to say about this. But here, specifically, Paul says, *from such withdraw yourself*, which means don't have communion with them, don't associate yourself with them.

> Now I urge you, brethren, note those who cause divisions and offenses, contrary to the doctrine which you learned, and avoid them. For those who are such do not serve our Lord Jesus Christ, but their own belly, and by smooth words and flattering speech deceive the hearts of the simple (Romans 16:17-18).

Second Thessalonians 3:6 is another verse that communicates a similar thought:

> But we command you, brethren, in the name of our Lord Jesus Christ, that you withdraw from every brother who walks disorderly and not according to the tradition which he received from us.

And this warning:

> But know this, that in the last days perilous times will come: For men will be lovers of themselves, lovers of money, boasters, proud, blasphemers, disobedient to parents, unthankful, unholy, unloving, unforgiving, slanderers, without self-control, brutal, despisers of good, traitors, headstrong, haughty, lovers of pleasure rather than lovers of God, having a form of godliness but denying its power. And from such people turn away (2 Timothy 3:1-5).

Titus 3:9-11 is also very clear:

> But avoid foolish disputes, genealogies, contentions, and strivings about the law; for they are unprofitable and useless. Reject a divisive man after the first and second admonition, knowing that such a person is warped and sinning, being self-condemned.

Titus 1:13 tells us even how to rebuke such people:

> Therefore rebuke them sharply, that they may be sound in the
> faith, not giving heed to Jewish fables and commandments of
> men who turn from the truth.

These passages make it clear that you must withdraw yourself from
these false teachers; avoid them, turn away from them, reject them,
and rebuke them sharply! Don't give them a listening ear.

You must ask God to give you discernment when you listen to
preachers and television evangelists. You might be saying to
yourself, "Well, this doesn't sound like Christ! I mean, where is the
love here?" My friend, this is the most loving thing to do! You can
search the Scriptures—and I hope you do—and you will never in
one instance see our Lord coddling the false teachers of His day.
He rebuked them sharply; He pronounced woes upon them; and He
called them names like "hypocrites," "fools," and "blind"! These are
not polite words! Our Lord defended His wholesome words and, my
friend, we must also!

What about you? When you look at your life, does it resemble the
characteristics of these evil men or the characteristics of our loving
Lord? Are you willing to stand up for the One who died for you and
defend His truth? Are you embracing the false ideas of our day?
Are you buying into every new wind of doctrine? One man tells
us a funny story which gives a pointed illustration of what we've
been talking about. He mentions an evening during which he went
to a party where a friend of his served dog food! Yes, that's right,
dog food! The dog food was served on delicate little crackers with
a wedge of imported cheese, bacon chips, an olive, and a sliver of
pimento on top. It was hors d'oeuvres *a la Alpo*. He goes on to
say how the hostess was a first-class nut, but the guests nonetheless
devoured her savory offerings. In fact, one guy just couldn't get
enough of them. The hosts finally broke the news to him, and when
he found out the truth, he probably barked and bit her on the leg! He
certainly must have gagged a little.

Ever since hearing that story—it is actually the truth—I've thought about how perfectly it illustrates something that transpires *daily* in another realm. I'm referring to religious fakes ... professional charlatans ... frauds ... counterfeit Christians who market their wares on shiny platters decorated with tasty persuasion and impressive appearance. Being masters of deceit, they serve up delectable dishes camouflaged by logical-sounding phrases! A glance at the silver platter and everything looks delicious: "apostles of Christ ... angels of light ... servants of righteousness." Through the genius of disguise, they not only look good, they *feel* good, they *smell* good! The media serve them under your nose. Testimonies abound! Listen to some: "This is new ... it has changed my life!" Others say, "I did what he said ... and now God speaks to me directly. I see visions. I can *feel* God." Over two million freely shout, "Eternity is now ... materialism is godly. Getting rich is a sign of spiritualty." They may have a "new" look—feel and taste like the real thing—but they are not. "Dog food is dog food, no matter how you decorate it." Or, as Paul put it so pointedly, "They are false ... deceitful ... disguising themselves as apostles of Christ." They may not look like it, but they are as phony as a yellow three-dollar bill. Unfortunately, as long as there are hands to pick from the platter there will be good-looking, sweet-smelling tidbits available. But some day, some dreadful day, the final Judge will determine and declare truth from error. There will be a lot of gagging and choking ... and it will no longer taste good. Nothing tastes good in hell.[53]

---

53 Charles Swindoll, *Growing Strong in the Seasons of Life* (Portland: Multnomah Press, 1983), paraphrase of account on pages 146-147.

Questions to Consider
Eleven Evil Characteristics of False Teachers
1 Timothy 6:3-5

1. (a) What qualities does Paul mention in 1 Timothy 6:3-5 that are characteristic of those who don't hold to sound doctrine? (b) How does this compare to the characteristics of the apostle Paul as he ministered? See 2 Corinthians 6:1-10 and Acts 20:33.

2. Memorize 1 Timothy 6:5.

3. (a) In what ways are 1 Timothy 6:3-5 and James 3:13-18 similar? (b) How would you try to help someone who exhibits these characteristics? (c) Why do you think these characteristics are more common in those who don't hold to sound doctrine? (d) Why is it important for us to get away from these types of people, as Paul mentions in 1 Timothy 6:5?

4. (a) According to the following passages, who tried to use godliness as a means of receiving material gain? 2 Kings 5:20-27; Jeremiah 6:13-15; Acts 8:14-24; 2 Peter 2:1-3. (b) What was the result for each one of them? (c) In what ways do you see people in our day using godliness as means to receive material gain?

5. (a) Are you guilty of any of the characteristics that Paul mentions in 1 Timothy 6:3-5? (b) According to the Scriptures, what is the best way to rid oneself of these things? (Use Scripture to back up your answer.)

6. In what ways do you need to be more diligent in holding on to wholesome words, the words of our Lord Jesus Christ? Based on your answer, write down a prayer request for yourself.

Chapter 19

Lovers of God or Lovers of Gold?

1 Timothy 6:6-10

The headline for a January 15, 2016 article in *The Washington Post* read, "'Boy Who Came Back from Heaven' actually didn't; books are recalled." The article went on to relate that

> The best-selling book, first published in 2010 purports to describe what Alex experienced while he lay in a coma after a car accident when he was 6 years old. The coma lasted two months, and his injuries left him paralyzed, but the subsequent spiritual memoir—with its assuring description of "miracles, angels, and life beyond This World"—became part of a popular genre of "heavenly tourism." Earlier this week, Alex recanted his testimony about the afterlife. In an open letter to Christian bookstores posted on the Pulpit and Pen website, Alex states flatly: "I did not die. I did not go to Heaven." Referring to the injuries that continue to make it difficult for him to express himself, Alex writes, "Please forgive the brevity, but because of my limitations I have to keep this short … I said I went to heaven because I thought it would get me attention. When I made the claims I did, I had never read the Bible. People have profited from lies and continue to. They should read the Bible, which is enough. The Bible is the only source of truth. Anything written by man cannot be infallible."[54]

What makes this so sad is that Alex's mother had been trying to alert the public for some time that Alex's story wasn't true. Other evangelicals, such as Phil Johnson and Justin Peters, had also been endeavoring to alert the church to the false nature of Alex's story, along with a great many other books chronicling people's fabricated experiences of going to heaven and back again. So once again, Christians are looked at as a bunch of nuts, and once again, we've blasphemed the Word of God and made it unattractive to the lost.

---

54 *The Washington Post*, January 16, 2015; article by Ron Charles.

What is the motive behind all this nonsense? Well, when you consider that this particular book has sold more than a million copies, need I say much else? I checked several of the other popular titles on Heaven (specifically, those books which relate the people's claims of having gone to Heaven and back) and the numbers of copies they've sold is in the millions, with one of those titles selling more than eight million. These authors and their publishers are making money off of innocent and ignorant people. In this particular case, with *The Boy Who Came Back from Heaven*, the publishing company had been alerted years before to the fraud of this particular book! In our last lesson, Paul warned us of this greed, and now as we move on to verses 6-10, he further describes the danger of loving money and how it has caused some their own destruction! Let's read together verses 6-10 of 1 Timothy 6.

1 Timothy 6:6-10

> Now godliness with contentment is great gain. [7]For we brought nothing into this world, and it is certain we can carry nothing out. [8]And having food and clothing, with these we shall be content. [9]But those who desire to be rich fall into temptation and a snare, and into many foolish and harmful lusts which drown men in destruction and perdition. [10]For the love of money is a root of all kinds of evil, for which some have strayed from the faith in their greediness, and pierced themselves through with many sorrows.

In our last lesson, we considered eleven evil characteristics of false teachers, and as we did, we contrasted those with eleven encouraging characteristics of our Lord. We also ended with Paul admonishing us to withdraw ourselves from them; we are to have nothing to do with them. If you recall, the last characteristic Paul mentioned was that these people think that they can gain financially (and they do) by their supposed godliness. In this lesson, Paul will draw out the fallacy of these false teachers' thinking as he writes that godliness is great gain when it is coupled with contentment rather than greed. In these verses, Paul will delineate the differences between lovers of God and lovers of gold. The two sections of this lesson will cover the

Lovers of God: Two Qualities and One Tremendous Result (vs 6-8), and the *Lovers of Gold: Two Qualities and One Tragic Result* (vs 9-10).

Let's read verse 6 and discover the first two qualities of those who love God over gold.

Lovers of God: Two Qualities and One Tremendous Result

1 Timothy 6:6-8

Now godliness with contentment is great gain. (1 Timothy 6:6)

Godliness is now presented in contrast to the ungodliness we learned about in our previous lesson. What is godliness? Godliness is defined as holiness, reverence, likeness to God. Obviously, this is a reference to the lovers of God; they desire godliness. *Godliness is the first quality about those who love God.* He goes on to say that godliness with contentment is great gain. *Contentment* is calm satisfaction that, quite frankly, cannot be bought with money. It comes from a term that means self-sufficiency, but not self-sufficiency in the way that we might think, because this person is does not find their sufficiency in themselves but in God. It's the idea of a person being unmoved or unruffled. *This is the second quality of lovers of God: they are content.* This should make us pause as God's daughters when we are using our mouths and inward thoughts to murmur and complain. Why aren't we content? What is it that we think we need so desperately? I remember Elisabeth Elliott saying in one of her conferences years ago that if you needed something, you'd have it, because God has promised to supply all your needs.

Now, Paul goes on to give the result for the God-lover, the person who possesses godliness and contentment, and he says *the tremendous result is that these things are great gain.* Notice it is not just gain, but *great* gain! *Great* means a huge degree of magnitude. And, contrary to what some would think, the *gain* here is not financial but spiritual. My friend, people can take your money, but they cannot take your contentment, the inner tranquility of your soul that comes from knowing God. Godliness is a relationship with our God, not a relationship with our gold, even though American culture constantly tells us otherwise. Sadly, even many Christians will tell you that if you will just live a holy life, then you'll surely be wealthy. It doesn't take long to look around and note that the most content people are not necessarily the wealthiest people. And the wealthiest people are usually the most discontented. In fact, my father-in-law was a wealthy man, and he was one of the most miserable people I knew until God saved him the year before he died. His favorite song quickly became *I'd Rather Have Jesus*. One of the stanzas of that song says, "I'd rather have Jesus than silver or gold; I'd rather be His than have riches untold; I'd rather have Jesus than houses or lands; I'd rather be led by His nail-pierced hand."[55] I remember my father-in-law often weeping and lamenting that his life was wasted by sin and sorrow. My dear friend, you either serve God or money, but you cannot serve both. You either seek godliness or you seek gold. Luke 16:13 is clear: "No servant can serve two masters, for either he will hate the one and love the other, or he will be devoted to the one and despise the other. You cannot serve God and money" (ESV). James is also clear in James 4:1-4,

> Where do wars and fights come from among you? Do they not come from your desires for pleasure that war in your members? You lust and do not have. You murder and covet and cannot obtain. You fight and war. Yet you do not have because you do not ask. You ask and do not receive, because you ask amiss, that you may spend it on your pleasures. Adulterers and adulteresses! Do you not know that friendship with the world is enmity with God? Whoever therefore wants to be a friend of the world makes himself an enemy of God.

Contentment is not dependent on circumstances or how much money one has; true contentment is a by-product of a godly life. Paul already wrote about the fact that godliness is profitable for this life and the life to come, and part of that profit is contentment (1 Timothy 4:8)! True contentment does not come from the junk

---

55 *I'd Rather Have Jesus*, words by Rhea F. Miller, 1922.

of this world, but from the joy of knowing God. Godliness is not a means to get material gain, but it is a means to gain contentment! Paul goes on to further illustrate this in verse 7.

> For we brought nothing into this world, and it is certain we can carry nothing out. (1 Timothy 6:7)

Those who truly know God realize that *they brought nothing into this world,* and they will *carry nothing out* of it. Therefore, why get all caught up in materialism? Statistics tell us that more than 108 billion people have been born since the inception of time. My friend, not one of those 108 billion babies have come out of the womb with a stitch of clothing on their little bodies or rings on their fingers! The same is true when every one of those 108 billion people die; they will carry nothing out with them! Of course, I realize that our bodies can be buried in our favorite outfits and be adorned with jewelry, and all kinds of things can be put in our caskets—and I've seen some odd things placed in caskets! In fact, I often tease that if my husband dies before me, I'll bury him with a book and yellow highlighter! Still, the fact remains that we aren't carrying any of those things with us to the next life because all that stuff will remain in the casket and be destroyed by time and worms! Psalm 49:16-17 states, "Do not be afraid when one becomes rich, when the glory of his house is increased; for when he dies he shall carry nothing away; his glory shall not descend after him." Job, in his distress, says in Job 1:21, "Naked I came from my mother's womb, and naked shall I return there. The Lord gave, and the Lord has taken away; blessed be the name of the Lord." Wise Solomon echoes both Job and the Psalmist when he writes in Ecclesiastes 5:13-15, "There is a severe evil which I have seen under the sun: riches kept for their owner to his hurt. But those riches perish through misfortune; when he begets a son, there is nothing in his hand. As he came from his mother's womb, naked shall he return, to go as he came; and he shall take nothing from his labor which he may carry away in his hand." Since we don't bring anything with us when we come into the world and we won't take anything out with us when we leave, then what is the logical conclusion? Verse 8 tells us:

> And having food and clothing, with these we shall be content.
> (1 Timothy 6:8)

Because what is said in verse 7 is true, then the logical conclusion is this: Be *content* with *food and clothing*. The word for *food* means nourishment that is sufficient. We certainly don't understand that concept in our culture because of the enormous amount of food we eat. Sometimes when I eat out, I look at my entree and think, "That is enough food for four people!" Not only do we overeat in our country, but we also throw out so much food. They say that the average American throws out about 25 percent of the food and beverages they buy. For the average family, that comes out to about $1500 a year that we simply throw in the trash! We might have difficulty understanding being content with what is sufficient for our basic needs, but the biblical world would have understood this because they didn't have the enormous amount or variety of food we have today. Ninety percent of the biblical world lived off their own land.

We should also be content with *clothing*, a word which refers to a covering over us and could include a roof over our heads. This, again, probably seems foreign to most of us because most of us have so many clothes that we think we have to get bigger closets, and many Americans even own more than one home! Again, the biblical world wouldn't understand us, and, quite frankly, I'm not sure any of us would understand their world, because most of them lived in a tent with very little furniture. The whole family lived together on a mud floor and slept in the same room. With sufficient nourishment and an item of clothing on our body and shelter over our heads we should be content. This is the joy of the godly woman—content with the basic needs of life! If you are not content with what you have now, you will never be content with what you want. This is something you should rehearse in your head often and train your children and grandchildren to rehearse, as well! Too often, we think statements like: "I would be content if I could get married"; or "I would be content if I could have children"; or "I would be content if my husband would get a raise"; or "I would be content if we could get a new car or go on a vacation." You fill in the blank. What is it that you are tempted to think would bring you contentment? The fact is that you wouldn't be content with that or with anything else because the more you get the more you'd want. Contentment is an inward tranquility of the soul that isn't dependent on material things or people or circumstances. One man said,

> I am reminded of the simple-living Quaker who was watching his new neighbor move in, with all of the furnishings and expensive "toys" that "successful people" collect. The Quaker finally went over to his new neighbor and said, "Neighbor, if ever thou dost need anything, come to see me, and I will tell thee how to get along without it." Henry David Thoreau, the naturalist of the 1800s, reminded us that a man is wealthy in proportion to the number of things he can afford to do without.[56]

Paul states in Hebrews 13:5, "Let your conduct be without covetousness; be content with such things as you have. For He Himself has said, 'I will never leave you nor forsake you.'" These words should cause us as women to pause when we're out shopping for food or clothing. Is this a necessary item I am purchasing? I wonder how much debt we would eliminate if we would stop to ask ourselves, "Is this a need or a want?" In fact, Luke 3 records for us an interesting account in which Jesus is preaching the gospel of repentance and some soldiers come to Him and ask what they should do. One of the things Jesus says to them is, "Be content with your wages" (Luke 3:14). This would be a good question to ask ourselves, as well: "Am I content with our wages?" Lovers of God are known for their godliness and their contentment, and the result is great spiritual gain. We turn now to lovers of gold and what they are known for, and it is certainly a stark contrast to the godly.

Lovers of Gold: Two Qualities and One Tragic Result

1 Timothy 6:9-10

> But those who desire to be rich fall into temptation and a snare, and into many foolish and harmful lusts which drown men in destruction and perdition. (1 Timothy 6:9)

56 *Bible Exposition Commentary, New Testament*; PC Study Bible-V5

As we have learned, *but* is a word of contrast. Instead of being content with food and clothing and godliness, gold-lovers want more. Notice that Paul doesn't say those who are rich but *those who desire to be rich*. There is no sin in being rich, but there is sin in the desire to be rich. The idea here is that getting riches is their aim in life and the context indicates that they are doing this by using "godliness" as the means of getting rich. Proverbs 27:24 says that "riches are not forever," so why do we pursue them as though they are? *So, the first quality of gold lovers is that they want to be rich.*

Instead of desiring God, they desire gold, and this desire to be rich brings about consequences. Instead of awesome contentment they have awful consequences. *This is the second quality of gold lovers.* These consequences are many, as evidenced by what Paul writes next. The first consequence, Paul says, is that they *fall into temptation and a snare*. *Fall* means to be entrapped or overwhelmed with temptation. A *temptation* is an enticement to do evil, and a *snare* is like a pit or trap that is dug in the ground and lined with sharp stakes. Because the pit is covered up, an animal doesn't see what is below and falls into it and is destroyed, which is what Paul refers to in verse 10. Those who are desirous of being rich and make money their aim in life are entangled in a web and they can't get out. They're stuck!

A second awful consequence for those who love money is that they not only fall into temptation but also *into many foolish and harmful lusts*. A *lust* is a longing for what is forbidden, and these lusts are both unwise and injurious. If it isn't bad enough that they fall into temptation and a snare, those who love money also keep spiraling downward as all of these temptations and snares *drown* them *in destruction and perdition*. Their fall leads them to *drown*, which means to sink in the deep, to be dragged to the bottom. And this finally leads them to *destruction and perdition*, which means they are completely ruined. The reference here is to eternal punishment. They have made shipwreck of their faith, like Hymenaeus and Alexander, whom we learned about back in 1 Timothy 1. You will learn of some sobering examples of this in the Questions to Consider.

Now, it's possible that you think that Paul is going a bit overboard here—money sending people to hell! Remember, Paul is not talking about money itself but loving money, which he again emphasizes in verse 10.

> For the love of money is a root of all kinds of evil, for which some have strayed from the faith in their greediness, and pierced themselves through with many sorrows. (1 Timothy 6:10)

Again, we see that those who are gold lovers love money, they desire to be rich. Instead of loving God, they love money! It is one thing to have money, it is another thing to love money. Being rich is not a sin. Abraham, Job, and Solomon were all rich. The Scriptures are clear from Proverbs 22:2, "The rich and the poor have this in common, the Lord is the maker of them all." But Paul says that loving money *is a root of all kinds of evil*. Notice that Paul doesn't say money is evil or even having money is evil but that the *love of money* is a root of evil. And he doesn't say that loving money is the root of *all* evil but all *kinds* of evil. Not all evil is because of money. When we think of a root, we think of a plant that has a root in the ground. From a root grows all kinds of usually good stuff. But when the root is the love of money, you can imagine what branches shoot up from that root—greed, selfishness, snobbery, pride, lying, and the list goes on. Even publishing a book to tell a fabricated story about going to Heaven, claiming that it was real, and then making money off gullible people demonstrates greed. Recently, I was walking with a friend and we were discussing how most popular singers and actors end up addicted to drugs or alcohol and end up ruining their careers, destroying their marriages, and in many instances taking their own lives. Doesn't sound like loving money worked out too well for them, does it?

The downward spiral here is similar to what's described in the previous verse. Because of their love of money and the evil which grows from it, *some have strayed from the faith*. The term *stray* comes from our English word planet, which means to wander. They wander from the faith, making a fatal departure from it. They have such an insatiable desire to be rich that they forget all rationale, their *greediness* gets the best of them, and before long they have *pierced themselves through with many sorrows.* Those sharp stakes lining the snare they fell into eventually pierce them through and they're destroyed. *This is the tragic result of loving material gain: great pain and sorrow.* Perhaps you are wondering what sorrows the rich could possibly have. One man says,

> Among the pangs are unrest, boredom, dissatisfaction, gloom, envy. In the pocket of a rich man who had just committed suicide was found $30,000 and a letter which read in part: 'I have discovered during my life that piles of money do not bring happiness. I am taking my life because I can no longer stand the solitude and boredom. When I was an ordinary workman in New York, I was happy. Now that I possess millions, I am infinitely sad and prefer death.[57]

Paul has already written that godliness is profitable both for this life and the life to come. So, it would only be theologically correct to say that ungodliness is unprofitable both for this life and the life to come, and in this case, it is destruction. The lovers of gold are known for their love of gold and for the awful consequences of that love, and the result is great pain!

Summary

The young man I referred to at the beginning of this lesson said it all: "The Bible is the only source of truth." Paul has just given us some pretty heavy truths. The reality is that you are either a God-lover or a gold-lover, and you cannot be both! What about you? Is your life characterized by becoming more godly or acquiring more gold? Do you desire more time so that you can spend it serving and loving the Lord and His people, or do you desire more time so that you can spend it making more money so you can buy more things? With loving God comes contentment; with loving gold comes terrible consequences. Are you content with what you have right now at this

---

57 William Hendriksen, *New Testament Commentary: Exposition of the Pastoral Epistles* (Grand Rapids, Baker Book House, 1957), 201.

moment, or are you still complaining about what you think you still need? Loving God produces awesome contentment, which is great gain. Loving gold brings awful consequences, which is great pain! What will you choose? You cannot serve God and money; you cannot have two masters! Which master do you serve? Maybe you're not sure which master you serve. Well, what if I offered you a thousand dollars for every verse you memorized or every chapter you read out of the Bible? Would that motivate you? If so, then perhaps you're a lover of money. But if I offered you a more intimate walk with the Lord through Bible reading and memorization of His Word, would that motivate you? If so, then it is likely that you are a lover of God!

The next time you make a purchase or the next time you think you might want to be a little wealthier than you are now, dwell on this acrostic, MONEY. Perhaps God will use it to prompt you to make the one right choice—to love Him supremely!

Money itself is not evil, but the love of it is.
Only a relationship with the living God is true gain.
Naked you came in, naked you will go out.
Evil consequences are the result of desiring riches.
Your eternal destination is at stake.

If you find that this cute little acrostic doesn't come to mind in your moment of need, remember the words of our Lord from Luke 12:15, "Take heed and beware of covetousness, for one's life does not consist in the abundance of the things he possesses."

Questions to Consider

Lovers of God or Lovers of Gold?
1 Timothy 6:6-10

1. (a) How do you see 1 Timothy 6:6-10 illustrated in the following passages? Joshua 7:1-26; Matthew 27:3-5; Luke 16:19-31; Luke 18:18-23; Acts 8:18-23; James 5:1-6. (b) In what ways are the truths of 1 Timothy 6:6-10 and these other passages warnings to you?

2. Memorize 1 Timothy 6:8.

3. (a) What are the challenges for the rich, according to Psalm 49:16-20; 62:10; Proverbs 23:4-5; 28:11; 30:8-9; Ecclesiastes 5:10-17; Matthew 13:22; 19:23-24; Luke 12:13-21; and James 5:1-6? (b) What do you think would be some temptations that the rich might have?

4. (a) Looking again at Luke 12:13-21, what does Jesus say about those who love money? (b) How do you see verses 17 and 18 carried out in our day? (c) Are you content with what you have, or are you continually wanting more things? (d) Why do you think we spend so much time buying and storing stuff that will burn up?

5. (a) What do you think should be the proper attitude regarding money for the child of God? (Use Scripture to back up your answer!) (b) Should believers save for the future?

6. (a) Are you content with what you have? (b) How can we train our children to be content with what they have in a materialistic world that desires the latest and newest item?

7. As you ponder this lesson, how are you challenged regarding your view of money and/or being content with what you have? Please write a prayer request based on your answer.

Chapter 20

What to Flee From; What to Follow After; and What to Fight For

1 Timothy 6:11-12

God in His kindness has allowed me for many years to disciple other women. It truly has been one of the greatest joys of my life. There have been some who have taken the baton and passed it on to others. There have been some who have grown leaps and bounds and their spiritual growth is intimidating. There have been some from other churches who have taken what has been taught to them and passed it on to the women in their churches.

But with the joy of discipleship comes also the pain of discipleship. There have been some who have defected from the faith. There have been some who seem to go nowhere but remain stagnant in their walk with Christ, and I've found myself wondering, "Do they really know the Lord?" There are times when my heart aches and burns for the spiritual welfare of the women I disciple. I see them making choices that I know will have serious consequences, and yet, no matter how much I pray and how hard I try to warn them from God's Word, they still choose disobedience. It grieves me, and I know it grieves the heart of God.

As we ponder discipleship, both its joys and its sorrows, we can learn much from our brother Paul. He knew the pain of discipleship, in all its sorrow—sorrow like Alexander doing him much evil; sorrow like Demas forsaking him and loving the world; sorrow like Hymenaeus and Alexander making shipwreck of their faith. But discipling others also brought joy to Paul: joy like Titus helping him on the isle of Crete; joy like Epaphroditus almost losing his life trying to get to Paul in prison; joy like having Timothy as a true son in the faith and a soul mate to him.

Just as any good discipler, Paul knew that the flesh is weak and that God's children must wage spiritual warfare daily. And to do so, there are certain things we must flee from, certain things we must follow after, and certain things we must fight for. Paul is coming to the end of his letter and his passion and concern for his son in the faith, Timothy, is strong and evident. Let's listen in as he writes to Timothy.

1 Timothy 6:11-12

> But you, O man of God, flee these things and pursue righteousness, godliness, faith, love, patience, gentleness. [12]Fight the good fight of faith, lay hold on eternal life, to which you were also called and have confessed the good confession in the presence of many witnesses.

In our last lesson, we contrasted lovers of God with lovers of gold. We learned that lovers of God are godly and content, and the result for them is great gain. That gain is not financial gain but the rich, spiritual gain of eternal life. In contrast, we learned that lovers of gold desire to be rich and reap the awful consequences of that desire, and the result for them is not great gain but great pain, the awful pain of piercing sorrows and eternal destruction. In the verses we'll look at in this lesson, Paul is continuing his admonition to Timothy, and like any spiritual father, he appeals to his spiritual son to not be like those he has just mentioned. He is pleading with Timothy not to fall into the sins that would cause him to defect from the faith. In these two brief verses, Paul will make clear to Timothy and to us

What to Flee From (v 11a);
What to Follow After (v 11b); and
What to Fight For (v 12).

He begins with the warning of what to flee from, in verse 11.

What to Flee From

1 Timothy 6:11a

But you, O man of God, flee these things (1 Timothy 6:11a)

The words *but* you introduce a contrast to those who love money. But you, *O man of God*, but you, O woman of God, *flee these things!* *O man of God* is interesting terminology because in other places Paul calls Timothy his beloved son, his faithful son, a brother, a servant, a fellow laborer, and a true son, but here he calls him a *man of God*. Even though Timothy was young physically ("Let no one despise your youth," 1 Timothy 4:12), he was to act like a man of God! As you read this, you can almost hear the passionate tone in Paul's voice: "O man of God! My son, be a man whose maturity in Christ will be so solid that you will flee such nonsense!" Yet, it isn't only the passion you can hear in Paul's voice but also the love he has for his son in the faith as he expresses his strong desire for Timothy not to make shipwreck of his faith. Paul doesn't want the love of money to ruin Timothy as it has ruined many a pastor. Many of us can identify with Paul's concern. We've poured our lives into someone, whether it's a spiritual daughter or a physical child, and we see them heading down paths of destruction and we want to cry out, "No! Don't go that way!" I am old enough to have watched many of the ladies I've mentored fall into terrible sin and my heart aches for them. It has often taken away the ability for me to eat and sleep because I am so burdened for them. A man or woman of God must be different than a man or woman of the world. Timothy must be a man after God, not a man after gold.

So Paul begs Timothy to flee these things, which brings to mind the question, "What things?" Paul is referring to the things we saw in our last lesson—the love of money and all the things that follow it, vain pursuits, foolish and hurtful lusts, temptations and snares. One man says,

A glance at Timothy's present life will show how possible it was, even for a loved pupil of Paul—even for one of whom he once wrote, "I have no man likeminded;" and again, "Ye know the proof of him, that, as a son with the father, he hath served with me in the gospel" (Philippians 2:20-22)—to need so grave a reminder. Since those days, when these words were written to the Philippians, some six years had passed. His was no longer the old harassed life of danger and hazard to which, as the companion of the missionary St Paul, he was constantly exposed. He now filled the position of an honoured teacher and leader in a rich and organized church; many and grievous were the temptations to which, in such a station, he would be exposed. Gold and popularity, gain and ease, were to be won with the sacrifice of apparently so little, but with this sacrifice Timothy would cease to be the "man of God"[58]

There is great danger for men of God to think more highly of themselves than they ought to think and to be swept away with earthly gain. Most of us have lived long enough to witness the fall of many a pastor whose pride brought him to destruction.

Paul tells Timothy to *flee* these things, which means to run away from these things, to get away from these things, to shun these things! The Greek tense indicates that Timothy is to keep on fleeing from these things, because these things will always be a temptation. In fact, Paul tells Timothy in 2 Timothy 2:22 to "flee youthful lusts." In 1 Corinthians 6:18, he tells the church at Corinth to "flee sexual immorality," and later on in 10:14, he says to "flee idolatry." Each of us has *things* that we must constantly run away from! It might be the love of money, the desire to be famous, the temptation to be a man pleaser, or sexual sins, wasting time, or some other idol of our hearts. We must constantly flee certain things in the same way that we see Joseph, in Genesis, fleeing from Potiphar's wife in response to her daily efforts to entice him. He finally had enough sense to flee and get out of the house! Timothy, too, must continually flee these temptations and remember that his pursuit must not be money but the Master. Timothy—and we—would be wise to remember what God said to Abraham, "I am your shield, your exceedingly great

---

58 *Ellicott's Commentary for English Readers*; Biblehum.com/commentaries

reward" (Genesis 15:1b). Even though Abraham was rich, it was God—not his riches—who was His real reward. We would also do well to rehearse what the Psalmist writes in Psalm 16:5: "O Lord, You are the portion of my inheritance and my cup; You maintain my lot." In fact, in this very same chapter of 1 Timothy, just a few verses away, in 6:17, Paul says, "Command those who are rich in this present age not to be haughty, nor to trust in uncertain riches but in the living God, who gives us richly all things to enjoy." We don't trust in money, dear friend, but we do trust in the living God! (The irony of this is, of course, that all our American money has "In God We Trust" imprinted on it!)

What to Follow After

1 Timothy 6:11b

and pursue righteousness, godliness, faith, love, patience, gentleness. (1 Timothy 6:11b)

Instead of pursuing the love of money, there is a different pursuit for the man or woman of God. Paul transitions from what Timothy should flee from to what he should follow after. He writes *pursue righteousness, godliness, faith, love, patience, gentleness.* The word pursue means to follow after, and the Greek tense is the same as we saw with the word flee. Keep on following after, keep on pursuing these five things. We will never arrive at perfection in this life and so we keep on pursuing the things of God. There have been times in my life that I have thought to myself, "Susan, you're doing pretty well in this area of patience or kindness or righteousness," and then, because I have forgotten to take heed lest I fall, all of a sudden, down I go! Dear one, we can never let down our guard!

The first quality to be pursued or followed after is righteousness. This would be doing what is right. This would be a man or woman of God who possesses integrity. Such a person is always asking the questions, "What would Jesus do?" "What did Jesus do?" "What does God say about this in His Word?" And then the righteous man or woman does those things. Paul wants Timothy to do the right thing—always! As one of my mentors often told me, "Susan, you will never regret doing what is right, but you will always regret doing what is wrong." Interestingly, Paul also mentions the importance of Timothy pursuing righteousness in his second epistle to Timothy, in 2 Timothy 2:22; he says, "Flee also youthful lusts; but pursue righteousness, faith, love, peace with those who call on the Lord out of a pure heart." Also, in Psalm 15, the Psalmist asks the Lord a question: "Lord, who may abide in Your tabernacle? Who may dwell in Your holy hill?" In other words, "Lord, who is truly Yours; who is truly religious?" The reply is given with several requirements, but listen to the first two: "He who walks uprightly, and works righteousness." Those who are truly God's are righteous. And they hunger and thirst for all the righteousness there is, as Jesus says in Matthew 5:6, in His Sermon on the Mount. Men and women of God are not satisfied with the "partial righteousness" we see among so many professing Christians today, who are content with just enough "religion" to get by.

The second quality Paul commands Timothy to follow after is *godliness*. This word means holiness or piety. Peter says in 1 Peter 1:15-16 that we are to be holy as God is holy. J.C. Ryle helps us here; he says,

> What then is true practical holiness? It is a hard question to answer. I do not mean that there is any want of Scriptural matter on the subject. But I fear lest I should give a defective view of holiness, and not say all that ought to be said; or lest I should say things about it that ought not to be said, and so do harm. Let me, however, try to draw a picture of holiness, that we may see it clearly before the eyes of our minds. Only let it never be forgotten, when I have said all, that my account is but a poor imperfect outline at the best.

And then he goes on to list 12 descriptions of holiness:

1. Holiness is the habit of being of one mind with God, according as we find His mind described in Scripture. It is the habit of agreeing in God's judgement—hating what He hates—loving what He loves—and measuring everything in this world by the standard of His Word. He who most entirely agrees with God, he is the most holy man.

2. A holy man will endeavor to shun every known sin, and to keep every known commandment.

3. A holy man will strive to be like our Lord Jesus Christ. He will not only live the life of faith in Him, and draw from Him all his daily peace and strength, but he will also labor to have the mind that was in Him, and to be "conformed to His image" (Romans 8:29).

4. A holy man will follow after meekness, long-suffering, gentleness, patience, kind tempers, government of his tongue. He will bear much, forbear much, overlook much, and be slow to talk of standing on his rights.

5. A holy man will follow after temperance and self-denial. He will labor to mortify the desires of his body—to crucify his flesh with his affections and lusts—to curb his passions—to restrain his carnal inclinations, lest at any time they break loose.

6. A holy man will follow after charity and brotherly kindness.

7. A holy man will follow after a spirit of mercy and benevolence towards others.

8. A holy man will follow after purity of heart.

9. A holy man will follow after the fear of God. I do not mean the fear of a slave, who only works because he is afraid of punishment, and would be idle if he did not dread discovery. I mean rather the fear of a child, who wishes to live and move as if he was always before his father's face, because he loves him.

10. A holy man will follow after humility.

11. A holy man will follow after faithfulness in all the duties and relations in life.

12. Last, but not least, a holy man will follow after spiritual-mindedness. He will endeavor to set his affections entirely on things above, and to hold things on earth with a very loose hand.[59]

The third thing Paul instructs Timothy to follow after is *faith*, which has the idea of faithfulness or dependability. Timothy is to be faithful to the Lord, first of all, but also to his duties as a pastor, to his family, and to all of his responsibilities. I remember one time a lady who used to work alongside me in women's ministry told me that I needed to have FAT women in leadership. I thought, "Fat women?! Why is that?!" Then she quickly explained to me what she meant by FAT: faithful, available, teachable. You know, she was right. That is the type of women (and men, I might add) that you want in leadership—those who are dependable, who are faithful. In fact, that's how the geyser "Old Faithful" in Yellowstone National Park got its name. It is unlike any other geyser in that it shoots up streams of boiling water every 65 minutes. It is dependable.

The fourth thing Paul urges Timothy to chase after is *love*. The Greek word for love here is agape. This means that I am to seek to meet the needs of others, and I am to do that above seeking the needs of myself. It means I am to die daily for others. This would

59 The full text of this list may be found at: http://www.iclnet.org/pub/resources/text/history/spurgeon/web/ryle.holiness.html.

be of utmost importance for Timothy as a shepherd of God's people, because the ministry can be exhausting and often the temptation is to neglect the pastoral duties for some self-seeking activity. We must always remember that we are to esteem others better than ourselves.

The fifth quality of a man of God needs to pursue is *patience*. This means sticking with it, enduring, even when things are rough and people are persecuting you. This is essential for all pastors and believers alike, and it is one of the fruits of the Spirit. This is not always an easy one, and I admit that I have to work on this often. As someone once said, "To live above with saints we love, that will be glory. To live below with the saints we know, that's quite a different story."

The sixth virtue to be sought after by the man or woman of God is *gentleness*. Gentleness is meekness—not weakness. This means strength under control. Paul will tell Timothy in 2 Timothy 2:24-26, "And a servant of the Lord must not quarrel but be gentle to all, able to teach, patient, in humility correcting those who are in opposition, if God perhaps will grant them repentance, so that they may know the truth, and that they may come to their senses and escape the snare of the devil, having been taken captive by him to do his will." Timothy must remember to not be argumentative but to have strength under control when dealing with people. I was just tested in this recently, and it is certainly a virtue that we must chase after! Having told Timothy what he must flee from and what he must follow after, Paul now turns to what Timothy should fight for, in verse 12.

What to Fight For

1 Timothy 6:12

> Fight the good fight of faith, lay hold on eternal life, to which you were also called and have confessed the good confession in the presence of many witnesses. (1 Timothy 6:12)

Paul instructs Timothy to *fight the good fight of faith*. This is what he is to fight for, and may I also say it is what you and I are to fight for, as well. The word *fight* means to agonize, and it was a term applied to athletes and soldiers who were agonizing to win—the athletes to win an Olympic medal, and the soldiers to win a battle. Such fighting is intense, not a casual walk around the block. It involves discipline and work, wrestling and praying. And the Greek tense indicates that we are to keep on fighting. We must not let our guard down for one moment. We're not to be like Hymenaeus and Alexander, who gave up the fight and made shipwreck of their faith. We're not to be like Demas, who loved this present world and quit fighting the good fight of faith. We must remember that this is a serious fight, because we are fighting the world, the flesh, and the devil, not our husbands, our kids, and our fellow church members. Our fight is far more serious than those latter things, as this, my friend, is the fight for our eternal soul! Paul writes of this in 1 Corinthians 9:26-27; he says, "Therefore I run thus: not with uncertainty. Thus I fight: not as one who beats the air. But I discipline my body and bring it into subjection, lest, when I have preached to others, I myself should become disqualified." Paul knew the seriousness of waging spiritual warfare in his own life and in the lives of others, as he had witnessed many defect from the faith. He did not want that tragedy for his spiritual son Timothy and, my friend, I don't want this for you or me either.

Notice that Paul calls this fight a *good* fight. This means it is beautiful, it is precious, it is virtuous. Maybe you don't think so and have often wondered if the fight of faith is worth it. Oh, dear one, it is worth it, because the alternative is eternal fire and separation from God. Fighting the good fight is doing something that has value; it is worthwhile; it is more precious than gold. Most of us have times in our walk when we can echo with the Psalmist in Psalm 27:13, "I would have lost heart, unless I had believed that I would see the goodness of the Lord in the land of the living." Or we can echo with Peter, "Lord, to whom shall we go? You have the words of eternal life" (John 6:68, which is the account when Jesus asked if the twelve would also leave Him as some of the other disciples had.)

Paul goes on to say that we fight this good fight so that we can *lay hold on eternal life*. To *lay hold* on means to seize, to attain, to get a grip on. And *eternal life* means perpetual life, a life that goes on and on forever. This earthly life is not eternal, thankfully. At the most, you might live to be 70-plus years old, and that's it. But there is life hereafter, and it is eternal, and it is either eternal in Heaven or in Hell. If you don't fight, then you don't win the prize. If you don't agonize, you don't win. Jesus says in Luke 13:24, "Strive to enter through the narrow gate, for many, I say to you, will seek to enter and will not be able." Paul says in Philippians 3:12-14,

> Not that I have already attained, or am already perfected; but I press on, that I may lay hold of that for which Christ Jesus has also laid hold of me. Brethren, I do not count myself to have apprehended; but one thing I do, forgetting those things which are behind and reaching forward to those things which are ahead, I press toward the goal for the prize of the upward call of God in Christ Jesus.

And in 1 Corinthians 9:24-25, he says, "Do you not know that those who run in a race all run, but one receives the prize? Run in such a way that you may obtain it. And everyone who competes for the prize is temperate in all things. Now, they do it to obtain a perishable crown, but we do it for an imperishable crown." James talks of those who have endured and who will receive the crown of life in James 1:12, and in Revelation 2:10 John speaks of those who have been faithful and who will receive the crown of life because of it.

Man has a responsibility to do his part, but all the while the mystery remains that God is sovereign in salvation. Paul puts it like this: *to which you were called*. Timothy was *called* to salvation. Paul speaks of this calling in 1 Thessalonians 2:12, where he urges the Thessalonians to "walk worthy of God who calls you into His own kingdom and glory." Again, in 2 Timothy 1:9, Paul says, "Who has saved us and called us with a holy calling, not according to our works, but according to His own purpose and grace which was given to us in Christ Jesus before time began." But Paul isn't the only New Testament writer who speaks of our being called by God. Peter writes, in 1 Peter 5:10, "But may the God of all grace, who called us to His eternal glory by Christ Jesus, after you have suffered a while, perfect, establish, strengthen, and settle you." My husband and I have a coffee cup in our home with a picture of Charles Spurgeon on one side and a quote of his on the other side, which says, "Some men hate the doctrine of divine sovereignty; but those who are called by grace love it, for they feel if it had not been for sovereignty, they never would have been saved."

One who is truly called by God will not only fight to lay hold on eternal life, but they will also, as Paul says, have *confessed the good confession in the presence of many witnesses*. The word *confess* is indicative of a covenant; it has to do with the confession of our faith, specifically that we are now in a covenant relationship with a new Master, the Lord Jesus Christ. This is probably a direct reference to Timothy's baptism; in the early church, when a person was born again, they were baptized, and this was done *in the presence of many witnesses*. It was a time when one publicly renounced his or her old life and confessed that they were embracing a new life, one in Christ Jesus. They were dead to the old and alive to the new!

Just as the fight of faith is good, so also is our confession. Paul says it is *the good confession*. To confess Jesus as Lord and to be in a covenant relationship with Him is good; it is beautiful; it is precious. Paul desires the same thing for his son in the faith as he desires for himself. Just before his own death, Paul will describe this desire when he writes to Timothy: "I have fought the good fight, I have finished the race, I have kept the faith. Finally, there is laid up for me the crown of righteousness, which the Lord, the righteous Judge, will give to me on that Day, and not to me only but also to all who have loved His appearing" (2 Timothy 4:7-8).

Summary

What is it that Timothy is to flee from? He is to flee from the love of money and all the things it leads to, such as vain pursuits, foolish and hurtful lusts, temptations and snares. What is it that Timothy is to follow after? He is to follow after righteousness, godliness, faith, love, patience, and gentleness. And what is it Timothy is to fight for? He is to fight to lay hold on eternal life.

What about you? How goes it with you this day? Are you fleeing from the love of money and following instead after love of God and others? As you go through your day are you driven by how you can make more money so that you can spend it on your pleasures, or are you driven by how you can love others better by spending your time serving them and meeting their needs?

Are you fleeing vain pursuits and following after righteous living? For example, when you look over your life as a believer and really examine your days and how you spend them, would the scale weigh heavier on vain living, pursuing things that are going to burn up, wasting time and money on things that have no value, or would the scale weigh heavier on righteous living, pursuing things that have eternal value?

Are you fleeing foolish lusts and following after godly living? Does your calendar for the week look like: pedicure, manicure, spa, work out, shopping at the mall, days of lunching with the purple hat society, watching your favorite reality show every night, and gossiping with your best friend at least once a day? Or is your calendar filled with purposeful activities, like grocery shopping for your family, visiting the widows, making a meal for a friend who is sick, spending time encouraging your friend through prayer and Scripture, enjoying time with your husband and family? (In case you think I am a legalist, I am not, and some of those things on the first list are not ungodly, but if that is how the majority of your days are spent, then it's time for some serious evaluation of your life!)

Are you fleeing greedy and hurtful lusts and following after gentleness? For example, as you deal with people in a given day, do you fight to have your own way, or are you looking for how you can please others? Do you find yourself arguing and manipulating so that you can fulfill all your desires, or do you tell yourself that it is more blessed to give than to receive?

Are you fleeing the cravings of your flesh and following instead after patience in your flesh? Do you have to have things you want right now? Do you patiently wait on the Lord's timing for that item you think you so desperately need? Do you get irritated when you can't dine out at your favorite restaurant or eat your favorite dessert, or are you patiently content with what the Lord has given you?

Are you fleeing the snares of the evil one and following after faithful living? For example, as you go through your day and you realize that the evil one is luring you with the lust of the flesh, the lust of the eyes, or the pride of life, do you follow his tantalizing call, or do you instead resist the evil one and put on your armor and choose to live faithful to the One who has called you? Do you saturate your mind with the Word of God so that you can withstand those days when the evil one is prowling around so that he can devour you?

The fight of faith is a serious one. I pray that you will examine yourself and ask, "What I am fleeing from, what am I following after, and what am I fighting for?" The stakes are high. It might just be the difference between spending eternity in the land of the living or spending eternity in the lake of fire. It is my desire as your teacher, as your discipler, that each of you examine yourself as to whether you are truly in the faith. And with my brother John, I would echo, "I have no greater joy than to hear that my children walk in truth" (3 John 4).

Questions to Consider

What to Flee From, What to Follow After, and What to Fight For
1 Timothy 6:11-12

1. (a) What is similar about 1 Timothy 6:11-12 and 1 Timothy 4:12-16? (b) Why do you think Paul repeats certain things in the same letter to Timothy?

2. Memorize 1 Timothy 6:11.

3. (a) Paul instructs Timothy to fight the good fight of faith. According to Paul, why is it important that we fight the good fight of faith? See 1 Corinthians 9:24-27; 2 Corinthians 10:3-6; Ephesians 6:10-18; 1 Timothy 1:18-20; and 2 Timothy 4:7-8. (b) According to these same verses, what means are we to use when fighting the good fight of faith? (c) What have you found to be helpful to you in persevering as you fight the good fight of faith?

4. (a) Paul says that Timothy is to pursue certain qualities mentioned in 1 Timothy 6:11. What are those qualities? (b) How does this list compare to the list in Galatians 5:22-23 and the list in 1 Timothy 3:1-7? (c) Would you say that you are pursuing the qualities mentioned in 1 Timothy 6:11? (d) If not, what is hindering your pursuit of these things?

5. (a) Recall a time in your life when you did not fight the spiritual battle as you should have. What was the result? What did you learn from that experience? (b) Recall a time when you waged good warfare. What was the result and what did you learn from it? (c) Why do you think waging spiritual warfare is difficult for the believer?

6. (a) Who are the believer's enemies, according to Ephesians 6:12 and 1 John 2:15-16? (b) How can we daily remind ourselves that these are our enemies, and why would that be important?

7. *As you prayerfully consider your answers to questions 4 and 5, what would be your prayer for your spiritual life? Please write it down to share with your group.

Chapter 21

Ten Things You Need to Know Today!
1 Timothy 6:13-16

Most of us listen to the radio or watch television to get the latest news. Some of us even get our news on our phones via news apps that often give us news alerts. I often hear on one local news station in the morning: "We will tell you the three things you need to know today." And yet, on another news station, I'll hear, "Here are five things you need to know." In fact, I've seen one that goes so far to list "Ten things you need to know today." I often chuckle when I read or hear the 3, 5, or 10 things that the world tells me I must know in order to get through my day. I think, "Really? Are you kidding me? This is something I need to know today?" Things like a blizzard is bearing down on the east coast, what was the best commercial of the Super Bowl, or the Democrats and Republicans have reached a stalemate on an important issue. Seriously?! These are the things I absolutely need to know today?!

In no way do I mean to diminish the importance of some of these things, but I often read headlines like these and think, "I would like to tell them what they really need to know today." I'd like to say, "The three things you need to know today are that Christ died for you according to the Scriptures, that He was raised from the dead, and that He is coming again to judge the living and the dead." Now, those three things would truly change someone's life today if they believed in and lived according to them!

As we think about the things we truly need to know today, let's consider what the apostle Paul would say to Timothy regarding what he needs to know. As we examine verses 13-16 of 1 Timothy 6, we'll see that Paul writes ten things that Timothy actually does need to know—ten motivations that will help him get through his days, his weeks, his life. And these ten things are also ten motivations for you and me as we endeavor to walk in obedience to our Lord. If genuinely pondered, these ten things will truly impact the way we live. Let's read these verses together.

1 Timothy 6:13-16

> I urge you in the sight of God who gives life to all things, and before Christ Jesus who witnessed the good confession before Pontius Pilate, [14]that you keep this commandment without spot, blameless until our Lord Jesus Christ's appearing, [15]which He will manifest in His own time, He who is the blessed and only Potentate, the King of kings and Lord of lords, [16]who alone has immortality, dwelling in unapproachable light, whom no man has seen or can see, to whom be honor and everlasting power. Amen.

As we consider the ten things we need to know, the ten motivations for living, we'll put them in the form of an acrostic: MOTIVATION. In our last lesson, we saw that there are certain things that Timothy is to flee from, follow after, and fight for. He is to flee from the love of money and all the things that leads to, such as vain pursuits, foolish and hurtful lusts, and temptations and snares. He is to follow after righteousness, godliness, faith, love, patience, and gentleness. He is to fight to lay hold on eternal life. Paul has just mentioned the many witnesses at Timothy's confession, which was probably a reference to his baptism when he made a public profession of his faith to follow the Lord Jesus. Paul goes on to remind Timothy of the One who also witnessed a good confession, in fact, the very One, Jesus, whom Timothy confessed as Lord. As we look at verse 13, we will see the first three of the ten things we need to know today! And all ten of these motivations are descriptions of God, the greatest motivation of all!

> I urge you in the sight of God who gives life to all things, and before Christ Jesus who witnessed the good confession before Pontius Pilate, (1 Timothy 6:13)

Paul begins by saying *I urge you*, which means I charge you. This is a solemn charge Paul is making. In biblical times, when someone made a charge before God, or a god, as a witness that charge was considered especially binding. This is similar to what we saw back in 5:21, where Paul said to Timothy, "I charge you before God and the Lord Jesus Christ and the elect angels that you observe these things without prejudice, doing nothing with partiality." Paul is saying, essentially, "I am doing this *in the sight of God*; He is present everywhere and He is watching me and you, Timothy." *This is the first O on your acrostic, the first thing you need to know: God is **Omnipresent**.* This means He is everywhere, and He not only sees this charge that Paul is making to Timothy, but He also is watching young Timothy's life and whether or not he will follow the commitment he made at his baptism. And, dear one, He is watching you and me as well. I think it odd that, somehow, we think we can escape the presence of an all-seeing God. As the Psalmist says in Psalm 139:7, "Where can I flee from your presence?" The obvious answer is: we can't flee from His presence! He goes where we go, and He sees all that we do! This is great motivation for living out our profession of faith.

Paul goes on to say this God who sees this charge Paul is making to Timothy is also the same God who gives life to all. *This is the I on your acrostic: He is the Imparter of life.* He *gives life to all things.* Paul speaks of this in his sermon on Mars Hill, in Acts 17:22-25, when he says,

> Men of Athens, I perceive that in all things you are very religious; for as I was passing through and considering the objects of your worship, I even found an altar with this inscription: TO THE UNKNOWN GOD. Therefore, the One whom you worship without knowing, Him I proclaim to you: God, who made the world and everything in it, since He is Lord of heaven and earth, does not dwell in temples made with hands. Nor is He worshiped with men's hands, as though He needed anything, since He gives to all life, breath, and all things.

This God who gives life is the One who will give Timothy—and us— eternal life on that day, if we fight the good fight of faith to lay hold on eternal life. We must remember that God gave us life, but

He can also take that life as well. This is, to me, great motivation to live uprightly.

This charge Paul gives to Timothy is not only before God but also *before Christ Jesus who witnessed the good confession before Pontius Pilate.* Just as Timothy made a good confession before many witnesses (verse 12), so Christ made a *good confession before Pontius Pilate.* As Timothy considers Christ, who in the face of death and suffering did not shrink from the truth of who He was, knowing that crucifixion was upon Him, so should Timothy not shrink from the truth of his profession of faith in God alone. Jesus confessed that He was the Son of God, and so must Timothy confess that Jesus is the Son of God! We, too, must not be ashamed that we belong to Him. *This is the M on your acrostic: Maintain your witness just as Christ maintained His witness.* My friend, we cannot fail in the day of adversity, even if it means we must go through intense suffering for the cross of Christ. Keeping our eyes on Jesus and His confession in the face of Pilate, with the cross ever before Him, is great motivation to remain steadfast in our faith and fight the good fight of faith. Paul now writes about what this charge is to Timothy, with yet another motivation to press on in verse 14.

> that you keep this commandment without spot, blameless until
> our Lord Jesus Christ's appearing, (1 Timothy 6:14)

Here is the charge, Timothy, the one that is given in the presence of God who has given you life: *keep this commandment.* What commandment is Paul charging Timothy to keep? Given the context, it would be the commandment to fight the good fight of faith and to remember the confession he made before many witnesses at his baptism that Jesus was his new Master. It is what Paul has just written in verses 11 and 12. Timothy must remember that he was renouncing his old life and saying yes to his new life; he must fight the good fight of faith. For Timothy to faithfully keep this charge it would mean he is also to endeavor to keep all the sayings of Christ and be committed to obeying His Word. The word *keep* means to guard or protect. And we do this *without spot* and *blameless*, which means we keep the commands of God unsullied, unrebukable, so that there will be no blight on our character or on our Lord's character. Paul has already written that elders are to be above reproach and blameless, and Timothy must remember that. Just as there should be no blight on the Word of God, there should be no blight on Timothy's life. His conduct should be exemplary. He should teach the truth and live the truth; he should teach the gospel and live the gospel.

How long must Timothy do this? Well, how long do you think you should live a blameless life, faithfully keeping what you have professed before others? *Until our Lord Jesus Christ's appearing,* Paul says. This is very similar to what John says in 1 John 3:2-3, "Beloved, now we are children of God; and it has not yet been revealed what we shall be, but we know that when He is revealed, we shall be like Him, for we shall see Him as He is. And everyone who has this hope in Him purifies himself, just as He is pure." My friend, the Lord's coming is a great motivator for holy living. *This is the A on your acrostic and the fourth motivation to live right: the Appearing of our Lord.* The fact that the Lord is coming and will judge the living and the dead should motivate Timothy to keep the charge that Paul is giving him. Timothy must remember that the Chief Shepherd will someday appear, and on that day, Timothy will give an account to Him, as Peter says in 1 Peter 5:4. Paul prays for the church at Philippi, "That you may be sincere and without blame until the day of the Lord Jesus" (Philippians 1:10b). The Lord's coming should give us motivation to fight the good fight of faith. As Paul continues writing regarding the Lord's return, he relates three more things Timothy—and we—must remember.

> which He will manifest in His own time, He who is the blessed and only Potentate, the King of kings and Lord of lords, (1 Timothy 6:15)

Paul writes that Jesus will come when it is the right time, *in His own time.* He will appear, *He will manifest,* when it is His time, not our time. There are days when I long for Heaven, when I long for Jesus to come and take us home, and I often say, "Even so, come Lord

Jesus!" Yet, I know my longings don't make it happen any quicker. Jesus makes it very clear in Matthew 24:26, "But of that day and hour no one knows, not even the angels of heaven, but My Father only."

While we wait for His return and we wage war in our members, we must remember *He who is the blessed and only Potentate. Blessed and only Potentate* is not a phrase we use often, but it means He is the only, happy, Sovereign ruler. *This is the second O on your acrostic and the fifth motivation for fighting the good fight of faith: He is the Only Potentate.* There is only One who is the sovereign ruler and it is He. We think we have some power, and we think we can control our lives, yet we cannot. When we are tempted to become smug and think we can rule our lives without Him, perhaps we should revisit Psalm 2, which says,

Why do the nations rage,

And the people plot a vain thing?

The kings of the earth set themselves,

And the rulers take counsel together,

Against the Lord and against His Anointed, saying,

"Let us break Their bonds in pieces

And cast away Their cords from us."

He who sits in the heavens shall laugh;

The Lord shall hold them in derision.

Then He shall speak to them in His wrath,

And distress them in His deep displeasure:

"Yet I have set My King

On My holy hill of Zion."

"I will declare the decree:

The Lord has said to Me,

'You are My Son,

Today I have begotten You.

Ask of Me, and I will give You

The nations for Your inheritance,

And the ends of the earth for Your possession.

You shall break them with a rod of iron;

You shall dash them to pieces like a potter's vessel."'

Now therefore, be wise, O kings;

Be instructed, you judges of the earth.

Serve the Lord with fear,

And rejoice with trembling.

Kiss the Son, lest He be angry,

And you perish in the way,

When His wrath is kindled but a little.

Blessed are all those who put their trust in Him.

He not only is the blessed and only Potentate, but He is the only *King of kings! This is the first T on your acrostic: He is The King of kings.* Numerous kings have come and gone since the beginning of time, but when time here on earth ends, He alone will reign as the one and true King. It will not be Nero; it will not be Caesar; it will not be Stalin or Hitler, or Obama or Bush or Trump; it will the King of Kings! This is certainly motivation for obedience, as we think about running the race and one day bowing before our King.

With this title comes often the title *Lord of lords. This is the second T on your acrostic: He is The Lord of lords.* He is the Lord of the universe, and so He is able to do as He pleases. The fact that He is King of kings and Lord of lords is motivation to fight the good fight of faith. One man says,

Why did Paul write so much about the person and glory of God? Probably as a warning against the "emperor cult" that existed in the Roman Empire. It was customary to acknowledge regularly, "Caesar is Lord!" Of course, Christians would say "Jesus Christ is Lord!" Only God has "honor and power everlasting" (1 Timothy 6:16b). If Timothy was going to fight the good fight of faith, he had to decide that Jesus Christ alone was worthy of worship and complete devotion.[60]

The fact that Jesus is Lord is a huge motivator for me to live right. Even though some don't acknowledge His Lordship in this life, the day is coming when every knee will bow and acknowledge Him as Lord. It is better to do it now than wait till that day! If He is not your Lord, then who is? Something or someone has Lordship in your life. Ironically, as I was studying to write this lesson, I spoke on the phone with a lady whose church I would soon be speaking at, and she mentioned that there were a number of people in her church who did not believe in Lordship salvation. We visited about the sad state of the church, and she said she had never heard of such nonsense, and that if Jesus wasn't their Lord, then who was? I agreed that the church is indeed in a sad state and that a professing believer's theology certainly will dictate how he or she lives. Timothy must remember, as he is fighting the good fight of faith, that Jesus is Lord and there is no other! What a great motivation! Paul now ends with verse 16 and writes concerning the last three things Timothy needs to know. These indeed will be great motivations to walk uprightly.

> who alone has immortality, dwelling in unapproachable light, whom no man has seen or can see, to whom be honor and everlasting power. Amen. (1 Timothy 6:16)

This verse may remind you of a hymn written by Walter Smith, entitled *Immortal, Invisible, God Only Wise*. The first stanza says,

"Immortal, invisible, God only wise,
in light inaccessible hid from our eyes,
most blessed, most glorious,

---

60 PC Study software, The Bible Exposition Commentary, New Testament.

the Ancient of Days,
Almighty, victorious,
Thy great Name we praise!"[61]

The song begins with the word immortal, which is also the idea Paul expresses in verse 16: *who alone has immortality*. *This is the second I on your acrostic and the seventh thing you need to know today: God is Immortal*. This means that He will never die. In Revelation 1:8, we read, "'I am the Alpha and the Omega, the Beginning and the End,' says the Lord, 'who is and who was and who is to come, the Almighty.'" He is not subject to death. I've heard it said that we should ponder our death every day. I think that might be a good exercise for each of us, because when we do so it motivates us to live each day as if it were our last. We also would do well to remember what Paul writes in 1 Corinthians 15:50-58,

> Now this I say, brethren, that flesh and blood cannot inherit the kingdom of God; nor does corruption inherit incorruption. Behold, I tell you a mystery: We shall not all sleep, but we shall all be changed—in a moment, in the twinkling of an eye, at the last trumpet. For the trumpet will sound, and the dead will be raised incorruptible, and we shall be changed. For this corruptible must put on incorruption, and this mortal must put on immortality. So when this corruptible has put on incorruption, and this mortal has put on immortality, then shall be brought to pass the saying that is written: "Death is swallowed up in victory." "O Death, where is your sting? O Hades, where is your victory?" The sting of death is sin, and the strength of sin is the law. But thanks be to God, who gives us the victory through our Lord Jesus Christ. Therefore, my beloved brethren, be steadfast, immovable, always abounding in the work of the Lord, knowing that your labor is not in vain in the Lord.

The fact that one day we will put on immortality should supply us with motivation to fight the good fight of faith here, knowing that our labor indeed will not be in vain.

Not only is God immortal, but He also *dwells in unapproachable light*. In fact, Paul says *no man has seen or can see* Him. *This is*

---

61   Words by Walter C. Smith, 1876.

the N on your acrostic: No one can see Him, because He dwells in unapproachable light. The Greek here means that He dwells in inaccessible light. Daniel 2:20-22 states,

> Daniel answered and said: "Blessed be the name of God forever and ever, for wisdom and might are His. And He changes the times and the seasons; He removes kings and raises up kings; He gives wisdom to the wise and knowledge to those who have understanding. He reveals deep and secret things; He knows what is in the darkness, and light dwells with Him."

Revelation 1:16 says of Him, "He had in His right hand seven stars, out of His mouth went a sharp two-edged sword, and His countenance was like the sun shining in its strength." And Revelation 22:5 says, "There shall be no night there: They need no lamp nor light of the sun, for the Lord God gives them light. And they shall reign forever and ever." Because God dwells in unapproachable light, no one can look upon Him. No one has seen Him, despite what you hear from some well-meaning people. I mean, think about it! Have you ever tried to look at the sun when it's right in your face? I have, and it hurts so bad it's blinding! God is a bazillion times brighter than the sun; how can we think we can look at Him? Jesus is clear in John 1:18 that "no man has seen God at any time." In the manifestation of His Son Jesus Christ and through His revealed Word, we are allowed to see what He has revealed to us about Himself, but to look on Him is impossible. I don't know about you, but it motivates me when I think about the enormity of our God! There is none like Him!

Paul finishes up this doxology with the tenth and final motivation for young Timothy to consider as he fights the good fight of faith, by saying *to whom be honor and everlasting power. Amen.* God alone is to be honored. God alone has everlasting power. *This is the V on your acrostic: Veneration is due to Him alone.* The word *honor* means esteem of the highest degree. It is imperative that Timothy remember that he must never glory in his flesh; instead, he must remember that God alone gets the glory. Together, these things are a motivator for holy living. The chief end of man is to glorify God and enjoy Him forever. No man, no woman, can glory in his or her flesh.

The words of Timothy's own spiritual father, Paul, in 1 Corinthians 1:26-31, expound on this thought:

> For you see your calling, brethren, that not many wise according to the flesh, not many mighty, not many noble, are called. But God has chosen the foolish things of the world to put to shame the wise, and God has chosen the weak things of the world to put to shame the things which are mighty; and the base things of the world and the things which are despised God has chosen, and the things which are not, to bring to nothing the things that are, that no flesh should glory in His presence. But of Him you are in Christ Jesus, who became for us wisdom from God—and righteousness and sanctification and redemption—that, as it is written, "He who glories, let him glory in the Lord."

Like Timothy, we too must remember that it is God who called us, not we who called God, and we owe Him our very lives. We must put the Lord on display in our lives and give Him all the glory. And Paul ends with *Amen*! This means so be it!

Summary

What are the ten things that Timothy needs to know? What are the ten motivations Paul gives him—and us—for carrying out the charge to fight the good fight of faith? What ten things do we need to know in order to remember the good confession we made to follow the Lord?

Maintain your witness as Christ maintained His.

Omnipresent—God is everywhere and sees everything.

The King of kings.

Imparter of life, He gives life to all things and He can take life as well.

Veneration is due Him alone.

Appearing of the Lord. He is coming to judge the living and the dead.

The Lord of Lords—every knee will bow, either in this life or the next.

Immortal—He has never died and never will; He is the beginning and the end.

Only Potentate—He is the blessed and only Sovereign.
No one can see Him—He dwells in unapproachable light.

What motivates you to get through your daily life as a Christian?
What ten things do you need to know today in order to fight your
good fight of faith?

- Do you need to know to **Maintain** your witness as Christ did,
  or do you need to know that the stock market is projected to
  go down today?

- Do you need to know today that God is **Omnipresent** and He
  is watching everything you do, or do you need to know that
  the president is proposing a 4-trillion-dollar budget?

- Do you need to know today that God is **The** King of kings,
  or do you need to know that a killer storm is heading to the
  east coast?

- Do you need to know today that He alone is the **Imparter** of
  your life and to make each moment count for Him, or do you
  need to know that increases in taxes are coming this year?

- Do you need to know that **Veneration** is due to Him alone to
  get you through this day, or do you need to know the how the
  latest vaccine debate is coming along?

- Do you need to know today that the Lord is **Appearing** one
  day soon, or do you need to know that Apple stocks are
  plummeting again?

- Do you need to know today that He is **The** Lord of Lords and
  that every knee will bow, either in this life or the next, or do
  you need to know the latest on the immigration debate?

- Do you need to know today that He is **Immortal**, or do you
  need to know that ISIS just beheaded another journalist?

- Do you need to know that He is the **Only** potentate, or that oil prices are skyrocketing?

- Do you need to know that **No** one can see God because He dwells in unapproachable light, or do you need to know NASA cameras captured images of solar flare?

What are the ten things that you think you need to know today?

Perhaps a better question is this: How does what you know today or think you need to know today change the way you will live today? May I lovingly suggest to each one of us not to buy into what the world thinks we need to know to get through each day, but to commit yourself to what God says we need to know to get through each day? By doing the latter we will keep our focus on the eternal life that Paul has told us to lay hold of, and not this temporal life that Peter says will one day be burned up.

Questions to Consider

Ten Things You Need to Know Today
1 Timothy 6:13-16

1. Read 1 Timothy 6:13-16. Why do you think that Paul gives such a solemn charge to Timothy while emphasizing some of God's attributes?

2. Memorize 1 Timothy 6:16.

3. (a)What do you notice about the end of each of the following passages? Romans 16:25-27; Ephesians 3:20-21; Philippians 4:19-20; 1 Timothy 1:17; Jude 1:25; Revelation 1:6; 7:12. (b) What do you think causes Paul to break forth in that way? (c) What attributes of God personally excite you, and why?

4. (a) What was the confession that Jesus made before Pontius Pilate, according to Matthew 27:11-26; Mark 14:53-65; and John 18:33-38? (b) Why do you think Paul makes this point in 1 Timothy 6:13?

5. (a) What does it mean to you personally that Christ is King of kings and Lord of lords? (b) How does it motivate you to hold fast to your confession of faith?

6. (a) As you read over 1 Timothy 6:15-16 and truly ponder these qualities of our Lord, how do you think it should impact the way you live? (b) The way you pray? (c) The way you behave in relationships? (d) The way you go about your daily duties?

7. Write a prayer of praise to God especially praising Him for at least one, if not more, of His attributes.

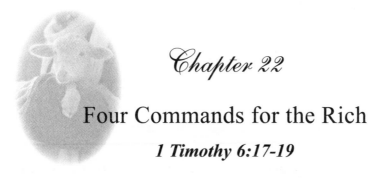

Chapter 22

Four Commands for the Rich
1 Timothy 6:17-19

Benjamin Franklin once said, "Money has never made man happy, nor will it; there is nothing in its nature to produce happiness. The more of it one has, the more one wants." That quote is more than 300 years old. And yet, as evidenced by the following true stories, it still rings true.

Chicagoan Urooj Khan found out the hard way that the lottery isn't always a winning game. The 46-year-old had sworn off lottery tickets, save for just one more in June, 2012, buying a scratch-off at his local 7-Eleven convenience store. And he wouldn't need a single ticket more after he revealed a $1 million jackpot on the ticket. Khan chose to cash out the reward in one lump sum instead of installments, waiting for his $425,000 check from the state. The check was issued on July 19, but Khan wouldn't have the chance to cash it — he was pronounced dead the very next day. Authorities determined his death was of natural causes due to hardened arteries and didn't conduct an in-depth autopsy since foul play wasn't suspected. Examiners did give Khan a simple toxicology test, the AP reports, which didn't show any traces of opiates, cocaine or carbon monoxide. But when a relative pressed for a more thorough autopsy in August, the Medical Examiner's office conducted an extensive chemical test. The subsequent result came as a shock: Khan had actually ingested cyanide, a lethal poison. Widely known as a poisonous substance, the bitter white powder can kill a person in minutes. Chicago police are now treating the investigation as a homicide though they have not yet revealed if there are any leads in the case. Someone did profit off of Khan's $425,000 though—his winnings were cashed on August 15, likely by his estate.

Billie Bob Harrell, Jr. thought his problems were over when he won the $31 million Texas Lotto jackpot in June, 1997. Nearly broke and constantly moving between low-paying jobs, with a wife and three children to support, the first of his $1.24 million annual payouts seemed like the light at the end of the tunnel. Instead, it was the beginning of a horrible existence for the 47-year-old Texan. It started out joyful: he quit his job at Home Depot, took his family to Hawaii, donated tens of thousands of dollars to his church, bought cars and houses for friends and family, and even donated 480 turkeys to the poor. But his lavish spending attracted unwanted attention, and he had to change his phone number several times after strangers called to demand donations. He also made a bad deal with a company that gives lottery winners lump-sum payments in exchange for their annual checks that left him with far less than what he had won. When Harrell and his wife Barbara Jean separated less than a year later, it was the straw that broke the camel's back. His son found him dead inside his home from a self-inflicted gunshot wound on May 22, 1999, shortly before he was set to have dinner with his ex-wife. While family members disputed the idea that Harrell could have committed suicide, he clearly wasn't happy with his life; he'd told a financial adviser shortly before his death that "Winning the lottery is the worst thing that ever happened to me."

William Post III proved the old adage to be true: more money, more problems. After Post won $16.2 million in the Pennsylvania lottery in 1988, he fell victim to crime, bankruptcy, tragedy and simply poor spending habits. In the two weeks after he received his first annual payment of nearly $500,000, he had already blown two-thirds of it, purchasing a restaurant, a used-car lot, and an airplane. His reckless spending continued, and within three months he was $500,000 in debt. But numbers were the least of his problems. According to Yahoo News, Post's brother was arrested for hiring a hit man to try to kill him and his sixth (yes, sixth) wife; his relatives convinced him to invest in worthless business ventures; and his landlady duped him into handing over a third of his cash. He ultimately filed for bankruptcy, and faced a stint in jail for firing a gun at a bill collector. "Everybody dreams of winning money, but nobody realizes the nightmares that come out of the woodwork, or the problems," Post said in 1993, according to the *Washington Post*. It seemed unlikely that the windfall could do anything but good for Post, who had already endured a hard-knock childhood in an orphanage and a nomadic young adulthood. According to the *Post*, he told reporters that he was surviving on disability payments and had a mere $2.46 in his bank account on the day he won millions. Still, the win did little to improve his lot in life, and Post allegedly claimed, "I was much happier when I was broke." Post died of respiratory failure in 2006 at age 66, leaving behind his seventh wife and nine children from his second marriage.

When British teenager Callie Rogers won £1.9 million ($3 million) in July, 2003, she showered her friends and family with gifts. The then-16-year-old from Cumbria, England treated her loved ones to presents such as cars, homes and lavish vacations. She also spent hundreds of thousands of dollars on partying, breast implants and designer clothing. But in 2009, the *Daily Mail* reported that Rogers was facing bankruptcy. "I've just wanted to make people happy by spending money on them," she told the tabloid. "But it hasn't made me happy. It just made me anxious that people are only after me for my money." She reportedly attempted suicide twice after winning it big and told the *Daily Mail* she was now ready to embrace her poverty. To make ends meet, she started working three cleaning jobs and moved in with her mother. "My life is a shambles and hopefully now that [the money] has all gone I can find some happiness," she said. "It's brought me nothing but unhappiness. It's ruined my life."[62]

Doesn't sound like a lot of happy, rich people to me. Does it to you? Perhaps you're thinking, "Yikes! I'm going to start praying to be poor!" That might not be such a bad idea. But, as believers in Jesus Christ, we know that God's Word is clear on the subject of money and, especially, on those who are rich. God is the One who gives the power to gain wealth and He is the One who possesses the ability to take that wealth away. He is Lord over both the rich and the poor.

---

62   Stories taken from: http://newsfeed.time.com/2012/11/28/500-million-powerball-jackpot-the-tragic-stories-of-the-lotterys-unluckiest-winners/slide/the-winningest-losers/

The fact of the matter is this: There have always been rich people and there will always be rich people. What should be the attitude of those who are rich? And specifically, what should be the attitude of those who are rich who belong to the Lord? Paul will answer that question for us in this lesson as he issues four commands to those who are rich—two positive commands and two negative commands. Let's read verses 17-19 of chapter six and discover what they are!

1 Timothy 6:17-19

> Command those who are rich in this present age not to be haughty, nor to trust in uncertain riches but in the living God, who gives us richly all things to enjoy. [18]Let them do good, that they be rich in good works, ready to give, willing to share, [19]storing up for themselves a good foundation for the time to come, that they may lay hold on eternal life.

As we learned in our last lesson, Paul is winding down his first letter to Timothy and he is writing to Timothy about the importance of Timothy fighting the good fight of faith. As he writes, Paul lays out ten motivations for carrying out the charge to fight the good fight of faith; ten things Timothy should keep in mind as one who follows the Lord and has made that confession before others.

In this lesson, Paul will issue four commands to the rich—two positive commands and two negative commands. I have put them in the form of an acrostic: RICH. Previously, Paul warned Timothy of the dangers for those who love money, but now he brings a warning for those who don't necessarily love money but whom, in God's providential design, have a lot of money. There were certainly rich people in the city of Ephesus, and Paul is going to briefly address them before he brings his letter to a close. He begins in verse 17 with the first three commands for the rich.

> Command those who are rich in this present age not to be haughty, nor to trust in uncertain riches but in the living God, who gives us richly all things to enjoy. (1 Timothy 6:17)

Paul has already dealt with the danger of loving money and the sorrows that can come because of it. But obviously, many people have money who don't necessarily have a sinful desire for it. They're either rich because of hard work and wise investments or because they've inherited money from a loved one. The city of Ephesus was known as the leading city of the wealthy in Paul and Timothy's day. So Timothy would have some wealthy church members. During biblical times, most riches were obtained by owning land and then renting it out to farmers or residents. Often, those landowners would take a percentage of the crop earnings. Another way the rich earned their money was through merchant ships. Even in Solomon's day, sailors brought back commodities such as gold, silver, and ivory— even monkeys—according to 1 Kings 10:22.

What are the rich to do, especially if they belong to the Lord? Paul tells Timothy what the rich are to do, and he begins by writing to Timothy to *command those who are rich in this present age not to be haughty*. The word *command* means to charge or transmit a message. Timothy is to give a charge *to those who are rich*. This would include those who were abounding with wealth, which is what the word *rich* means. Some of you may already be tuning me out because you think, "Well, this lesson won't apply to me because I'm not rich." But, my friend, we are! When we consider that 80% of the world lives on less than $10.00 a day, and almost half the world lives on less than $2.50 a day, it is clear that we are rich! If you have ever traveled to a third world country, then you know this lesson applies to you! When I have gone to India and Honduras in my travels, I often find myself sobered by what my fellow American Christians (and myself) think that we need in order to live.

The first command to the rich is that they are not to be haughty. *This is the first negative command and the H on your acrostic: Haughtiness is forbidden.* The word *haughty* means to be high-minded. People who have an abundance of money are not to think that their riches are all that matters. They are not to think that their value in life comes from their money. They are not to be snobs, which usually occurs among those who have more than others. A number of years ago, when my husband wanted to move to a new neighborhood, I graciously appealed to him not to move us there. I did not want to move to that particular neighborhood because it would be a step up for us. He had inherited some money from his parents and thought it would be a good investment. I loved where we had been living because there was a sweet sense of community in the neighborhood. We did move, and we lived in that house for more than 13 years. But snobbery was exactly what I discovered among my new neighbors. It was difficult to live there because there wasn't a sense of community and even though we endeavored to be friendly and neighborly, even having our neighbors over for dinner and such, we were never welcomed in that neighborhood. In all those years, I never even felt comfortable asking any of my neighbors to get our mail when we were out of town! We are now living elsewhere, and the difference is amazing. Our new neighbors are friendly and welcoming.

Paul gives a second negative command for the rich. I guess it's nice that he gets the negative out of the way! Not only are the rich not to be haughty, but they also are *not to trust in uncertain riches. This is the R on your acrostic: Riches are not to be trusted!* We are not to put our confidence in riches. Riches are not trustworthy; you can't bank on them. This too has been illustrated to me in my life, as I'm sure it has in yours. In 2008, I was away on a speaking engagement when my husband called me. I knew from the tone of his voice that something was terribly wrong. As I already mentioned, he had inherited some money when his parents died, so much so, that we were financially independent at the time and didn't even take a salary from the church he was pastoring. He proceeded to tell me the dilemma he was in and asked me what I thought we should do about it. Of course, I had no idea at the time that this wasn't just an isolated incident that had affected only us. It was far from isolated and ended up becoming the worst financial crisis since the Great Depression. It is known today as the Financial Crisis of 2007-2008 or the Global Financial Crisis. At the time, numerous banks were in danger of collapsing but were eventually bailed out by the government. The stock market plummeted, the housing market crashed, innumerable foreclosures took place, and many, many people were unemployed for long periods of time. It was a difficult time for many. We lost 2/3 of our assets, which we never regained (which is why we moved yet again and why my husband now takes a salary).

Ladies, I share this with you as a living illustration that we cannot trust in riches. Proverbs 23:5 says, "Will you set your eyes on that which is not? For riches certainly make themselves wings; they fly away like an eagle toward heaven." Psalm 62:10 warns, "Do not trust in oppression, nor vainly hope in robbery; if riches increase, do not set your heart on them."

There is something so much better for you to trust. As Paul moves from the negative to the positive, he gives his first positive command to the rich. Instead of trusting in riches, the rich are to trust *in the living God. This is the C on your acrostic: Confidence for the rich must be in God alone.* Why should those who are rich trust in the living God over riches? Because riches come and go, but God does not. Money is not the same yesterday, today, and forever, but God is the same yesterday, today, and forever. In fact, Paul describes money as *uncertain* but God as *living*. Money is not alive; it will one day be burned up with the rest of the earth. But God is alive and will live forever! Just recently, I went into our local tax office to pick up our tax returns. The man who was totaling the bill for payment said, "I see you purchased the Peace of Mind policy." I replied, "There is no amount of money that can buy peace of mind." He quickly responded, "That's a very wise statement!" My friend, only God can give you peace; money can never buy you peace.

Paul gives a reason for why the rich must trust in God over their riches, and he puts it like this: God *gives us richly all things to enjoy.* The phrase *gives us richly* means He furnishes abundantly, and the word *enjoy* means to have full enjoyment. Without knowing the One who has given us the ability to get wealth, as Deuteronomy 8:18 reminds us, it is difficult to enjoy the things He has given us. It is God who even allows us to enjoy things like having money and the blessings it provides for us—blessings like food, clothing, shelter, and even the ability to use our money to bless those who are less fortunate. The *all things* would also include anything God has made, like creation and life. He is the giver of life and He has created all things for our enjoyment. Our Father wants to give us good things and He wants us to enjoy both them and the life He has given us. Consider Jesus' own words in Matthew 7:7-1:

> Ask, and it will be given to you; seek, and you will find; knock, and it will be opened to you. For everyone who asks receives, and he who seeks finds, and to him who knocks it will be opened. Or what man is there among you who, if his son asks for bread, will give him a stone? Or if he asks for a fish, will he give him a serpent? If you then, being evil, know how to give good gifts to your children, how much more will your Father who is in heaven give good things to those who ask Him!

Wise, rich Solomon said in Ecclesiastes 5:18-20,

> Here is what I have seen: It is good and fitting for one to eat and drink, and to enjoy the good of all his labor in which he toils under the sun all the days of his life which God gives him; for it is his heritage. As for every man to whom God has given riches and wealth, and given him power to eat of it, to receive his heritage and rejoice in his labor—this is the gift of God. For he will not dwell unduly on the days of his life, because God keeps him busy with the joy of his heart.

Without a relationship with the living God it is truly hard to enjoy the blessings of life. Isn't it ironic that most rich people are also most unhappy, because they haven't learned how to enjoy what God has given them. John Rockefeller, who was once one of the richest men in the world, said, "I have made millions, but they have brought me no happiness. I would barter them all for the days I sat on an office stool in Cleveland and counted myself rich on three dollars a week."[63]

Maybe you're wondering what the rich should do with all their money? According to the next verse, instead of heaping it up for

---

63 *The New Encyclopedia of Christian Quotations* (Grand Rapids: Baker Book House, 2000), 1106.

themselves, they are to help those who are less fortunate. Paul now gives the second positive command for the rich.

> Let them do good, that they be rich in good works, ready to give, willing to share, (1 Timothy 6:18)

The fourth and last command is the I on your acrostic: Involvement in good works is a must for the rich. Paul says *let them do good,* which indicates that they are to do good things with their money, and then he goes on to define how the rich are to be involved in doing good in three ways. First, he says, they are to *be rich in good works.* Just as they are known for having earthly riches, so they should be known for being rich in good works. Others should be able to watch their lives and see that they indeed have a lot of money but that they also use it to do a lot of good things. They are not to be like the rich men in James 5 who live in pleasure and luxury while oppressing those less fortunate than them.

The second way the rich should be involved in doing good is to be *ready to give,* which means they should be good at imparting; they should not be stingy. I remember meeting a woman at one of my speaking engagements who was obviously very wealthy. Over the years, we've become friends and I have learned to be careful about saying, "Oh, I like this!" or "I don't have that book," because she will purchase it for me almost immediately! In fact, one evening when my friend and I were staying in her house, my friend happened to mention how much she liked Skittles, and the next day there were some waiting for her! That's the idea of being ready to give.

The third way the rich are to show benevolence is by being *willing to share,* which specifically refers to having a willingness to share what God has given to them with others. Paul has already written about the need to care for the widows and for the elders in the church, so these would be at least two things a rich man could do with his money that have eternal value. But he might also do something like pay a college student's tuition who, perhaps, wants to be trained for the pastorate. He could support missionaries. He could give to support orphans in foreign countries or even here in America. There are numerous things that rich Christians can do with their money that have eternal value.

Being willing to share means not only giving of what one has but also includes fellowshiping with those who are of a lower socio-economic class. The Scriptures are clear that the rich are not any better than the poor. The rich must remember that Christ died for the poor as well, and in glory there will be no financial distinctions because God owns it all. I love the passage in Acts 2, where it says, "Now all who believed were together, and had all things in common, and sold their possessions and goods, and divided them among all, as anyone had need" (Acts 2:44-45). Paul even mentions in Galatians 6:10, "Therefore, as we have opportunity, let us do good to all, especially to those who are of the household of faith." And in Hebrews 13:16, we read, "But do not forget to do good and to share, for with such sacrifices God is well pleased." Having said all this, Paul now ends this section on the rich with a reason why they should help others with their money instead of hoarding it.

> storing up for themselves a good foundation for the time to come, that they may lay hold on eternal life. (1 Timothy 6:19)

Instead of storing up treasure here, the rich are to store up treasure in Heaven. Jesus warns in the Sermon on the Mount, "Do not lay up for yourselves treasures on earth, where moth and rust destroy and where thieves break in and steal; but lay up for yourselves treasures in heaven, where neither moth nor rust destroys and where thieves do not break in and steal. For where your treasure is, there your heart will be also" (Matthew 6:19-21). Paul says that by doing this they are *storing up for themselves a good foundation*, a foundation that is not set on the sinking sand of money which comes and goes but on the solid rock of Christ who is our glory to come. By doing so, they will surely *lay hold on eternal life*, the life to come! This is the second time Paul has mentioned this idea; he first mentioned it back in verse 12. Those who are rich and use their riches to help others show that their real foundation is in glory, not in their money here and now. They realize that God gave them wealth and they want to use it to help others and not to spend it on their own pleasures. Thomas Brooks once said, "There are three things that earthly riches can never do: they can never satisfy divine justice, they can never pacify divine words, nor can they ever quiet a guilty conscience. And until these three things are done, man is undone."[64]

Summary

R*iches are not to be trusted.* Since every one of us is more than likely rich in comparison to the rest of the world, I would ask you, "Are you trusting in riches?" We have no guarantee that the economy of the world won't collapse, and, according to the Scriptures, it will again someday. Will such a world event shake you to the point of doubting the goodness of God? Are you even now trusting in your bank account, your IRAs, your 401Ks, your stock investments, your life insurance, or any other of your investments?

I*nvolvement in good works is a must for the rich.* Biblically speaking, involvement in good works is a must for all of God's children. We've already learned that the widows who are to be listed for financial support by the church must have had a history of doing good works. What good works are you involved in now? Does a part of your good works include endeavoring to relieve those who are less fortune than yourself?

C*onfidence for the rich must be in God alone.* Do you trust in God alone? Is He enough for you even when times are tough financially? Do you trust Him to provide for your needs as He has promised?

H*aughtiness is forbidden.* Do you think you are better than those who are on welfare due to no cause of their own? Are you proud of your husband's well-paying job and do you look down upon those whose husbands barely make enough to support their families? Do you associate with those who are of a different social class than you?

---

64 Ibid, 1106.

The lyrics of a song written several years ago came to mind while I was writing this lesson. The song is entitled *Psalm 62:10* and its lyrics come from that same verse: "Do not trust in oppression, nor vainly hope in robbery; if riches increase, do not set your heart on them." The words I want to close this lesson with are only a brief part of that song; I challenge you with them as we close.

Find rest, my soul, in God alone, amid the world's temptations
When evil seeks to take a hold, I'll cling to my salvation.
Though riches come and riches go, don't set your heart upon them;
The fields of hope in which I sow are harvested in heaven
O praise Him, Hallelujah, my delight and my reward;
Everlasting, never failing, my Redeemer, my God.[65]

---

65 Words by Aaron Keyes, 2007

Questions to Consider
Four Commands for the Rich
1 Timothy 6:17-19

1. What differences are there between 1 Timothy 6:17-19 and 1 Timothy 6:6-10 as it relates to the subject of money?

2. Memorize 1 Timothy 6:17.

3. (a) According to Deuteronomy 8:18; 1 Samuel 2:7; and 1 Chronicles 29:12, where does the ability to get rich come from? (b) Why would it be important for those who are rich to keep in mind what is written in Psalm 50:10-12? (c) What happens if we trust in riches, according to Proverbs 11:28 and Proverbs 23:4-5?

4. (a) What does 1 Kings 10:23 say about Solomon's wealth? (b) Read again 1 Timothy 6:17-19, noticing the commands to the rich. As you skim 1 Kings chapters 9-11, make note of the ways in which Solomon failed to heed the commands of this passage in 1 Timothy. (c) What warnings do you learn from Solomon's life? (d) What valuable lessons can you learn for yourself and pass down to your children, grandchildren, or others regarding riches and using them wisely and for the glory of God?

5. (a) Give at least five reasons why it is better to trust in God than in riches. (b) How could these reasons give perspective when you might be tempted to think that money is the answer to all your problems? (c) What are some ways that the rich could use their money that would have eternal value?

6. Endeavor this week to give away something you value. It might be as small as a piece of jewelry or as large as a piece of furniture. It might be inexpensive, like a favorite coffee cup, or it might be expensive, like a piece of crystal. (Of course, ask your husband if you're in doubt about giving it away!) How did doing this affect you and what did you learn about yourself regarding money and if and how tightly you hold on to it?

7. (a) How can you avoid the lie of our age which tells us that "having money is the key to happiness"? (b) What should be the truth we tell ourselves regarding money? (c) As you think on these two questions, please write a prayer request for yourself.

Chapter 23

Guarding the Truth by God's Grace

1 Timothy 6:20-21

For the past twenty years, I have been writing and teaching ladies' Bible studies. It has been a joy for the most part, but it is a task that requires disciplined study and hours of tedious work. When I consider the many women I've taught, I am both humbled and sobered at the responsibility that is laid upon me, now and in the life to come, because James 3:1 assures me that teachers will receive a stricter judgment. However, I'm also sobered at the responsibility that lies upon the ladies I teach, for their lives now and in eternity. We know that to whom much is given much is required (Luke 12:48) and that to be a mere hearer of the Word without being a doer of it is to be deceived and lost (James 1:22). I confess that I often become burdened and discouraged when I see that women aren't taking the truths of God's Word seriously and applying them to their lives, for the purpose of being conformed to the image of Christ.

In some ways, this is where we find ourselves as we come to the end of Paul's first epistle to Timothy. Paul has poured out his heart in this letter to his spiritual son and to the church at Ephesus, and he has one last punch, so to speak, before ending his letter. He is burdened for Timothy as any spiritual father should be. Paul's writings, unlike mine, are inspired by the Holy Spirit of God, and we too would do well to heed his final words. Let's listen in to Paul's final plea to Timothy!

1 Timothy 6:20-21

> O Timothy! Guard what was committed to your trust, avoiding the profane and idle babblings and contradictions of what is falsely called knowledge—[21]by professing it some have strayed concerning the faith. Grace be with you. Amen.

In our last lesson, Paul has just finished explaining how imperative it is that the rich use their wealth for that which has eternal value rather than temporal value. And he writes that this is important so that they may lay hold on eternal life. In this same line of thinking, Paul now turns his thoughts back to Timothy, knowing that it will be imperative for Timothy to guard certain truths in order that he also may lay hold on eternal life! As we consider Paul's final words to Timothy, we will see the importance of

> *Guarding the Truth* (v 20a) and
> *Getting Away from Error* (v 20b).

We'll also see the

> *Grievous Result of Those Who Don't Guard Truth* (v 21a) and that
>
> *God's Grace Alone Keeps Us in the Truth* (v 21b).

Let's look at Paul's charge to Timothy to guard the truth in verse 20a.

Guarding the Truth

1 Timothy 6:20a

O Timothy! Guard what was committed to your trust,
(1 Timothy 6:20a)

As we know, Paul is now coming to the end of his first letter to Timothy and it is proper that he wants Timothy to pay special attention to his final words, as evidenced by the words *O Timothy!* We noticed something similar just a few verses back, in 1 Timothy 6:11, where Paul said, "But you O man of God, flee these things." This was Paul's plea to Timothy just after he had warned him of the love of money. Here, he issues a similar plea just after his warnings to the rich. We can only surmise that this may have been a temptation for Timothy, or perhaps that Paul knew it would be a temptation for any man or woman of God, one that we must always keep a check on lest we too be swept away by the love of money.

The word *O* would be a point of exclamation and emotional affection. The name *Timothy* means dear to God. By now, we've come to know that Timothy was dear to the apostle Paul; he was to Paul a like-minded genuine son in the faith. In this first epistle to Timothy, Paul has only used Timothy's name two other times: first, in the introduction in 1:2, and then again in 1:18, where he encourages Timothy to fight the good fight of faith. Here, in chapter 6, verse 20, we find the third use of his name. When one uses a person's name, it is often for the purpose of getting their attention. For example, if I were to write, "What do you think God would have you do in this situation?" compared to "Susan, what do you think God would have you do in this situation?" which of these would get your attention the most? Of course, the one in which the person's name has been used!

Having gotten Timothy's attention, Paul then charges him: *guard what was committed to your trust.* This is much like Paul's instructions to Timothy in his second epistle, in 2 Timothy 1:13-14, "Hold fast the pattern of sound words which you have heard from me, in faith and love which are in Christ Jesus. That good thing which was committed to you, keep by the Holy Spirit who dwells in us." The word *guard* means to keep. Just as one would guard or keep money or valuable items in a safe place, Timothy is to guard or keep Paul's instructions to him in a spiritual safe place, the deposit of his heart. He is to guard what was committed to his trust. One man says, "It is as if God had made a 'deposit' in Timothy's bank."[66] We can certainly relate to this, because we've all made deposits in the bank. When you deposit your money in the bank you trust that they will keep it safe! That's the idea here. Paul has entrusted quite a bit of knowledge to Timothy in this first epistle and he wants Timothy to keep it safe. Timothy must guard the truth! These things that Timothy must guard would include everything Paul has written in

---

66 William Hendriksen, *Exposition of The Pastoral Epistles* (Grand Rapids: Baker Book House, 1957), 211.

this epistle, the gospel, and the way he conducts himself as a pastor!

But Timothy isn't only to keep what Paul has entrusted to him; he is also to pass these things on to faithful men, as Paul will tell him in 2 Timothy 2:1-2, "You therefore, my son, be strong in the grace that is in Christ Jesus. And the things that you have heard from me among many witnesses, commit these to faithful men who will be able to teach others also." We have a spiritual responsibility to take what has been entrusted to us and teach it to others, who will be able then to teach others also. What a beautiful pattern the Lord has set for His children! We even see in the gospels that Christ mentored His disciples and then left earth with a command for all of his disciples to be involved in disciple-making (Matthew 28:18-20).

Getting Away from Error

1 Timothy 6:20b

> avoiding the profane and idle babblings and contradictions of what is falsely called knowledge (1 Timothy 6:20b)

Timothy is to guard the truth, but he is to do so by keeping away from error. This is Paul's second charge to Timothy: get away from error. Paul puts it like this: *avoiding the profane and idle babblings and contradictions of what is falsely called knowledge.* One of the many ways one guards truth is by avoiding error. The word *avoiding* means turning away. The same man says, "It should be avoided like the pestilence ... today, far too much attention is paid to the 'empty jabberings' of men [and might I add women?] who, in the final analysis, reject God's infallible revelation!"[67] I've often wondered why some believers spend so much time listening to and reading all the false ideas out there. Do they spend as much time in the Word and prayer as they do hunting down all the novel ideas in Christendom today? It is disturbing! Why would anyone desire to spend so much time listening to such nonsense when they could enjoy the pure milk of the Word and communion with the living God?!

---

67 Ibid, 212. Parenthetical comment mine.

This is not the first time Paul has warned Timothy in this epistle about the dangers of listening to such nonsense. Consider 1 Timothy 1:3-7:

> As I urged you when I went into Macedonia—remain in Ephesus that you may charge some that they teach no other doctrine, nor give heed to fables and endless genealogies, which cause disputes rather than godly edification which is in faith. Now the purpose of the commandment is love from a pure heart, from a good conscience, and from sincere faith, from which some, having strayed, have turned aside to idle talk, desiring to be teachers of the law, understanding neither what they say nor the things which they affirm.

And in the same chapter, 1 Timothy 1:18-20, Paul wrote of two who had defected from the faith, having gotten caught up in some novel idea:

> This charge I commit to you, son Timothy, according to the prophecies previously made concerning you, that by them you may wage the good warfare, having faith and a good conscience, which some having rejected, concerning the faith have suffered shipwreck, of whom are Hymenaeus and Alexander, whom I delivered to Satan that they may learn not to blaspheme.

Then in 1 Timothy 4:6-7, Paul mentioned once again the danger of rejecting good doctrine for junk doctrine: "If you instruct the brethren in these things, you will be a good minister of Jesus Christ, nourished in the words of faith and of the good doctrine which you have carefully followed. But reject profane and old wives' fables, and exercise yourself toward godliness."

Paul clarifies what some of these nonsense ideas are that should be avoided. He says they include *profane and idle babblings. Profane* means heathen, worldly, wicked. And *idle babblings* are fruitless discussions, utter emptiness, empty talk. In addition to these, Paul also says to avoid *contradictions of what is falsely called knowledge. Contradictions* are oppositions, which in the original language means a placing over against; the implication is that those who participate in such things are involving themselves in things that are in opposition to the truth. Essentially, these people just want to argue about the Word of God. Today, we might call these things psychobabble or marrying the Word of God with new age or gnostic ideas. Oh, my sister, we have so much of this in Christendom that it is mind-boggling! Sometimes I'm asked what I think of this teacher or that teacher, and so I'll watch or listen to some of their teaching, and I often find myself in utter shock that people who call themselves believers actually think that what they are listening to is healthy for a genuine believer. When Paul writes his second epistle to Timothy, he warns of this again, mentioning Hymenaeus again, whom he has already mentioned in his first epistle. Listen to 2 Timothy 2:16-19:

> But shun profane and idle babblings, for they will increase to more ungodliness. And their message will spread like cancer. Hymenaeus and Philetus are of this sort, who have strayed concerning the truth, saying that the resurrection is already past; and they overthrow the faith of some. Nevertheless the solid foundation of God stands, having this seal: "The Lord knows those who are His," and, "Let everyone who names the name of Christ depart from iniquity."

These things are *falsely called knowledge*, but it is not the knowledge of God's Word. Verses like these should push us to read, study, memorize, meditate on, and obey the Word of God! Timothy is to guard the truth and one of the ways he does this is by getting away from error. But for those who do not guard the truth, Paul now deals in the next verse with the grievous result of their failure.

The Grievous Result of Those Who Don't Guard the Truth

1 Timothy 6:21a

> by professing it some have strayed concerning the faith.
> (1 Timothy 6:21a)

The meaning here is that some who were *professing* believers got caught up in false teaching, that is, in vain conversation and idle babblings, and the grievous result is that they have strayed from the faith. The sad thing is that we have many in the church today who are professing believers and yet are leading many away from truth. But there is nothing new under the sun; John says in 1 John 2:18-19, referring to those who teach heresy,

> Little children, it is the last hour; and as you have heard that the Antichrist is coming, even now many antichrists have come, by which we know that it is the last hour. They went out from us, but they were not of us; for if they had been of us, they would have continued with us; but they went out that they might be made manifest, that none of them were of us.

By getting involved in doctrinal error, they *have strayed concerning the faith*, which means they have erred from the truth, they have missed the mark. They have joined the ranks of Hymenaeus and Alexander, who have been turned over to Satan. Getting caught up in dangerous doctrine has eternal consequences—eternal damnation. This grievous result is frightening indeed and should be a challenge for us all to pray and study the Scriptures. But ultimately, there is only one thing that will keep Timothy and us from becoming an apostate; Paul mentions it in closing.

God's Grace Alone Keeps Us in the Truth

1 Timothy 6:21b

Grace be with you. Amen. (1 Timothy 6:21b)

In contrast to the grace that is not with those who have strayed from the faith, *grace* is to be with Timothy and grace is to *be with you*, my friend. Here, the pronoun *you* is plural, so it points not only to Timothy but also to the church at Ephesus, as well as the church universal. This is the shortest of Paul's benedictions. But though it is short, it is rich with truth! *Grace* is divine influence upon the heart and its subsequent reflection in the life. It's as if Paul is saying, "May the grace of God keep you from these errors, my son, Timothy." I would echo, "My dear sister, may the grace of God keep us from these errors!" It is only by the grace of God, dear friend, that you and I are not swept away by error. Paul himself knew this when he wrote to Timothy in his second epistle, in 2 Timothy 1:12, "For this reason I also suffer these things; nevertheless I am not ashamed, for I know whom I have believed and am persuaded that He is able to keep what I have committed to Him until that Day." Interestingly, he follows that verse with the charge we just looked at in 2 Timothy 1:13-14: "Hold fast the pattern of sound words which you have heard from me, in faith and love which are in Christ Jesus. That good thing which was committed to you, keep by the Holy Spirit who dwells in us." Yes, we must do our part by the grace of God, but all the while realizing that it is God who keeps us.

A similar thought is found in Paul's words in Philippians 2:12-13: "Therefore, my beloved, as you have always obeyed, not as in my presence only, but now much more in my absence, work out your own salvation with fear and trembling; for it is God who works in you both to will and to do for His good pleasure." We do our work, and God does His work. God is sovereign, and yet man is responsible. The grace of God will keep us from error, and it will keep us in the truth of His Word. And because of that, we can echo with Paul a hearty *Amen*, which means so be it!

Summary

As we close out our study of Paul's first epistle to his spiritual son Timothy, we learn from these last two verses to *Guard the Truth* (v 20a). Timothy is to guard the truth, the things which have been entrusted to him. What about you? Are you also keeping the things that have been entrusted to you in the safety of your own heart? Do you meditate on those truths and have they changed your life? With this command, Paul is essentially pointing us back to our responsibility toward all the many things he's taught us in this epistle. So, before we go on to remind ourselves of the last three points Paul makes in these final verses, I want us to remind ourselves briefly of the things we've learned in this epistle and the ways we must be diligent to guard those truths.

In Lesson 1, Paul introduced Christ as our hope. Is He your hope? Have you submitted to Him as Lord over your life? Is that truth tucked away in your heart?

In Lesson 2, we learned that a right use of the law results in our pursuit of God's Word, which leads to obedience, which leads to eternal life. Are you banking on that truth, and are you taking heed to yourself to make sure that is really your passionate pursuit for living each day?

In Lesson 3, Paul gave us a glimpse into both his sinful past and God's abundant grace that saved him. Are you keeping tucked away in your heart and mind the truth that you are a great sinner and Christ is a great Savior?

In Lesson 4, we saw the tragic ending of Hymenaeus and Alexander, who made shipwreck of their faith. Because they did not wage spiritual warfare, the results were tragic! Are you waging war in your members, or have you become spiritually sluggish? Keep tucked away before your mind's eye the tragedy of Hymenaeus and Alexander.

Lesson 5 was personally difficult for me, and it is one I have gleaned much from and am endeavoring to heed by praying for my governing leaders, knowing that it is God's will for my life and that He considers it excellent. I learned that by doing so I can lead a quiet and peaceable life. Have you pondered your responsibility to pray for your leaders, and are you doing that each time you are frustrated with the downward spirit of our nation?

Each of us as women should have especially guarded what was entrusted to us from Lesson 6 as we looked at a woman's attire and attitude in the house of God. Have you taken heed to the truth that women are not to teach or usurp authority over the men in the local assembly? What about your attire in the house of God? Are you making sure that each time you enter the house of God you are wearing what pleases the Lord?

As we worked through Lessons 7 and 8, we considered the qualifications necessary for elders and deacons. Are you remembering the importance of not only praying for your church's leaders but also making sure your church has leaders who are truly biblically qualified? Have you tucked this truth away deep into your heart? Too many churches have leaders who are not qualified biblically and are leading their sheep astray by their compromised lifestyles. Guard this precious truth, dear one!

Lesson 9 taught us to guard a truth that is imperative for us, but also to share with others. God was manifest in the flesh, justified in the Spirit, seen by angels, preached among the Gentiles, believed on in the world, and received up in glory. My dear sister, believe this, live this, and preach this truth to others!

Perhaps Lesson 10's truth is an obvious one, but it is nonetheless one we should guard. If it isn't the demonic doctrines of forbidding marriage and the eating of certain foods, then it will surely be another doctrine of demons that attempts to lure us away from the truth. Are you praying that God will alert you to any new doctrines of demons that might be on the horizon?

The need for a disciplined life may not be popular among many professing believers, but it is a biblical truth. We learned in Lesson 11 that bodily exercise profits a little, but godliness is profitable both for the life now and the life to come. Are you not only keeping this truth safe in your spiritual bank but also endeavoring to become more spiritually disciplined now than when we started this study? In what disciplines have you grown? What disciplines do you still need to improve upon?

As we worked our way through Lesson 12, we learned that Paul instructed Timothy to be an example to other believers and to make sure that he was taking heed to himself and to his doctrine. We also learned that these mandates are for each of us as well. As you go through the day, are you mindful that others are watching your life, especially your family, and learning what Christianity is by how you live out what you profess? Have you lived out this truth?

Lesson 13 got some of us squirming as we learned that it is not just the pastor and his wife who must confront sisters and brothers in Christ, but it is the responsibility of all of us. Are you being faithful to do this when it is needed among those in the family of God? This is a truth that we must remind ourselves of often so that we don't do the alternative, which is to become either embittered toward others or to gossip about them.

In Lessons 14 and 15, we studied a command that is often neglected in the church today, and that is caring for its widows. Every one of us women should have double motivation to guard this truth, since we are likely to be widowed at some point in our lives, and we will be hoping at that point that some of our fellow church members have heeded this truth and are willing to practice it. What widow have you blessed since you learned of your responsibility to the widows around you?

Paul again touched briefly on the office of elder in Lesson 16, and we learned what we are to do about his salary and his sinning. Are you guarding this important truth in an age in which we not only gloss over our own sins but also the sins of our spiritual leaders? This is a truth that must be kept and practiced.

As we began the final chapter of 1 Timothy, we studied in Lesson 17 the responsibilities of slaves and masters, and we learned that it is not so much the job or the boss that is important but the attitude. We learned that we must have proper dispositions of honor and service toward those who employ us.

Eleven evil characteristics of false teachers was our focus in Lesson 18. Do you know these characteristics? Do you know the other characteristics of false teachers that the Word of God clearly gives us? If you don't tuck the truths of this lesson away in your heart and mind, my friend, what will be the result? What will keep you from being swept away by error? Hide these in your heart! Guard them!

Lovers of gold or lovers of God was our focus in Lesson 19. Have you been seriously evaluating your life to see if it is characterized by desiring more gold or desiring more of God? Have you guarded the truth that money is not godliness and that the error of our age, the prosperity gospel, is a heresy that is sending people to hell?

Paul teaches Timothy in Lesson 20 to flee, follow, and fight for things that are crucial to his faith. This is a spiritual battle! How is that battle going for you? Do you awaken each morning remembering that you can't fight without your spiritual armor? Are you wearing it in preparation for each day and for the darts the enemy will hurl at you? This is not a truth you can ignore because as soon you do, you will be undone. Memorize this truth, guard it, and teach it to your children and grandchildren and others!

We considered ten motivations for righteous living in Lesson 21, and they all had to do with our Lord and His attributes. Do you dwell upon the attributes of God and are they motivators for you to live righteously in this evil age? Are you teaching your children a balanced doctrine of who God is so that they don't develop the erroneous ideas that He is some loving grandpa in Heaven doting on his grandchildren, on the one hand, or that He is some dictator with his whip out ready to zap our every failure?

Lesson 22 was another reminder from Paul regarding the dangers of money, especially for those who are rich. This must be an important truth we must guard, but also heed for ourselves. It is easier for a camel to go through the eye of a needle than for a rich man to enter into the kingdom of Heaven. If there is a truth that is needed in our Americanized Christianity, this one surely is it, for we are all rich!

Last, but not least, in this lesson, Lesson 23, Paul has impressed upon us the importance of *Guarding the Truth* (v 20a). By doing so, we will spare ourselves the grievous result of apostasy and the grace of God will keep us as we depend upon it. Meditate on this day and night!

From these final verses in Paul's epistle to Timothy, we also learned that we must *Get Away from Error* (v 20b). Since you began this study of 1 Timothy, what have you done to get away from the errors of the day? Do you still entertain novel ideas, or are you endeavoring to avoid them? Are you endeavoring to help others who are caught up in false teaching? Do you love them enough to tell them the truth? This is the day of apostasy, this is the day of great heresy, and this is the day of false doctrine. Stay with the pure milk of the word, my friend.

We also learned *The Grievous Result of Those Who Don't Guard Truth* (v 21a). We learned in an earlier lesson about Hymenaeus and Alexander, who departed from the faith due to doctrinal error. Paul ends his letter by warning Timothy once again of the dangers of those who don't guard truth, the danger of straying from the faith. Are you guarding the truth with tenacity? Have you swerved, even just a tad, from the doctrines you once held so dear? One swerve is all it takes to go off the doctrinal cliff and fall headlong into destruction.

Finally, we learned that *God's Grace Alone will Keep Us in the Truth* (v 21b). Are you depending on the grace of God to keep you in the truth? Are you trying to pull yourself up by your own spiritual bootstraps? My dear sister, it is God's grace alone that keeps any of us! It is that same grace that has saved any of us. We are saved not by works and not even by keeping any of these truths we have studied; we are saved by His grace alone through faith in Him alone! Amen!

It has been my great joy to shepherd you through this study of 1 Timothy. And as delightful as it has been for me, truly it is the great Shepherd, our Lord Jesus Christ, who has been our real teacher as we have learned what it means to be *With the Master Shepherding His Sheep*.

Questions to Consider

Guarding the Truth by God's Grace
1 Timothy 6:20-21

1. Read 1 Timothy 6 and summarize it in a few sentences.

2. Memorize 1 Timothy 6:20.

3. Paul tells Timothy to guard what has been entrusted to him; this would include the totality of this entire epistle that Paul has written. Read all of 1 Timothy and write down one truth from each chapter that you would especially like to keep secure and safe in the deposit of your heart.

4. (a) How does one keep what has been committed to them, according to 1 Timothy 6:14 and 2 Timothy 1:13-14? (b) How do you personally keep those things that have been spiritually passed down to you?

5. (a) What would be some of the "profane and idle babblings and contradictions" of our day that we should avoid? (b) How do you personally deal with those when you encounter them?

6. (a) If you still have your first lesson's homework, look at question number 7, which asked "What would you like to gain from this study?" Considering your answer to that question, would you say that you gained what you hoped you would gain from this study? (b) What other things have you learned or gleaned from our study of 1 Timothy?

7. What has been most impacting to you personally in your study of 1 Timothy? Please come with a prayer of thanksgiving to God for the things He has taught you through this study.

Endnotes

1   Jay Adams, *The Christian Counselor's Commentary: I & II Timothy and Titus* (Hackettstown: Timeless Texts, 1994), 3.

2   Susan Heck, *A Call to Discipleship* (Bemidji: Focus Publishing, 2012), 3.

3   William D Mounce, *Word Biblical Commentary* (Nashville: Thomas Nelson Publishers, 2000), 3.

4   George W. Knight III, *The New International Greek Testament Commentary: The Pastoral Epistles* (Grand   Rapids: Wm. B. Eerdmans Publishing Co., 1996), 67.

5   Charles Haddon Spurgeon, *Metropolitan Tabernacle Pulpit*, 39:434.

6   William Hendriksen, *New Testament Commentary: Exposition of the Pastoral Epistles* (Grand Rapids: Baker Book   House, 1957), 58-59.

7   Ibid, 63.

8   John Calvin, *Calvin's Commentaries, Volume XXI* (Grand Rapids: Baker Book House Co., 1981), 33.

9   Mounce, *Word Biblical Commentary*, 51.

10 Words by Julia H. Johnston, 1911.

11 Kenneth W. Osbeck, *Amazing Grace* (Grand Rapids: Kregel Publications, 1990), 170.

12 Richard Hartley-Parkinson. "Video: Doomed South Korea ferry school kids sing Titanic theme tune as they lark around during alert warning." *Mirror*. May 2, 2014. https://www.mirror.co.uk/news/world-news/south-korea-ferry-video-inside-3486916#ixzz39v1tRDfx.

13 Donald Guthrie, *The Pastoral Epistles* (Grand Rapids: Wm. B. Eerdmans Publishing Company, 1979), 68.

14 T. De Witt Talmage. "Wrecked Through Losing a Good Conscience." *The Biblical Illustrator*. 2011. www.BibleSoft.com.

15 Theron Brown and Hezekiah Butterworth, *The Story of the Hymns and Tunes* (New York: American Tract Society, 1907), 374.

16 Words by Edwin S. Ufford, 1988.

17 E. F. & L. Harvey, *Kneeling We Triumph: Book One* (Shoals: Old Paths Tract Society, Inc., 1982), 16.

18 See chapter 22 of *With the Master in Fullness of Joy*, by Susan Heck (Bemidji: Focus Publishing, 2011).

19 Albert Barnes, *Barnes' Notes: Ephesians to Philemon* (Grand Rapids: Baker Book House, 1873), 129.

20 Calvin, *Calvin's Commentaries*, 54-55.

21 Matthew Henry, *Taking Hold of God*. Edited by Joel R. Beeke and Brain G. Najapfour. (Grand Rapids: Reformation Heritage Books, 2011), 141.

22 Harvey, *Kneeling We Triumph*, 62.

23   Hendriksen, *New Testament* Commentary, 107.

24   Ibid, 107

25   Guthrie, *The Pastoral Epistles*, 74.

26   Ibid, 75.

27   John MacArthur, *The MacArthur New Testament Commentary: 1 Timothy* (Chicago: Moody Press, 1995), 88.

28   MacArthur, *MacArthur New Testament Commentary*, 103.

29   *The Homiletic Review: Volume 5* (New York: I.K. Funk, 1881), 462.

30   Mark Water, *The New Encyclopedia of Christian Quotations* (Grand Rapids: Baker Book House Co., 2000), 600.

31   Paul Lee Tan, Th.D., *Encyclopedia of 7,700 Illustrations: Signs of The Times* (Rockville: Assurance Publishers, 1979), 1234.

32   MacArthur, *MacArthur New Testament Commentary*, 127.

33   Tan, *Encyclopedia of 7,700 Illustrations*, 1630.

34   MacArthur, *MacArthur New Testament Commentary*, 143.

35   Clarke. *Adam Clarke's Commentary on the Bible*. PC Study Software: Version 5. 1988-2008. http://www.bmsoftware.com/pcstudybiblecompletelibrary.htm

36   Renee Jacques. "Ten Reasons It's Totally Fine to Never Get Married." *Huffington Post*. December 7, 2017. http://www.huffingtonpost.com/2014/05/14/reasons-not-to-get-married_n_5274911.html.

37   Clarke, *Commentary on the Bible*.

38   MacArthur, *MacArthur New Testament Commentary*, 159-160.

39   Mayo Clinic Staff. "Exercise: 7 benefits of regular physical activity." *Mayo Clinic*. https://www.mayoclinic.org/healthy-lifestyle/fitness/in-depth/exercise/art-20048389.

40   Donald S. Whitney, *Spiritual Disciplines for the Christian Life* (Colorado Springs: NavPress, 1991), 19.

41   Richard J. Krejcir. "Statistics on Pastors." *Into Thy Word*. http://www.intothyword.org/apps/articles/?articleid=36562.

42   John F. MacArthur, Jr. and Wayne A. Mack, *Introduction to Biblical Counseling* (Dallas: Word Publishing, 1994), 178.

43   MacArthur, *MacArthur New Testament Commentary*, 190.

44   R.C.H. Lenski, *Commentary on the New Testament: The Interpretation of St. Paul's Epistles to the Colossians, to the Thessalonians, to Timothy, to Titus, and to Philemon* (Peabody: Hendrickson Publishers, 1937), 661.

45   Frank E. Gaebelein, *The Expositor's Bible Commentary* (Grand Rapids: Zondervan, 1981), 377.

46   As cited by George P. Landow. "How Doth the Little Bee." *The Victorian Web*. October 15, 2005. http://www.victorianweb.org/authors/rands/ajrbion1.html.

47 Pulpit *Commentary Homiletics.* https://biblehub.com/sermons/1_ timothy/5-14.htm.

48 MacArthur, *MacArthur New Testament* Commentary, 220.

49 As quoted by Floyd Doud Shafer in "And Preach As You Go!" *Christianity Today*, March 27, 1961.

50 Lenski, *Commentary on the New Testament*, 694-695.

51 *The Bible Exposition Commentary: New Testament.* PC Study Bible: Version 5.

52 MacArthur, *MacArthur New Testament Commentary*, paraphrase of points found on pages 234-235.

53 Charles Swindoll, *Growing Strong in the Seasons of Life* (Portland: Multnomah Press, 1983), paraphrase of account on pages 146-147.

54 Ron Charles. "'Boy Who Came Back from Heaven' actually didn't; books recalled." *The Washington Post*, January 16, 2015. https://www.washingtonpost.com/news/arts-and-entertainment/wp/2015/01/15/boy-who-came-back-from-heaven-going-back-to-publisher/.

55 *I'd Rather Have Jesus*, words by Rhea F. Miller, 1922.

56 Bible *Exposition Commentary, New Testament.* PC Study Software: Version 5. 1988-2008. http://www.bmsoftware.com/pcstudybiblecompletelibrary.htm

57 Hendriksen, *New Testament Commentary*, 201.

58 *Ellicott's Commentary for English Readers.* https://biblehub.com/commentaries/ellicott/.

59 J.C. Ryle, "Holiness: A Sermon by J.C. Ryle." Bath Road Baptist Church. http://www.iclnet.org/pub/resources/text/history/spurgeon/web/ryle.holiness.html.

60 *The Bible Exposition Commentary*, PC Study Software.

61 Words by Walter C. Smith, 1876.

62 "The Unlucky Winners: The Tragic Stories of the Lottery's Unluckiest Winners." *Time.* November 28, 2012. http://newsfeed.time.com/2012/11/28/500-million-powerball-jackpot-the-tragic-stories-of-the-lotterys-unluckiest-winners/slide/the-winningest-losers/.

63 *The New Encyclopedia of Christian Quotations* (Grand Rapids: Baker Book House, 2000), 1106.

64 Ibid, 1106.

65 Words by Aaron Keyes, 2007.

66 Hendriksen, *New Testament Commentary*, 211.

67 Ibid, 212. Parenthetical comment mine.

About the Author

Susan Heck, and her husband Doug have been married for over 40 years. She has been involved in Women's Ministries for over 30 years. This includes teaching Bible Studies, counseling, and leading Ladies with the Master women's ministry at Grace Community Church in Tulsa, Oklahoma. (www.gccoftulsa.net)

Susan is a certified counselor with the Association of Certified Biblical Counselors (ACBC, formerly NANC). She is the author of "With The Master" Bible Study Series for women. Previously published books in that series are,

- With the Master on the Mount:
    A Ladies' Bible Study of the Sermon on the Mount

- With the Master in the School of Tested Faith:
    A Ladies' Bible Study of the Epistle of James

- With the Master in Heavenly Places:
    A Ladies' Bible Study on Ephesians

- With the Master on our Knees:
    A Ladies' Bible Study on Prayer

- With the Master in Fullness of Joy:
    A Ladies' Bible Study on the Book of Phillipians

- With the Master Before the Mirror of God's Word:
    A Ladies' Bible Study on First John

She is also the author of five published booklets:
- Putting Off Life Dominating Sins
- A Call to Scripture Memory
- A Call to Discipleship
- Assurance: Twenty Tests for God's Children
- The Liberating Gospel: A Call to Salvation

Susan's teaching ministry is an outgrowth of her memorization work on the Bible. She has personally memorized 23 books of the New

Testament word-for-word (The Gospel of Matthew, The Gospel of John, Romans, Second Corinthians, Galatians, Ephesians, Philippians, Colossians, First and Second Thessalonians, First and Second Timothy, Titus, Philemon, Hebrews, James, First and Second Peter, and First, Second, and Third John, Jude, Revelation), one book of the Old Testament (Jonah), and several other portions of Scripture.

Susan and her husband have two grown children and seven grandchildren. Both children and their spouses are in full-time ministry. Because of the enthusiasm of ladies who attended Susan's Bible studies, she has been invited to speak to ladies' groups both nationally and internationally. (www.withthemaster.org)